D0074820

*Peasant Economic Development within
the English Manorial System*

Challenging a hundred-year tradition that English peasants were serfs at the disposal of their lord, J.A. Raftis argues that tenants were in considerable control of the manorial regime and were able to take advantage of what most scholars have considered to be exploitive and negative aspects of the medieval agricultural economy.

Offering a revisionist theory that shifts the focus from labour services required by the lord to capital required by the customary tenant, Raftis reveals that "peasant economic development" and "manorial economy" are not mutually exclusive terms. Using account rolls, charters, court rolls, and lay subsidy rolls, he demonstrates that lords subordinated their power to tax and to extract labour services to a policy of capital maintenance. This breakthrough allows him to develop a more rational explanation for the growth of markets and wealth in a countryside not exclusively dependent on the economy of lords.

Peasant Economic Development within the English Manorial System is a ground-breaking analysis that redefines the social and economic history of rural medieval England and changes the direction of medieval scholarship.

J.A. RAFTIS is professor of medieval social and economic history, University of Toronto.

Peasant Economic Development within the English Manorial System

J.A. RAFTIS

Sutton Publishing

McGill-Queen's University Press
Montreal & Kingston • Buffalo

© McGill-Queen's University Press 1996
ISBN 0-7735-1403-1

HC
254.3
.R33
1997

Legal deposit fourth quarter 1996
Bibliothèque nationale du Québec

First published in the United Kingdom in 1997
Sutton Publishing Limited
Phoenix Mill • Thrupp • Stroud • Gloucestershire

ISBN 0-7509-1348-7

All rights reserved. No part of this publication may
be reproduced, stored in a retrieval system, or
transmitted, in any form or by any means, electronic,
mechanical, photocopying, recording or otherwise,
without prior permission from the publishers and
copyright holder.

Canadian Cataloguing in Publication Data

Raftis, J. A. (James Ambrose), 1922–
  Peasant economic development within the English
  manorial system
  Includes bibliographical references and index.
  ISBN 0-7735-1403-1
  1. Farm tenancy – Economic aspects – England –
  History. 2. Manors – Economic aspects – England –
  History. 3. Peasantry – England – History. I. Title.
  HC254.3.R33 1996   330.942'02   C96-900277-7

British Library Cataloguing in Publication Data

A catalogue record for this book is available from the
British Library.

This book has been published with the help of a
grant from the Humanities and Social Sciences
Federation of Canada, using funds provided by
the Social Sciences and Humanities Research
Council of Canada. Funding has also been received
from the Pontifical Institute of Medieval Studies.

McGill-Queen's University Press is grateful to the
Canada Council for support of its publishing
program.

Typeset in Palatino 10/12
by Caractéra inc., Quebec City, Canada
Printed in Canada by Friesens

Contents

University Libraries
Carnegie Mellon University
Pittsburgh, PA 15213-3890

Preface

Though often hidden from view by the theoretical scaffolding that crumbles with time, the new subdisciplines that sparkle and glow in their adolescence, the schools of thought that surface and fade as academic fashions change, and the imprint that passing geniuses leave upon an ever shifting surface, there has been a steady growth in the social and economic history of rural medieval England over the past one hundred years. The endeavours of many scholars, attracted by the multitude of extant records, have led to England's having the best-developed historiography of medieval western Europe.

That this study has found it convenient at almost every stage to contradict many conclusions of the work of M.M. Postan and E.A. Kosminsky as the most representative exponents of the classical liberal and Marxist doctrines does not qualify my respect for the contributions that these scholars have made to the growth of economic history. Michael Moyse Postan was first and foremost a historian. For those of us who were privileged to have been his postgraduate students at Cambridge University, for the wider circle still whom he engaged in national and international conferences, he is a gifted imaginative historian. Never was I aware of an imposition of structured views as he vetted my PhD thesis. The seminars were noteworthy for the variety of approaches among those invited to present papers. Over extended periods of time the points raised in his conference papers remained ongoing topics for debate. I remain convinced that he would have welcomed this study with that characteristic chuckle by which he introduced debate on the "intellectual feasts," as he called his seminars.

The work of E.A. Kosminsky in bringing the 1279 Hundred Rolls into the mainstream of historiography must be recognized as a classic. His critical assessment of these rolls has provided questionnaires for a generation of scholars. Despite my disagreements with the form of his many conclusions, the substantive contributions of his data stand on their own. Along with the works of Rodney Hilton, Kosminsky's Marxist alter ego in England, these research achievements must remain an essential part of economic historiography.

Other acknowledgments are of a different order. Upon rereading the works of Edward Miller after completing the first version of this study, I was delighted to find how fully my findings corroborated many of his insights. Only then did I appreciate how the "gentle reasonableness" of his approach had caused the significance of his contributions to be eclipsed by those with an ideological flair. The assistance of the work of several others of the same sort may be found acknowledged in notes. Perhaps I should add that the recent volume by Richard Britnell became available only after this study had been completed. Although my study is on an entirely different scale, I was pleased to discover how much my research complemented his innovative theme of commercialization.

This study would not have been possible without the detailed contributions of many individual scholars, among them many of my former students. I have tried to give full acknowledgment to these contributions at appropriate places. But the growing comprehension of any field of endeavour is accomplished by a range of communication wider than direct reference to the written word. This is particularly true for the influence of Edwin B. DeWindt, whose editions have created a cumulative substantive base, a virtual literature of their own, for study of the English peasant. At the other end of the source spectrum, conversations with James Masschaele about the emerging knowledge of the peasant market economy have developed insights well in advance of published village market studies.

J.A.R.

PART ONE

An Evolution within the Manor

Introduction

Historical research into the social and economic life of rural medieval England has shared in that explosion of specialized research and the non-ideological quality of such research that have been the characteristics of the later twentieth century. One has the impression that the unequivocal notions of productive organization and *a priori* value judgments, as to be found, for example, in nineteenth-century capitalist and Marxist theories, are on the whole being allowed to wither and to be quietly ignored. In addition, many grand concepts of "system" and "corporate organization" have simply become obsolete. There is, for example, a discernible line of progression from the dismantling of the large-scale open-field-system concept by such means as emphasis upon furlongs, sowing courses, and the local relativization of two and three courses to the current recognition of local decision-making as necessary to efficient productivity. Over much the same period the individual peasant has been brought into the light of history, especially through the study of local court rolls, so that the socio-economic life of the peasant could begin to be seen from the peasant's own perspective.

Most significant of all may be the analysis of local markets. By comparison with the scores of studies that lay behind the developments sketched above, analysis of rural markets, trade, and commerce has hardly begun. And yet the rural economy is finally beginning to have a role alongside foreign and urban trade in the "commercialization of England."[1]

It is no longer considered an anomaly that the English rural economy produced wealth sufficient to attract proto-modern taxation methods and maintain costly wars against a much larger opponent. Steps are being taken to elucidate the local and regional commercial infrastructure so that our knowledge of such trade may be integrated with the developments noted in the previous paragraph. For example, the efficient costing of local and regional road and river transport has now been determined,[2] and work is under way to assess the related efficiencies of the small-scale commercial turnover and to identify the personnel of such operations.

The potential for such studies has been recognized for the medieval period. The expert in Domesday Book has come to the conclusion that "the best returns could usually be got by these small local producers" and "small producers were effective and efficient across a wide range of activities."[3]

Nor is the potential for recent studies surprising in view of the role of the peasant during the expansion period of the twelfth century. Evidence varies from place to place, following such variables as programs of drainage and forest clearing, and, as David Farmer has stressed, our sources are lamentably thin for this century. By and large, however, the peasant seems to have moved with the "frontier" action and advanced his economic status through net increases of revenues and lands. As records become more available by the early thirteenth century, peasants are found to have taken advantage of commutation opportunities and, whether free or villein, to have been engaged in an active land market. On the whole, a peasantry with initiative and productive capacity has been given a recognizable role by historians in the economic development that centred about the twelfth century.[4]

In striking contrast, the peasant has not been accorded a positive role in the main body of analysis of economic development, that is, interpretations of the direct farming of estates by the lord over the thirteenth and fourteenth centuries, or, as it is often called, the high farming period. The reason for this neglect is obvious. According to the high farming thesis, the resources of the peasant, and, most importantly, the labour resources of these peasants, were henceforth directly manipulated to the profit of the lord. One significant sector on the local economic scene, the customary tenants, have quite simply been blocked out of the economic picture by traditional theories. According to M.M. Postan: "But whatever may have been the division of land between the landlord and his tenants in the dim beginnings of manorial history, it was bound to evolve to the disadvantage of the tenants in later centuries."[5] Even when we allow for the difference in approach, E.A. Kosminsky's premises were the same: "But the organization of serf labour on the demesne demanded the strict subjection of the peasant to manorial discipline."[6] Both the person and the resources of the peasant were at the disposal of the lord according to these classical theories. The customary peasant could no longer be expected to have a role in economic development, above all when the lord was exploiting the demesne directly.

These theories easily won the day among economic historians since they conveniently interpreted the lords' records, above all detailed customaries or surveys and the voluminous account rolls, which formed the heart of studies of large estate complexes that have appeared frequently over the past fifty years. To this point apparently even market studies are failing to challenge the traditional thesis. The liberating role of markets in classical capitalist economic history does not seem to have come into play for the medieval English peasant. Rather, as R.H. Britnell reports, the currently accepted doctrine follows more along the lines of Marxism as described by E.A. Kosminsky.[7] That is, whether in the twelfth-century farming context or in the high farming thirteenth century, the peasant is supposed to have been forced to obtain cash for the lord's needs by marketing his produce. He was being forced to be efficient, to develop markets, to gather profits for the lord. The collective farms of modern communist Russia, even with the coercive power of the Gulag Archipelago, would have liked to know how this was done!

More pointed dissatisfaction with the high farming thesis has been growing rapidly over recent years. There are indications that a complete review of the field would be of some benefit. Such a review might well begin with a return to an earlier historiographical perspective. For the old monastic complexes, and no doubt for comparable lay estates as well, an administrative reform that would bring ordered control over revenues was the first priority from the late twelfth century. As R.A.L. Smith pointed out in his pioneer studies of Canterbury Cathedral Priory long ago, the central financial system was the first objective in reorganization.[8] It is arguable that sensitive attention to the central financial system remained the first priority over succeeding centuries. Funds now made available from this more efficient system could be employed in a wide variety of ways. Among these was the investment in arable productivity and animal management along with the purchase of more properties in order to augment the rent rolls. This financial responsibility and large-scale investment do not indicate a genuine capitalist mentality. The dominance of consumer requirements and the lack of flexibility in adjustment to market conditions assured that the lords' involvement in the market scene would often be of brief duration. Lack of investment by the fourteenth century has been an accepted historical fact, but more clarification is long overdue about the degree to which this was lack of investment by lords and was something new.

It might also be rewarding to subject the concept of farming to a thorough review. In order to make direct investments in their demesnes and to have direct access to profits, the lords themselves displaced farmers who by and large traditionally had administered estates under contracts calling for a fixed annual payment during the term of the contract. Beyond correcting abuses of the lord-peasant relationship that may have been allowed by farmers, there is no overriding evidence that the lords introduced new policies vis-à-vis peasants as farmers were displaced. Indeed, Kosminsky was struck by the failure to rationalize, that is regroup, manors over the two centuries after Domesday.[9] In the same fashion, those who have probed into the comparable detail of manorial service structures have been struck by the complex differences in tenurial structures and service obligations even between contiguous manors belonging to the same lord.

Furthermore, those various manuals that became available later in the thirteenth century very likely reflected traditional practices. As Dorothea Oschinsky has stressed in her definitive edition,[10] such manuals were instruments for the use of the auditing-legal staff of the lord. One would hardly expect such personnel to be capable of innovative experiments! By contrast with the flexible "hands on" running of the rural economy that is now being emphasized, such manuals again remind us largely of the existence of an efficient central administration. *Prima facie* the policy involving customary tenants in the thirteenth-century manuals would not appear to differ from twelfth-century arrangements expected of farmers.

Nevertheless, it is doubtful that such revisions in themselves will offer a definition of the role of the peasantry. The vast bulk of manorial records are still the record of decisions by the lord and his officials. Will further studies of the same policies change the picture? An updating of the evidence by Miller and Hatcher does not appear to support this possibility. Rather, fresh analysis of the same type of evidence merely introduces more variety and hence more ambiguity: "At the same time, while these efforts at improvement were real enough, it must also be admitted that their impact was less than dramatic."[11] "The likelihood that livestock farming was in any significant respect more efficient than arable farming is not high."[12] "The tendencies which had undermined manorial structure during the preceding century were checked. Some demesne land which had been alienated was resumed and some claims to agricultural services which had been released for money were revived."[13] "At the same time, it is dangerous to exaggerate either the extent or the durability of the thirteenth-century manorial reaction."[14]

Clearly, a general interpretation of the context for recent peasant studies cannot be derived as a spin-off from traditional theses. Rather, it has to be discovered within manorial records themselves and as policy of the lord. In short, the built-in exclusion of peasants from thirteenth- and fourteenth-century economic development must be unblocked where it began. It began with the estates of Ramsey Abbey. We may take E.A. Kosminsky's own words about the significance of these estates for traditional theories: "the estates of the old Benedictine house of Ramsey provide an example of the purest type of manor cultivated by servile tenants, with a large area of villein land and an insignificant percentage of free holdings."[15] "The classical picture of the manorial order, based on serfdom and serf labour, was to no small extent created on the basis of the material from the Ramsey cartulary."[16] Throughout his study, Kosminsky illustrates this point by the many references to what we may call the purest of the pure Ramsey evidence, the estates of Hurstingstone Hundred.

That the main illustrations for the following study are taken from the estates of Ramsey Abbey ought to be seen, therefore, in the wider context of the role of the history of these estates as the model for traditional theories. The selection of estates for this volume goes even further by analysing those estates that are right under the nose, as it were, of the lord's headquarters, that is right next to the abbey. Since the evolving role of the customary tenant traced in this study was largely within the manorial structure, analysis has had to be confined to the internal organization of each manorial village. The framing of our investigations about individuals and families became such an extremely complex operation that it was decided to limit such detail to the one village group of Abbots Ripton, Broughton (and King's Ripton), Upwood, Warboys, and Wistow when it was found that this group adequately demonstrated conclusions emerging from the study. Comparable sets of clusters about St Ives and Godmanchester-Huntingdon introduce quite different sets of variables. Concluding remarks to this volume will discuss the possibility of extending to such comparable clusters the historical profile of the customary tenant emerging from this study. At that time it will also be noted that this story evokes significant parallels with the neighbouring estate complexes of Ely and Peterborough.

Where this study should begin is, therefore, obvious. But how it should and did begin was not so obvious in our sources. So, a few words about how this book "happened" may be of assistance to the reader, for it was neither anticipated nor pre-planned. In the spring of 1990 I began to review the work accomplished by many scholars on the villages of medieval England in order to determine where I might best expend the research time accumulated over a decade of senior administration. It was gratifying to see the productivity of a wide variety of scholars trained in differing ways in Britain and North America, but not an easy task to determine where my own experience could best be invested.

Finally, I settled upon the need to investigate further the reasons for mobility over the pre–Black Death century. Evidence for considerable mobility about Ramsey Abbey manors had been presented some thirty years ago in *Tenure and Mobility*. But neither in that volume nor in my own studies and those of others since that time had there emerged a coherent explanation for such mobility in the heart of the manorialized Midlands. Following the fact-finding methodologies of our time, it appeared that some further clarification ought to be obtained by a more thorough documentation of the context of those moving about. Accordingly, a grant was sought and obtained from the Social Sciences and Humanities Research Council of Canada enabling me to pursue this direction in 1991.

Much to my surprise, the first phase of this investigation brought consistently to the fore a number of major questions with which I was unfamiliar, since these questions did not issue from traditional manorial economic analysis. During the period of a veritable population explosion, why did so many continue to move into these manors in order to become tenants of larger customary holdings? Why were formal entry arrangements not extant for these new customary tenants? Why did the burden of labour services appear irrelevant to the attraction Ramsey customary holdings held for these new tenants? Why did the decline and virtual disappearance of labour services have no close correlation to the retention of customary tenure?

Ultimately, the consistency of such questions could only be explained by the priority given to customary tenant capital in manorial management policies. The "bottom line" behind the movement of wealthier tenants into Ramsey estates was the maintenance of capital resources; scions of wealthier tenants moved from Ramsey manors because of the prospect of improvements in their capital; even adjustments to labour-supply management were conditioned by the concern for capital. The ensuing study really became an investigation into capital and the customary tenant.

To provide an analytic framework for such observations was another matter. Economic rationality required that if capital had such a recognizable function in the manorial scene, major customary tenants must have been attracted by a potential profit margin. But how could such information be derived from records drawn up to determine the lord's profit or loss position? Happily, sources recently published from records whose purpose originated from beyond the lordship – that is, lay-subsidy inventories – gave indirect evidence for such a profit by providing an inventory of taxable surplus. Chapter 1 begins with a summary of this information about capital. The names of these wealthier tenants then made it possible to interpret manorial administration with respect to entry fines and the appearance from beyond the village of new tenants on major customary lands. Smallholders were excluded from this economic activity and hence from consideration in this volume.

The families of more substantial customary tenants were also entities distinct from the lord's account-roll calculus. Inasmuch as lay-subsidy rolls supplied invaluable information about family-wealth settlement, a context was provided for chapter 2. Furthermore, from the practice of common response to the requirements of manorial administration, these tenants gradually took on the characteristics of a corps with its own self-interests. Indeed, it is this group that may be credited with introducing more orderly patterns to movements from the manor. Such patterns followed upon the devolution of responsibility for the tithing organization and the pledging system. Internal structural flexibilities were introduced to the manorial system that would allow significant mobility of both labour and capital.

The most challenging part of this study lay in the matter of labour services. In extents and account rolls such services were quite simply personal obligations owed to the lord. How could one penetrate behind the scenes of the apparently unequivocal sets of records? Increasing awareness of the emerging group structure formed by major customary tenants proved to be the key to the resolution of this problem for chapter 3. Data available from account and court rolls about personnel of the wealthiest customary-tenant group revealed that flexibilities in the allocation of customary labour were deliberately designed to benefit this corps. That is to say, the rewards of official positions, the opportunities of *ad hoc* or yearly commutation, and the benign acceptance of refusal to work were policies implemented to benefit major customary tenants.

In the light of the developments described in the first three chapters, changes in manorial policy after the Black Death would not be found innovative in part two of this study. In fact one of the more intriguing aspects of the major customary tenants as the most active economic agents in the manor would be the degree to which these tenants, supplemented by additional wealthy members from abroad, would actually maintain the form of the traditional demesne economy over the latter half of the fourteenth century. Detailed information now for the first time available about marriage patterns and other personal family information would finally reveal that, by the fifteenth century, this was a social as well as an economic group or class. As such, the major tenants would continue together although no longer functioning as customary tenants with substantial obligations to the lord's demesne.

But what of the lord throughout this period? After all, Ramsey Abbey retained as many feudal jurisdictions and powers by the fifteenth century as it had held two centuries earlier! The various estates under consideration here were directly administered rather than farmed from the thirteenth century until demesnes were farmed in the fifteenth century. The answer to this apparent contradiction lies in the distinctive pragmatic qualities of the English landed aristocracy. This phenomenon has long intrigued continental scholars, such as Marc Bloch, who found a striking contrast with the idealism of the French nobility. Yes, the lords of Ramsey, or their agents, understood well the economy of their day since they were careful not to employ their authority to thwart the system. They knew that the total village economy was more productive than the demesne economy; they knew that the supply and demand for capital moved on a wider plane than the manor-village ambience; they knew that the market system extended below, above, and beyond manorial control. In consequence, they were sufficiently intelligent to tap into the system whenever and wherever licensing profits could be obtained. Hence, an evolution would take place under the lordship umbrella. Whatever may have been the case prior to the period under study here, from the late thirteenth century the active agents on the economic scene would not be the landlords.

It must be admitted that the study of customary tenants has not offered a very attractive proposition to the economic historian. The tangled terminology designating such tenants, the variety of customary obligations, the question of whether oppressive lordship was the rule or the exception, and the increasing evidence "on the ground" for "independent" economic activity by such tenants are all part of the historiographical picture.[17] In order to avoid such complexity, we take as a point of departure in this study the customary tenant as he is so designated in the records – that is, simply the tenant owing full customary services. The structure of this volume is then determined by the story of these tenants that unfolds in our records.

1 Capital and the Customary Tenant

Paradoxical though it may seem in the light of traditional historiography, a true economic perspective on the customary tenant must begin with the question of capital rather than labour. In this chapter we shall see that capital gave an economic status to customary tenants that received the support of the lord, since this status was deemed essential to the maintenance of the manorial system. Indeed, the demand for an adequate pool of capital would force the lord to accept wealthy tenants from beyond the manor throughout our period.

That early, and one might properly say primitive, notion that the lord simply employed his feudal monopoly power to exploit tenants has gradually been discarded.[1] In the case of the lords of Ramsey, the most telling evidence for economic wisdom has been seen in their management of the great international fair of St Ives. As with any intelligent landlord and jurisdictional authority, they realized that they would benefit from encouraging rather than thwarting economic prosperity.[2] This chapter isolates some ways by which the same economic rationality was applied to the preservation of the capital base of the village manorial organization, although it may be noted that this same theme of rationality underlies all subsequent chapters.

It has long been recognized that the critical need for capital on the lord's demesne was central to the manorial economy. Estate records spelled out capital resources as the most prominent feature of the manor. Domesday Book recorded the value of estates after listing the number of tenants, properties of varying sizes, animals, ploughs, and ploughlands. For centuries, extents and surveys repeated this formula. Concern for the volatility of capital resources owing to seasonal crop failures, disease among animals, and the wearing out of ploughs and other equipment was an ever- present fact of life. In consequence, twelfth-century farming contracts were careful to guarantee the maintenance of capital.[3] When account rolls become extant, from the thirteenth century, evidence for the cost of capital maintenance can best be appreciated from the annual inventories of replacement and repair costing. Villagers must have been equally sensitive to the fundamental need for capital since, until the late fourteenth century, tenants were rarely accused in local courts of allowing deterioration in their properties.

There are coherent historiographical explanations[4] for the failure of economic historians to perceive that the economic welfare of demesne and customary tenants were so intricately dovetailed that one could not survive and prosper without the other. But it must also be said that historians have not focused on the worth of the customary tenant for another very good reason. There is not one shred of direct evidence about the economic wealth of these tenants in manorial records. For example, customary tenants were tenants of virgates, semi-virgates, and lesser land units, each with well-defined obligations in the generously detailed extents or customaries of the mid-thirteenth century for Ramsey Abbey estates.[5] But, unlike the list of animals to be found for the lord's demesne, there is nothing about the capitalized state of these customary units. And one can easily analyse extents and account rolls without adverting to the fact that virgates and semi-virgates are in a sense microcosms of the manor. That is to say, these units assessed to indicate obligations to the lord actually embody a whole bundle of resources. There was the physical homestead proper, that is the messuage with its main house, outbuildings such as granges, along with gardens and orchards. The tenant arable holding signified by the virgate or half-virgate also embodied rights to common in fen, marsh, and meadow. The last section of this chapter illustrates the intense competition for these resources. Even for the arable units themselves manorial extents do not reveal that virgates and their subdivisions were actually composed of numerous small units spread throughout the open fields and easily detached for subletting.

Once alert to these features of the customary tenurial complex, we become aware of the potential for variety in the economic actions of individual tenants. But it will come as no surprise that the best index to this variety is provided by non-manorial sources – that is, those local lay-subsidy inventories that list and evaluate surplus items taxable by the crown. For example, this is the list of evaluations for Wistow[6] in 1290:

- £4.11s.; 62s.; 37s.1d.ob.; 7s.6d.; 62s.; 35s.10d.; 61s.6d.ob.q.;
- 61s.4d.ob.; 68s.9d.ob.; 76s.4d.; 11s.; 60s.6d.; 60s.2d.; £4.17s.6d.ob.;
- 17s.8d.; 75s.1d.; 29s.8d.ob.; £4.8s.2d.; 48s.; £7.5s.4d.; 57s.10d.; 72s.4d.; 70s.8d.; 79s.6d.; £10.10s.2d.; 9s.2d.; £4.5s.2d.; £4.22d.;
- 70s.8d.; 65s.2d.; 72s.8d.; 74s.10d.; 20s.; 12s.6d.; 20s.6d.; 9s.

It will be immediately apparent that these lists do not at all reflect the neat manorial-extent categories of virgates and semi-virgates. Although we do not know the size of the holdings of these individuals at Wistow in 1290, the review of tenemental structure for our whole period given in chapter 4 suggests continuity of the manorial-extent arrangement until the later fourteenth century. As we shall see in chapter 2, these lay-subsidy lists do not even confine themselves to the man or woman in charge of the traditional home property. Ostensibly, then, these lists indicate that the lord did not have a monopoly on the capital of the village in the same fashion that he had a feudal monopoly on land.

As work has progressed on lay-subsidy rolls, the attention of scholars has increasingly been drawn to the realities of the extensive capital base of the manorial economy.[7] Detailed local rolls are particularly revealing for this purpose. Such local rolls are extant for the banlieu of Ramsey Abbey and among the villages to be studied here, including Upwood, Wistow, and Great Raveley. The records for 1290 are particularly useful. At this time the taxable surplus at Upwood was £206.9s.7d.ob., of which nearly 60 per cent (£98.14s.1d.) belonged to villagers. At Wistow, where the taxable goods of the lord were not listed, villagers had £111.13s.ob.q. in surplus wealth.

For the most part, lay-subsidy lists detail readily marketable farm produce such as various grains and animals. The capital equipment required to make a village holding viable, such as buildings and heavy equipment like ploughs, are not given in these records. Even axes, hoes, and other lighter tools are rarely noted. Apparently all these were exempted as essential to productivity and livelihood. The formula for exemption from assessment would be the traditional "lock, stock, and barrel" found, for example, in twelfth-century farming contracts.[8] By these agreements a property was to be maintained as when received. That is to say, essential buildings, equipment, regular field rotation, and so forth were to be in a normal or standard state of productivity. In an entry from the 1307 court roll of Graveley, reference to a fairly common type of arrangement, the letting of land

for services (*ad opus*), illustrates how this capital-maintenance question would be ever present:

Graveley,[9] 1307: William Shepherd, who twelve years ago surrendered a
messuage and [?] acres of land into the lord's hands to be held for services
by William the son of Dyke, comes with his wife and they ask permission of
the lord for re-entry to that messuage and land. And the said abbot ordered
inquiry to be made as to how much cost and [expenditure] the above William
Dyke had invested and spent in the above messuage and lands since the time
he fined for them, both in buildings and lands. Upon the evidence of the
appointed clerks they say that from all costs and expenses made by the above
William to the said messuage and lands it is now truly worth sixty shillings
more than its value at the time he fined for it, in addition to his fine of one-
half mark paid to the lord for entry to the above messuage and land, etc.

That type of arrangement seen here for Gravely would seem to
have been common throughout Ramsey estates. At Ellington in 1299
specific note was made of building a house for 6s.8d.[10] At Over in
1308 an incoming tenant was charged with payment of 1s.6d. for
improvements by the former tenant.[11] At Elton in 1308 Robert of
Teyngton recovered from the incoming tenant recompense for deterioration of the property during his tenure.[12] Note again that these
changes in capital were a matter for contractual arrangements among
tenants rather than with the lord. For this reason we have had to
search beyond our five villages in order to find rare examples of such
agreements. The lord was content to leave the expense of these rather
normal adjustments of capital to agreement among the tenants. Only
with the total decay ("dilapidation," in the words of the records)
would the lord invoke his authority and order the reeve to seize the
property, a rare event before 1348.

What was the actual "value" of a normally capitalized virgate? The
great variety in lay-subsidy assessments and entry fines makes clear
that actual capital values would vary widely from one virgate or half-
virgate to another. However, the administrative system does provide
us with one index for an answer to this question by a note appended
to the mid-thirteenth-century extent of Warboys by a later hand.[13]
This entry records the custom whereby the mobile and immobile
goods of a customary tenant escheated to the lord if the tenant died
without heir born to him and his wife. One-third of these goods (that
is, no doubt, of their estimated value) remained with the lord. The
entry then concludes that upon the death of Richard Plumbe, virgater,
without issue, his widow Margaret pays 5 marks (66s.8d.) to the lord
as was entered in the entry fine for "25 Abbot John" (of Sawtry: 1311–

12). If one-third of the capital was worth 5 marks, then 15 marks, or 200 s. (£10), would seem to have become the standardized formula for the value of the capital on a virgate. These nicely rounded figures were of course a practical accounting device in order to avoid a complex detailed inventory. Such a device was common at this time, for example in accounting royal farms, accounts, and escheat rolls. The £10 total does make creditable capital improvements of 32s. and 60s. given in entries above.

At Warboys, the Hundred Roll of 1279 tells us that there were 36 virgate units and 14 one-half units at 30 acres per virgate. If Richard Plumbe's property may be taken as typical, then the capital value of Warboys virgates would have been £430. These virgates are exclusive of the 34 messuages and one-acre units at Warboys, 5 messuages and two-acre units, 4 messuages and curtilage (½-rod) units, 6 other small units, and 10 freehold units of various sizes. All of the latter were calculated at 10½ virgates in the mid-thirteenth-century extent. Following this calculation, the capital value of the villagers' virgates at Warboys would be in excess of £500. Virgates of the neighbouring villages were likely valued around this same level, since the customary acreage sizes of virgates at Broughton, Upwood, and Wistow were about the same as Warboys (32, 30, 30), though Abbots Ripton and Little Raveley were only 20 acres per virgate.

These figures may be minimal, since we do not know whether the "mobile and immobile" goods of Richard Plumbe included important elements such as sown acres. Nor do we know whether such arrangements included surplus accumulated by Plumbe or were calculated as the "working operation" of the virgate. The fact that the widow would be expected to continue the operation and still pay this "death duty" would suggest the latter. That is to say, 66s.8d. would be an ordinary surplus in lay-subsidy rolls, and it may have seemed logical for this amount to escheat to the lord. That this amount could be borne by the virgate is further indicated, as we shall see below, by the fact that the 66s.8d. figure appears to have been a normal entry fine for the virgate ca 1300. On the whole, the £10 value of Richard Plumbe's virgate can only provide us with a useful estimate of the order of magnitude of the capitalized virgate. Corporate capital values of around £500 would seem too low when, as we have seen above, surplus at Upwood and Wistow averaged around £100 for villagers.

Data about fines paid by customary tenants upon entry to their properties are only infrequently listed in the revenue sections of account rolls. But there are enough data to show the basic policies behind the administration of these fines. First, entry fines tended to be standardized according to the manorial property designation of virgate, semi-virgate, and so forth, rather than, as was the case with royal taxes, according to the assessed individual wealth. That is to say, around 1300 fines were usually expressed as some multiple of the mark. Thus we find the five-mark fine for entry to one virgate twice at Warboys and once at Broughton. Around 1300 the three-mark fine was usual for entry to a one-half virgate unit (Warboys: 3; Wistow: 3; Broughton: 1). One mark was paid for one-quarter virgate at Wistow in 1311. One-half mark was paid for the further subdivision (cotland) at Wistow in 1307 and Broughton in 1312.

Secondly, entry fines were sensitive to the issue of capital maintenance on the customary tenement. When properties became under-capitalized, entry fines were lowered from these standard rates. Two rather than three marks were paid for entry to one-half virgates at Wistow in 1310 and 1316, at Broughton in 1312, and at Warboys in 1336. Deterioration of properties could vary quite widely. At Wistow entry fines of only one mark (13s. 4d.) for one-half virgate were paid in 1298 and again in 1324. At the same village one-half virgate was entered for one and one-half mark (20s.) in 1297 and a virgate for only three-quarters of a mark (10s.) in 1316. A slightly better series of entries for Broughton indicates the trend for capital values of property to fall as the fourteenth century progressed. This vill had entry fines to virgates twice for 40s. in 1314 and entries to one-half virgates for 20s. in 1314, 13s.4d. in 1318, and 10s. in 1326. Again, only 40s. was paid for a virgate in 1319, 20s. for one-half virgate in 1326, and only one-half mark (6s.8d.) for another one-half virgate during the latter year.

Some corroboration of this interpretation of entry fines can be made by relating the size of the entry fine to the payment of lay-subsidy taxes. Even well into the fourteenth century the larger fines meant capital was there for production of a taxable surplus. Godfrey, the son of Richard le Noble, entered a virgate at Warboys for 40s. during the year 1318–19 and in 1327 had 30s. taxable surplus. At the same village Hugh Lone entered one-half virgate for 30s. over 1324–25, and three years later this young successor to the Lone family had 10s. in taxable goods. During the same year, 1324–25, John Palmer entered one-half virgate for 40s., and this scion of the wealthy Palmers had 16s.8d. in taxable goods in 1327 and 30s. in 1332. In other instances at Warboys taxes can be identified with well-capitalized properties at the time of entry, although one cannot be certain that the tenant is the same member of the family. Thus Godfrey Gerold paid 40s. for entry to one-half virgate over 1306–07, and a Godfrey Gerold had 26s.8d. in taxable goods in 1327. John le Rede also paid

40s. for one-half virgate over 1306–07, and he or a son with the same first name had 16s.8d. in taxable goods in 1327 and 27s. in 1332.

For well-capitalized estates there is no evidence that entry fines and lay-subsidy taxes debilitated the family enterprise. For example, the affairs of the Beneyt family of Warboys are fairly well traceable in the second quarter of the fourteenth century. A young Hugh Beneyt began his career as a customary tenant by receiving a mondaymanland croft for a 2s. fine over 1318–19. By 1327 Hugh was about as wealthy as his father Roger, since their relative taxable subsidies were 35s. and 33s.6d.ob. In 1332 Roger and Hugh were assessed equally at 25s. A Hugh Beneyt junior did not make the 1332 tax list, but by 1335–36 was able to enter the half virgate formerly held by Hugh senior for a 26s.8d. fine. At Wistow, Andrew Outy represented a family that moved into that village at the turn of the century. The surname does not appear in the 1290 and 1295 lists. Andrew thrived and by 1327 had turned over property to his son William so that their taxable wealth was fairly comparable (Andrew, 25s.; William 20s.). By 1332 Andrew has passed on from our records but, his son William benefited so that his taxable wealth was now 35s. Andrew may have sublet the home property, or the entry fine was not collected at the time of entry, for only over 1335–36 does William, son of Andrew Outy, pay the substantial entry fine noted above for land "once of his father."

By contrast, smallholders pay entry fines but do not garner taxable surplus. For example, John, son of John Bronning, who entered one-quarter land at Warboys for 10s. in 1325–26, is not on the 1327 tax list. William Smart, who in 1329–30 entered a smallholding once held by his father Robert for 5s., is not listed as a Warboys taxpayer in 1332.

Undercapitalization of a tenement could follow individual family fortunes as well as general economic trends. At Wistow the Herod family continued for several generations but could not seem to improve their lot. Robert Herod entered an obviously impoverished one-half virgate for a low fine of 20s. in 1297, but the Herod name does not appear in tax records during the 1290s or later. Also at Wistow, the Puskere (buckle-maker) family name appears in the 1290s as associated with the tenancy of one-half virgate. But the name does not appear in either the 1290 or 1295 tax lists. The reason becomes apparent in 1298, when Godfrey Pusker entered his father's one-half virgate for the low fine of 13s.4d. But Godfrey prospered, perhaps as a tradesman, and by 1327 had 10s. in taxable goods. At Wistow, too, smallholders were less likely to progress. John le Heringmonger entered one cotland (⅛ virgate) for 6s.8d. in 1307. But by

1316, when Robert le Heringmonger entered this cotland, he paid only 2s. for entry. This old family never made the tax lists.

These few glimpses at relative successes and failures of families will be more fully supplemented in chapter 2. But it is logical now to address a more critical issue. What happened when customary tenants on well-capitalized properties failed to replace themselves? Historians have long been conditioned to assume that the lord could find a sufficient number of tenants on his own estates in the late thirteenth century. The lord was expected to allow preference for traditional tenant families.[14] And the wide acceptance of M.M. Postan's overpopulation theory has meant that no significance has been given to the possibility that tenants for customary land would be encouraged from beyond the manor.

In consequence, the significance of startling statistics about the disappearance of traditional main family names and the appearance of new main family names has passed over the heads of historians. Since main family names can normally be identified with considerable certainty,[15] the accuracy of these data can be considered secure.

A study[16] of a cluster of Ramsey estates has found that main family names disappear from our records at rates varying from 10 per cent in Upwood to 16 per cent in Warboys, 22 per cent in Broughton, 23 per cent in Wistow, to 24 per cent in Abbots Ripton. New names appearing vary from 5 per cent in Broughton to 8 per cent in Upwood, 11 per cent in Warboys, 12 per cent in Abbots Ripton, to 18 per cent in Wistow. These data from Ramsey estates do not seem surprising when compared with the same phenomenon on estates of neighbouring Peterborough Abbey. On the home group of the latter lord, 30 of 54 entry fines were paid by apparent strangers,[17] while on the western group of estates 21 of 50,[18] and on the northern group 17 of 41 fines were paid by strangers.[19]

Demographic evidence for the difficulty many families had in replacing themselves from the thirteenth to the sixteenth centuries has now become readily available.[20] Apparently this phenomenon of very uneven replacement rates might be expected for a pre-industrial society, even when, as in the late thirteenth century, the English countryside was well populated. But the question is not only about the disappearance of families but also why other families either from that same manor or from elsewhere on the lord's domain failed to take their place. The fact that other families were there and did not enter customary holdings vacated by main families may be presumed from data given in the previous paragraph, although the point can also be readily established from information available about lesser tenants.[21]

Branches from families who had more than one son were not the answer to this demographic dilemma. As we shall see in the next chapter, families strove to establish branches, and many did so successfully. But in nearly all instances these did not become major customary tenants. Branches could be established in a cottage or shop on the main family messuage as bakers, butchers, or in other trades. Lesser branches often survived by rewards from such posts as beadles, tasters, and herdsmen. But in all such instances, when we do find evidence for agrarian holdings, these secondary branches held something like one-quarter virgates or crofts. By and large, therefore, these were lesser tenants, and although many of these would continue, it would be as lesser tenants only.

Subdivision was not the answer for family branches, since this was a region governed by impartible inheritance. In addition, as already noted, manorial administrators were determined to retain a fixed tenurial mould. This continuation of the basic profile of customary tenure with its varying proportions of large and smaller holdings, dramatized by the magisterial study of E.A. Kosminsky[22] and generally confirmed by other scholars,[23] would seem to argue against recruitment for vacancies among major tenants from the ranks of smallholders. That is to say, over the several generations from the late thirteenth to the mid-fourteenth centuries, evidence accruing from surveys, hundred rolls, account rolls, and *opera* allocations indicates relatively constant numbers of units of virgates, semi-virgates, and smaller holdings. Unlike the post–Black Death period of failure in the supply of tenants both from at home and from beyond the village, the lord obviously turned to recruiting main tenants from abroad over the pre-plague generations.

The best explanation for this recruitment of tenants from abroad must be found in the realities of demography and capital. Many families were simply unable to replace themselves after a generation or two. Other families could not find the capital to enter these expensive enterprises. As we have seen, the lord would take smaller entry fines as the fourteenth century progressed in order to encourage his villeins to remain in their traditional customary holdings. But the nub of the matter was the financial capacity to enter and maintain valuable holdings. The lords of Ramsey, as no doubt lords elsewhere, gave priority to prospective tenants who could furnish the entry fines and maintain well-capitalized properties.[24]

Let us turn to Warboys in illustration of this demographic phenomenon. It may not seem surprising that many more modest smallholders disappeared from the Warboys scene in the early fourteenth century: Agath, Alan, Bolby, Baseley, Bishop, Brandon, Ponder,

Sculle. But the evidence is equally compelling for those recorded in tax records with a surplus: Long, Moke, Palmer, Puttok, Tymme, Unfrey. Some, like the Thurbernes, who held more than one virgate, were from among the largest landholders. Others, like the Herbert and Le Noble families, had more than one branch paying towards the lay subsidy but still disappeared well before 1348. In short, there is no evident economic explanation for this stark demographic reality. The fact that none of the members of these families was cited for moving from the lord's demesne further corroborates the demographic explanation.

Of course, the Black Death brought more dramatic changes. Warboys families of one unit (Nel, Pilche), of one unit and noticeably wealthy (Chycheley, Segeley), with three sons (Nicholas, Top), and with several substantial branches (Wodekoc) disappeared from the scene. But some of these families can be seen weakening before 1348: only Christine Chycheley and Beatrice Pilche, for example, represented their respective families during the 1340s. Data from Warboys describing varying periods of illness for which allowances were made from the early 1340s also demonstrate that ill health, like death, did not discriminate according to wealth in land. Again, many families were weakened by the plague and ended within a decade or two: Fot, Haugate, Lone, Outy, Richard.

Between 1300 and 1348 some forty new families appeared in Warboys.[25] Like the families that disappeared, these newcomers varied from petty tradesmen to smallholders to more substantial tenants. No record of their entry appears to have been kept. Nor was there need for such a record, since the pledging system and the entry-fine roll fully covered acceptance of status in the village and control of property conveyance. By the fourteenth century, surnames were firmly in place for ordinary people of the Hunts region, so place-name surnames do not give us clues to the provenance of these newcomers to a village. No doubt these immigrants came from near and far, as maps for the late thirteenth-century place-name surnames indicate. But, in any case, concern for provenance was not of interest to this land-market system. Newcomers brought money and human resources to a village as merchants and others brought greater wealth to the fairs of St Ives.

The exclusive legal designation "outsider" or "stranger" employed for the legal rationale of medieval manorial records is somewhat misleading. Prospective tenants must have received some information about available properties from someone in the manor and must further have had sufficient personal contacts to be acceptable to pledges. As has been amply demonstrated, court orders to find pledges indicate the voluntary nature of the system. How this could work is shown below for the manor of Elton. Through the pledging system the lord could be fully confident that his property would not be abused by outsiders:

Elton[26] 1300: Because it is testified in full court by free tenants as well as others, that Richard Turne who held of the lord one cottage with a curtilage in the vill of Elton is a native of the vill of Fodringeye from the land of the abbess of Northampton, and that upon the death of the said Richard a certain Gilbert his son entered the said cottage to hold it of the lord by the services therefrom due and accustomed for an entry fine which he made with the lord, and because it was found and proved by all present in the same court that the said Gilbert is not a naif of the lord but rather the son of a newcomer from the homage of another, the said Gilbert was told by the steward that he should surrender the said cottage and seek an abode for himself where he should see more fit, or that he should find four safe and substantial pledges that he the said Gilbert and all those issuing of his blood will do in all things to the lord abbot and his successors all manner of unfree customs as any cottar or naif does more fully in the same vill. Wherefore the said steward at the request of the above Gilbert received the underwritten pledges that he will fully perform all the aforesaid things, to wit John Trune, Richard Gosselyn, Andrew Gamel and Reynald de Brynton, each of whom is a pledge and surety in all the aforesaid things.

The economic factor in these land contracts was so strong that there was something of the impartiality of a market system. Outsiders and strangers were obviously not villeins of the lord but freemen. On their part, when it came to property, such free folk did not cavil at holding villeinage for services, to become in effect villeins. Even a relative of the lord abbot would enter villein property in the manor of Hemingford Abbots, though the land could not be enfeoffed without the consent of the lord:

HEMMINGFORD ABBOTS,———[27] 1307: And they say through the jurors that a certain William Gapup in the time of King Henry [III] held of the lord a messuage and two virgates in the above vill without a charter, and for entry fine at the will of the lord abbot that time, and for the above land he was at law with all of the above vill just like any others who hold servile land in that vill. And they say that the said William begot of his wife Lyn a certain daughter Agnes who is still living, [and] who married a certain Thomas of Acolt brother of the lord William of Acolt, abbot. From her Thomas begot Thomas Onpron and his sister Agnes who are still living, while the said Thomas of Acolt died. William Gapup died, and after his death his daughter

Agnes fined to hold that land at the will of lord William of Godmanchester, abbot. Afterwards a certain Simon Byle Whyt, naif of the lord, came and fined for two marks of silver to enter that land by marriage to the above Agnes, so that he should hold that land by such services as others who hold by service in that vill. And they say that the said Simon and Agnes then enfeoffed by a charter to one-half of that messuage and land Thomas Onpron, which charter the same Thomas shows and it is identified. And they say that afterwards the said Thomas enfeoffed to a certain part of the above messuage the said Agnes his sister, by a charter that the said Agnes shows. And they are told that it was at the grace of the lord that the above lands were held at the will of the lord, and they hand over their charters <   > in open court <   >. And therefore it is directed that all the above land be taken into the lord's hands both that land as well as the part held by Simon and Agnes because they enfeoffed by charter so as to disinherit the lord to [the advantage of] Thomas with servile land to which the same Thomas was by them enfeoffed, etc.

The great concern expressed in entries such as this for the maintenance of the customary status of their lands and tenants logically followed the open-door market policy. Once the lord found that he could not be isolationist in choice of tenants, he was forced upon a regional tenant market and had to articulate his control more clearly.

It is questionable whether a vast estate complex such as that of Ramsey Abbey ever was an economy closed by the jurisdiction of the lord. The farming practice of earlier centuries exposed such estates to the feudal competition for lands. Administrative demands often forced compromise arrangements that took lands totally or partially out of the customary system according to twelfth- and thirteenth-century extents. But the attraction of customary holdings on these estates cannot be readily traced in these earlier records.

Only with the availability of court rolls do we begin to acquire direct information on this topic. Our most conclusive evidence for the identification of newcomers with capital requirements comes when their wealth is indicated by lay-subsidy rolls. But from court rolls we know William Baret came from outside because in 1294 he was charged as an *extraneus* with having married Elina, the daughter of Agnes Barun, without licence, and Agnes was charged with receiving him while he was not at tithing. Agnes, apparently a widow, had £4.5s.2d. in the lay-subsidy assessment of 1290. Customary tenants were as sensitive as any group in society to the status bestowed by wealth and were not likely to marry beneath their "class." William Baret, not noted of course in 1290, had 28s.8d.q. in taxable goods by

1295. His stay at Wistow was brief, since he murdered Agnes in 1299 and fled.

Records are too sparse to be able to trace the development of more permanent surnames after the time of the mid-century extents. All that can be suggested is that there are indicators that wealthy newcomers were among the newly fixed surnames. Although noted at Warboys and Wistow, there were no members of the Frere family at Upwood according to the 1251 extent. However, by 1290 a Thomas Frere was found to have £4.15s.10d. in assessable goods at Upwood. In similar fashion, there was no family with the surname Warboys at Upwood in 1251, but an Augustine de Warboys had 75s.4d. in taxable goods there in 1290. There was no Bigge family in the mid-thirteenth-century extent for Upwood, but by 1290 John Bigge was assessed there for 32s.4d. in taxable goods, and by 1295 two branches were assessed, Thomas (28s.6d.q.) and John (116s.11d). There were no Aylmers, Horsebonders, or Randolfs in any villages of the mid-thirteenth-century extents. By 1290 Wistow had a Thomas Aylmer (£4.8s.2d.ob.), Robert Horsebonder (60s.2d.), and Thomas Randolf (60s.6d.). Profits from occupations may have backed the entry of some outsiders to costly customary tenements. Robert Flemyng, a surname not in the extents, was noted as a tanner at Upwood in 1278. A Robert Flemyng, probably a son of the former (from the pattern of court roll entries), had a substantial 24s.7d.ob. in assessable goods in the lay-subsidy assessment of 1295. The Haring (Hering) family may have been of the same type. Although this family name cannot be found in the extents, a Richard Haring was assessed for £4.18s. assessable goods in 1290.

As we shall see in the following chapter, the concentration of goods under one name depended very much upon the stage in the family cycle at the time of the assessment. The above examples by no means include all wealthy new families. At Wistow, for example, the Haukyn family first appeared in Ramsey estates in 1290, but in this first occurrence it was represented by assessable goods spread through four members of two generations (61s.4d.ob.; 76s.4d.; 11s.; 9s.).

By the time of the lay-subsidy records of 1327 and 1332, assessed wealth seems to have been "normalized" at about 2s., or 6 to 10d. From later records, it is difficult to establish as clearly as in the local lay-subsidy inventories of 1290 and 1295 a good appreciation of the surplus wealth of the villagers. However, well-endowed virgaters and even semi-virgaters provided long-term jury representation in the manor courts. Through jury lists, therefore, we can collect information on wealthy new members of our villages. All the new names noted in the passage following surface over the decade after the famine (1316). Some were co-opted almost immediately for jury duties, but others did not serve until the 1330s:

Wistow – Robert de Cotes, Robert Lacy, John Mowyn, John de Wennington, John Willeson, Alexander Willeson;

Broughton – John Attedam, Ralph Atehile, Thomas ad Crucem, John Bigge, John Gernoun, Simon Nel;

Upwood – John le Carter, John Kyng, William Othewold, John Pappeworth, John Robyn, William Sabyn, Hugh Thatcher, William Wadilond;

Warboys – John Palmer, John le Rede, Godfrey son of Richard, Collesons (from 1340s);

Abbots Ripton – Philip Colle, John Maggeson, Thomas le Neve, Nicholas Ode, John Ode, Thomas Aylmar (1313).

Customary tenants usually did not serve as jurors in consecutive years, with the result that the scattered survival pattern of court rolls could miss many individuals who had done jury service frequently. As we shall see, larger customary tenants also tended to display clearly recognizable patterns of dereliction in work service. Newcomers after 1320 with this pattern were frequent at Upwood: John Elyot, John Hyche (juror once in 1313), John Hobbe, and in the Hirne family; and at Warboys, the families of Dike, Godfrey, Mold, Tymme, Vicory, and Wilkes.

As has already been suggested in note 20, the significance of these new replacements for customary tenants comes from their continuing and thereby cumulative pattern. Economic conditions would not always favour a ready supply of potential new tenants. Nor could demographic variables be anticipated. For such reasons, no doubt, there was no exceptional immigration of wealthier tenants after the Black Death. At Abbots Ripton, for example, only four new jurors appeared after 1350: John Brewster, Robert Carter, Thomas Frere, and John Hickes. At Wistow, court records show Stephen Ategate, John Driver, Nicholas Herron, John Vernoun, and John Wryghte as important tenants appearing for the first time at the end of the 1340s.

Evidence presented in this chapter indicates that by encouraging substantial customary tenants, Ramsey was encouraging villagers with liquid capital who were active in markets. Lay-subsidy payments and entry fines presuppose ready conversion to cash. It has also been suggested that the lord was following the same economic rationale in his relations with these tenants as with the merchants from far and near at the fair of St Ives. Presumably, then, there were economic opportunities on these Ramsey estates that attracted investment in customary land by natives and newcomers. The scope of local market analysis is immense, as may be seen by the splendid study of David Farmer, "Marketing the Produce of the Countryside, 1200–1500."[28] The purview of this study only allows space for brief indications of such potential peasant attractions. We begin by providing a possible general perspective on villagers' market activities.

Although the lord realized he did not have jurisdictional control over regional markets and certainly did not control the capital supply of the region, he was still a major producer through the well-organized demesne economy. How did the sale of his own demesne produce fit into this order of things?

The best evidence on this point is available for Upwood. Only for Upwood do we have a calculation in the local tax assessment for the "manor of the Lord Abbot," giving the value of taxable goods as £82.19s. in 1290. The valuation comes nowhere near the actual value of produce sales recorded in the account rolls for Upwood. Those nearest in time to 1290 – that is, for the years 1297 and 1303 – record respectively sales of around £15 and £16. The earlier accounts – that is, for the mid-thirteenth century – range slightly below these amounts.[29] By contrast, although we do not know what produce tenants sold from their taxable goods, the value of such goods was almost £121. Potentially, therefore, these tenants could play a role in the markets as much as eight times the role of the lord's demesne. The huge taxable assessment of the Upwood demesne does make some sense if the produce sent to the abbey is evaluated. This suggestion gives further credence to the recent trend to identify large estate complexes as consumer rather than producer economies.

A rare peep at the actual herds of some customary tenants, rather than just the numbers considered to be taxable, further sharpens our perception of their capital resources. In 1299 three tenants of Abbots Ripton were fined for not folding sheep with the lord. Andrew Attechirche and Oliver atte Dam were each fined for the improper folding of 25 sheep and John Andrew for 39 sheep. There is no way of ascertaining whether they owned other sheep that were folded with the lord. J.P. Bischoff has calculated in his 1982 *Agricultural History* article "Fleece Weights and Sheep Breeds in Late Thirteenth- and Early Fourteenth-Century England" that average fleeces weighed around 2 pounds per animal; thus 25 sheep would produce about 50 pounds and 39 sheep 78 pounds of wool.[30] In his *Agrarian History of England and Wales* study,[31] David Farmer gives 3s. per stone

(14 pounds) as the average price of wool at this time. Hence the cash value of fleeces from these flocks would be around 10s.6d. for 25 sheep and 15s.8d. for the larger flock of 39 sheep.

More credibility will be given to the central role of major tenants when we see below in chapter 4, section iii, their tendency from the early fourteenth century to take over substantial portions of demesne arable. A brief digression here on the sale of produce from the commons would suggest that major tenants were aggressive on the local markets by at least the last decades of the thirteenth century.

Mid-thirteenth-century account rolls indicate that the lord was engaged in commercial exploitation of the commons, most notably by the selling of turf and pannage. Why this entrepreneurial venture ceased by the time of the account-roll series from the 1290s we do not know. The lord had replaced a quota system by regular annual licensing. But even this licensing had been abandoned by the 1330s if account rolls may be taken as our source of information. When later fourteenth- and fifteenth-century sources finally make more detailed data available, this system may be seen as providing a powerful resource for the tenants. Except for Wistow in the 1390s, the flocks of tenants paying pannage would much exceed the flocks on the lord's demesne at Broughton, Upwood, Warboys, and Wistow.[32]

The aggressive spirit of the customary tenants is well illustrated at Upwood at the turn of the century. A pasture called Assedych may have been recently drained and developed, since there was no mention of this pasture in the mid-thirteenth-century extent. In the court of December 1299 all the customary tenants of the Wistow hamlet of Little Raveley were charged with "not yet having procured a survey of the lord's separate pasture as Assedych," although these customaries had been pasturing there for two years. The court threatens the tenants with a 20s. fine unless they pay for the pasture by their beasts or seek some arrangement with the lord. By October 1301 the customaries are charged with three years' pasturing and the reeve is ordered to levy the 20s. fine. The suit has disappeared by 1307, the year of the next court roll. Nor is there any reference to Assedych in account rolls that might indicate the nature of the settlement.

Whether the lord won this battle we do not know. But the villagers may have won the war. For there was a clear shift in administrative emphasis to by-laws over succeeding decades. That is to say, those who trespassed wrongly would be charged with breaking the by-law establishing the time of entry to pasture or, if they had pastured beyond their quota, with infringing on the rights of fellow villagers. Previously the emphasis had been upon infringing on the rights of the lord. The most telling evidence of this administrative shift comes with evidence for lighter fines.

Selling turf to outsiders was another active part of the local market scene and thereby engaged local commercial personnel as well as major tenants. The scope of involvement in the turfing operation is seen at Upwood in 1307, when 34 individuals, largely from outside the vill, were charged with damage to the marsh by turves to the number of 3,000 (by 2 individuals), 2,000 (10), 1,000 (19), 500 (2), plus one uncertain amount condoned. Furthermore, 27 individuals were listed as also having damaged turf, though no specifics were given. Such commercial activities also attracted non-tenants. Among the eight individuals fined for selling turves to outsiders from the same vill in 1333 were three women, and all eight were associated with local trades rather than customary tenements.

The commercial operation in the marsh at Warboys was centred on the trade in reeds. Again, we do not find the lord engaging directly in this commerce, although it must have been profitable. In a failed lawsuit during the 1240s the free tenants of Fenton and Pidley charged that Ramsey had destroyed reeds they had collected to the value of £60.

Offences for cutting turf wrongly were only significant among the fines for the one year of 1307. The sale of reeds seems to have been acknowledged as a legal right for tenants since, in the court of 1299, the wealthy Ivo de Hirst, who was from Woodhurst, was forbidden further entry to the marsh with the ruling that neither Ivo nor anyone else not having their home (*mansio*) in Warboys could "give sell or carry reeds from the marsh." In 1294 John Ballard of Broughton was distrained for cutting more reeds than he had purchased (*ultra emptionem suum*). Ralph Scut was overseer of the reed operation and in that same year sixteen prominent tenants were fined for buying reeds beyond their quota from Ralph and his associates. No doubt such purchases were for resale to outsiders. The by-law was honoured thereafter except by the occasional individual. Only in 1334 were several main tenants fined for cutting reeds illegally.

This summary overview of the intense competition for commercial exploitation of the commons is presented here to illustrate one of the many elements in the complex of a customary tenement that would have attracted investment from home or abroad. This also introduces a pattern that will become familiar throughout this study as we observe prominent tenants virtually licensed to extend their control over many resources of the village by their capacity to pay the attendant fines.

2 The Disposition of Capital within Customary Tenant Families

It has long been an anthropological axiom that the life of the peasant is best revealed through the family. So, too, for late medieval Huntingdonshire the main access to knowledge of the villagers' management of capital comes to us through various modes of capital management for the benefit of the family. This must not be taken to mean that the families of Huntingdonshire functioned in some fashion as one corporation or one co-operative unit. Nuclear families remained central to family structures. The frankpledge system isolated the individual as an independent and personally responsible adult. The system of primogeniture established the ongoing family as a unit of its own. If at all possible, branch families were encouraged for the other siblings. The independent structure of branch families and the readiness of landless siblings to seek their fortunes abroad underline the lack of evidence for pooling of capital and labour in the common cause of family aggrandizement. That allocation of family resources to be studied in this chapter is, then, the study of a one-generation policy, the launching of new units from their natal stem.

Broad patterns of family-wealth settlement can be seen in the lists of the lay-subsidy rolls. The method of recording such tax assessments is of special assistance. For these taxes as for other collections such as rents and frankpledge fines, assessors simply moved along the streets from house to house. In consequence, for well-established families these records often show individuals with the same surname listed next to one another but with vastly different surplus valuations.

In such instances we are dealing with individuals likely living on the same messuage. And in this fashion we can identify sons or daughters who have been given some resources, some surplus, to start them on their way towards independence. That is to say, the chronology of these individuals with smaller surpluses can be clearly seen in records as pointing to a new generation.

The detailed local record of 1290 for Wistow can be used to illustrate this type of listing. Thomas, son of Simon Palmer, is listed right after Simon. While the latter had nearly £5 of taxable goods, his son Thomas had less than £1 (one two-year-old foal, five quarters of drage, four sheep). Thomas Palmer is noted in tax records as late as 1327. Robert Haukyn, with only 11s. assessment (one cow, one two-year-old mare, one yearling calf, and four sheep), is listed right after Margaret Haukyn, who has goods to the value of nearly £4, and Margaret is but one entry away from Robert with more than £3. The assessed chattels are listed above because of the interesting number of young and potentially productive animals that have been given to children.[1]

Other villages illustrate this same family-wealth settlement in lay-subsidy lists. Next to Thomas atte Snap, with £4 assessable chattels in Upwood, were John atte Snap with 23s.10d., Richard atte Snap with 17s., and Roger atte Snap with 9s.10d. The Prepositus family had impressive wealth. Simon, son of Nicholas Prepositus, was assessed at nearly £6. Seven entries away was William, son of Nicholas Prepositus, with an assessment of £12.8s.6d., and next to him John, son of Nicholas Prepositus, with an assessment of only 7s. (two quarters of barley and one sheep). In the hamlet Great Raveley of the same village, William son of Gode had £4.7s.4d. in assessable chattels. Listed separately from William, and likely therefore on his own tenement, was Godfrey Godesone with an assessment of 23s.3d.

There is another tell-tale pattern revealed by the method of recording various rents and taxes. This is the entry at the end of the roll of names of those with few assessable chattels who have been missed by the main inventory. Clearly some of these were young people who very likely had only recently been given some chattels by their families. At Wistow in 1290, for example, John, son of Adam Prepositus, was assessed at more than £4. Near the end of the roll came John, son of John Prepositus, who is listed simply as having 20s. in "chattels," and Agnes, daughter of John Prepositus, with 12s.6d. (three quarters of grout and one quarter of malt). It is interesting that Matilda, widow of John Prepositus, would seem to have "retired" to Great Raveley, since she is listed near the end of the Great Raveley roll as having assessable goods to the value of 9s.4d.ob. Apparently the maintenance arrangements for this widow of a former reeve allowed for some surplus above and beyond her living expenses.

Lay-subsidy rolls also show shifts occurring at other stages in the family cycle. Again at Wistow, for example, Robert Attebrok is listed with more than £7 of taxable wealth in 1290. By 1295 he would appear to have passed some of his wealth on to Christine Attebrok, who is listed next to him with 27s.11d.ob.q., while the value of Robert's chattels has fallen to 37s.7d. A parallel pattern may be found for the Haukyn family. William, whom we have met above with more than 60s. in taxable wealth, has less than 30s. by 1295, while listed next to him in the latter year is Robert, with 43s.4d., a fourfold increase since 1290. Further evidence will show that the transmission of capital from one stage of the cycle to another does not always coincide with extant tax records. Scholars must be careful not to argue for the decline in wealth of a family from the negative evidence of one roll.

The 1327 and 1332 tax records for Wistow pose some problems because of the inclusion of Wistow with Upwood. So it is not possible to discern succession patterns between Andrew and William Outy (1327), John and Alice Martyn (1332), and Mariota and John Catelyne (1332). Although these three family name-sets were listed next to one another, their assessments were relatively equal and may have represented dual family branches. At Upwood there is plenty of evidence for family branches not listed next to one another: Prepositus (all years), Wenyngton (all years), Bedel (1295), Aspelon (1327), Warin (1327), Clervaux (1332). Prepositus (or Reve) had become family names by 1300, although one cannot exclude the possibility that one of these entries may have indicated an officer for that year. Again, extant tax records do not always coincide with intra-family wealth-conveyance patterns. In 1290 Thomas Frere of Upwood had the substantial taxable surplus of £4.15s.10d. His assessment was less than £2 in 1295. In 1327 a William Frere appeared near the end of the roll with almost the minimum (10s.10d.) in assessment. Yet by 1332 William had clearly inherited, since his assessment had now risen to 45s., while later in the roll another Frere with the traditional family name of Thomas, perhaps a younger brother of William, had made the list for the first time with the substantial assessment of 35s.

No local detailed inventories are extant for Warboys, but the village was so populous that several transition arrangements for family property can be seen between the 1327 and 1332 tax records. The Gerold family had four names in 1327, one at the beginning of the roll, two together half-way through, and a Simon beginning at the end. By 1332 Simon was more fully established. Roger Raven also moved from the end of the roll to an earlier position as one of those with higher taxes. Some other examples could be the following. Emma and Godfrey Wodekoc, with separate substantial wealth, are listed next to one another in 1327, with a Richard Wodekoc close by only having the minimum taxable wealth. By 1332 Emma has been replaced by a William, who is likely of the next generation and has only one-half of Emma's taxable wealth. In the meantime, Richard too has increased his taxable wealth. The large Berenger family had four branches, with two members next to one another, for both years.

The capital base for taxes paid by our villagers in 1327 and 1332 does not show anything like the range and variety to be found in the lay-subsidy rolls of the 1290s. One suspects that uniformity was being introduced to conform to properties of given sizes. That is to say, the practice that would lead to the compromise of a fixed quota system by 1334 was already moving into place.[2] In any case, in this instance as will be seen with the *capitagium*, administrative control by villagers meant the loss of more information about their families in our records.

Secondary[3] (less wealthy in lay-subsidy lists) branches were very often more totally committed to the commercial enterprise of brewing. Since brewing depended upon farm produce, this might explain the proximity of family branches. However, in total contradiction to multiple-family settlements would be petty service operations. The independent location of Faber shops is particularly obvious in lay-subsidy lists of villagers. At Wistow, for example, in 1290 a Robert Faber with more than £7 in taxable wealth, and Godfrey Faber, with £3.12s.8d. in taxable wealth, were listed at some distance from one another. In 1295 there were listed at some distance apart, very likely to indicate shops on three different streets, Robert Faber, Robert son of Thomas Faber, and Godfrey Faber, each with chattels worth around 30s.

The very fact that sons or daughters of a new generation are listed so early in their careers in lay-subsidy rolls raises an interesting question. Given the terms of reference of these assessments, does this mean that the young member already has enough independent wealth for his or her livelihood so that a surplus can be generated? Or does it mean that the assessors considered adequate livelihood as having home and maintenance with another so that chattels given to the young could therefore be taxed as surplus? The question is not without contemporary analogy as tax experts seek to shift residential taxes upon all earning members of a "family" residence!

While the question cannot be answered from Huntingdonshire records, well-established families certainly encouraged the provision of lands for their children as soon as possible. This meant that lands had to be purchased. For example, in the previous chapter we saw how William Outy of Wistow only entered the property "once his father's" in 1335–36, although in so far as taxable subsidy was concerned, William was as substantial a tenant as his father Andrew in 1327. In the same village a Thomas Arnold, who would appear to be new to Wistow in the late thirteenth century, owned nearly £4 of assessable chattels in 1290. Thomas might have been encouraged to become a tenant because his mother was from Wistow. Yet it was only in 1309–10 that Thomas entered one-half virgate that "once belonged to his mother Dionysia" for the entry fine of 26s.8d. The same arrangement may be seen taking place for the Noble family when, over 1318–19, Godfrey succeeded to the virgate of Richard le Noble and five years later John le Noble entered a mondaymancroft. John, son of John Bronning, entering a one-quarter unit of land (1325–26), William Smart entering a smallholding once his father's (1329–30), and William, son of Albyn Semar, entering a messuage once his father's (1306–07) are other examples of initial support for secondary sons at Warboys.

Wealthier families could afford to pay the largest entry fines and still establish more than one branch. For example, at Warboys the old family of Thurberne had a father, Ralph, holding the traditional family virgate by the 1290s, and a son, William, holding a one-quarter unit of land. In 1303 William succeeded to the family virgate, and his brother Robert paid a 10s. entry fine for the quarter once held by William. Other family members were not always available. In 1316 John Lanerok gave up one-half virgate that was entered by Thomas Palmer for 26s.8d. John Lanerok then entered the more valuable family one-half virgate (formerly held by his father) for a fine of 40s.

By far the greater number of substantial villagers did not have the capital and labour to establish two well-endowed branches simultaneously. More often the villager took advantage of the scattered smallholdings to add to the home properties by lease or purchase of an available rod or two. Custom allowed short-term renewable land leases without recourse to the courts. Villagers left no record of these dealings, nor did they enter the routine detail of account and court rolls. What may be evidence for this practice is revealed by the complete "still shot" to be found in the mid-thirteenth-century extents. At Abbots Ripton, for example, twenty-one units were attached to regular larger units: nine of 2 rods, four of 3 rods, a ½-rod, three of 1 rod, one 1½ rod, a 1-acre unit, a 2-acre unit, and a 2½-acre unit. At Upwood, twenty-eight small pieces of land were listed with major tenants in the 1251 extent.

By another accident of record-keeping – that is, the more detailed land entries to be found for King's Ripton because it had been an ancient demesne[4] – we obtain a more complete record for this type of tenure. King's Ripton was administered with Broughton throughout much of our period, and main Broughton tenants invested liberally in the former village. Among customary tenants at Broughton were the following with the size of their King's Ripton holdings in brackets: Thomas Aspelon (1 rod + 1 rod), John Aspelon (1 rod), John Balde (1 acre), Thomas Attebrigge (1 acre), William Attebrigge (1 rod and 3 rods), Henry, son of John (1 house and ½ acre), Thomas ad Portam (1 rod), Ralph Attehill (1½ acres), Andrew Outy (1 rod of meadow). Other villages had less representation in the King's Ripton land market, such as William Smart of Warboys, with a cottage and 1 acre. This is just a minimum list and could be lengthened by including land pleas and freeholders with customary land.

It may have been common practice among more substantial villagers everywhere to allocate these small units of land as support for sons and daughters who were not main heirs.[5] Godmanchester records provide excellent detail for this phenomenon in a royal manor of Huntingdonshire.[6] There is no reason to expect matters to have been different among Ramsey villages. The simple fact is that we have no evidence, since villagers would not go through the courts and pay fines in consequence when there was no need. As we shall see below, manorial records acknowledge that non-inheriting siblings have acquired property when it is always noted that those withdrawing illegally from the manors brought chattels with them. Assuming that some at least of these chattels were animals, as has been indicated above from lay-subsidy rolls, we are still unable to determine whether the parent leased small units of land for the maintenance of animals given to children.

When the home village did not provide adequate opportunities for a member of a family, he or she would go beyond the village to seek his or her fortune elsewhere. As far as our sources reveal information, for daughters this usually meant marriage abroad. Evidence for this shall be treated later in this chapter. But for both sons and daughters from substantial families there was no logical break with the policy we have seen for children remaining in the home village. Their homes would offer resources to start their careers either as dowry or in other forms of moveable wealth. Furthermore, in that age of unpredictable lifespans the homestead might offer some future financial prospects with the death of older members of the family. In consequence, members of these families would tend to leave their home villages only after arranging to retain their legal status within the customary-tenant system. This whole process has been much misunderstood[7] because of the traditional literary image of villeins fleeing from the lord's jurisdiction. So we must digress in order to explain the proper functioning of this movement from home manors or villages.

The fundamental control system over the mobility of people in the villages of medieval England was a part of the national government organization called the tithing system. By law, boys coming of age (variously designated as fourteen, fifteen, or sixteen years) must be in tithing. The tithing was a group, nominally ten, as the term suggests, but usually more, presided over by a headman or chief pledge. The operative principle of the organization was pledging, that is, being mutually responsible for maintaining law and order. At the same time, this principle operated much more widely than the tithing system. Entry to a manorial village of Ramsey Abbey was in the first instance entry to a community by finding pledges. Prospective customary tenants entered this way, as has been noted in chapter 1. In this respect they did not differ from those who entered (for a fine) the liberties of the borough of Huntingdon[8] or the royal manor of Godmanchester[9] and obtained pledges. Just as freeholders entering these towns did not have to be in tithing since they were bound by the customs of the liberty, so anyone entering customary land in these Ramsey villages was not required to be in tithing since he would be bound by the customs of the manor.

Although in origin the tithing system may have envisaged a rather static society, when combined with the wider practice of pledging, the system was adaptable and familiar to a mobile society. An example will demonstrate how this worked for a tradesman without property in Upwood. In the February 1307 court of Upwood it was noted that William le Combere was in the village but not in tithing. William apparently claimed that he was in a tithing at Huntingdon, so he was not fined. A prominent customary tenant, John Bigge, pledged that William would produce some warranty that he was in tithing at Huntingdon. No mention was made of William le Combere in the court of late 1307. However, by the court of November 1308 John Bigge is fined sixpence because William le Combere never produced warranty for being in tithing elsewhere. By now John Bigge had had enough of his charge, and the court ordered that William be distrained to be in tithing at Upwood before the next court, when the tithings would be reviewed (the so-called view of frankpledge). A parallel case was reported at Upwood in 1299, when John Taesens, *cissor*, was pledged to be in a tithing at Somersham.[10]

Although unusual in the amount of detail, the case of Combere represents dozens of references to outsiders having been "received" illegally – that is, without someone pledging for the newcomer. In most instances these newcomers were very likely casual labour, since their names do not reappear in the context of land or occupation. The point to be stressed is that there was an interim stage before an outsider need be received in a tithing. This parallels the proceeding whereby landless sons were ordered to be in tithing by the next view of the frankpledge. This interim stage of less formal commitment to a village would be of convenience for many tradespeople and of course for tenants who wished to recruit labour from abroad.

The most regular obligation of chief pledges was to enrol sons of villagers as these came of age. There is plenty of evidence throughout the court rolls to verify the wisdom of the system. Time and again boys who would later become local leaders as jurors and reeves first come into the light of history for frequently breaking laws, either by trespass, quarrelling, or some other disregard for neighbours. More adult people who violated the rights of neighbours and their neighbours' property could be assessed financial penalties and damages. But the delinquent early teenager would not be likely to have property.

In the mid-thirteenth-century extents tenants and their sons over twelve years of age paid an annual tax, called variously *in capita* or the English equivalent, "hedsilver." The amount of this payment varied from a half-penny per person at Broughton and Warboys to a penny at Abbots Ripton and Wistow and one and one-half pence at Upwood. By the time of the court rolls, emphasis had shifted to children as landless, under the rather exotic name of *anileppimanni*.

Perhaps paucity of evidence has discouraged study of these landless individuals.[11] Studies now under way for some estates of Glastonbury Abbey[12] make the picture incontestably clear for one estate complex. The court rolls of the Deverill manors list those in tithing as in residence, usually with mother and father. When an individual from the tithing acquires property, an action that can be verified from full lists of conveyances, his name is removed from the tithing list. This may well be the same organization that developed on the manors of Ramsey Abbey. Without rent rolls, court rolls for villages of Ramsey supply little evidence for such conveyances, since villagers did not have to be coaxed to take up land. In the rare instance of Abbots Ripton in 1292, three men were notified that they should take up lands, and again in 1306 it is noted that John, the son of Simon le Gothyrde, is coming of age to take up land. On these occasions the court employed the denomination *anileppimanus*.

The court is usually more concerned to secure identification of those coming of age by stressing family relationships of these possible future tenants. Among those listed not in tithing at Upwood in 1294, sons with patronymic identification, such as Robert and Henry, sons of Nicholas, and William, Nicholas, and John, sons of Philip, are predominant. Among the eleven not in the tithing of John de Higney for Warboys in 1301 were Ralph, William, and Stephen, sons of William de London, Hugh, son of Richard Catoun, Maurice, son of Robert, William, son of John Berenger, and John, son of Alexander Tortorin.

F.W. Maitland stresses that the grants of privileged jurisdiction over such matters as the frankpledge system were very much a grant of profits.[13] The actions of the lords of Ramsey with respect to the frankpledge system certainly support Maitland's observation. Some-time before the extant court rolls, Ramsey had absolved itself of the tedious task of counting new boys coming of age by an agreement with the villagers. For the payment of a fixed sum every year the villagers would themselves collect the tithing penny or head tax from everyone in tithing. Henceforth, each village paid a fixed tax called the *capitagium*:[14] Abbots Ripton (13s.4d.), Broughton (6s.8d.), Upwood (6s.8d.), Warboys (13s.4d.), and Wistow (6s.8d.).

The rounded mark and half-mark figures underline the neat administrative convenience of these figures. But they must have represented some reality at the time of the arrangement. Assuming the mid-thirteenth-century tax quotas for these manors remained the same throughout the century, the *capitagium* payments were fixed to indicate 160 (71) individuals at Abbots Ripton, 80 (44) at Wistow, 55 (27) at Upwood, 80 (50) at Broughton, and 160 (43) at Warboys (the figures in parentheses indicate the number of tenants to be found for each of these manors in the previous generation – that is, the mid-thirteenth-century extents). By this calculation, total quotas for what was to be the permanent head tax varied widely, from less than double at Broughton to roughly twice the number of tenants at Abbots Ripton and Wistow, to three times at Upwood and four times at Warboys. However, if one assumes that each person in frank-pledge for all of these manors paid the same tax of one penny, totals become: Abbots Ripton 160 (71), Broughton 80 (50), Upwood 80 (27), Wistow 80 (44) and Warboys 160 (43). One would not expect family sizes to vary so greatly from one contiguous village to the next, so these data give more credibility to the suggestion that landless indi-viduals alone were paying the head tax from the late thirteenth century. Furthermore, the large number of these at Warboys may not seem extravagant when, as we shall see below, there were 33 (licensed and non-licensed) away from this manor in 1294, 17 in 1306, and 25 in 1313.

The villagers must have been content with running their own affairs by the *capitagium* agreement, just as they would themselves collect lay-subsidy taxes for the Crown after 1334. But by the 1290s at least a serious flaw had appeared. All those in tithings were expected to be present at the annual view of frankpledge, but for two of our five villages the chief pledges were not able to produce all those in their tithing. For this failure, chief pledges were fined. In turn, chief pledges rebelled against the system.

Evidence from the five villages suggests that the thirteenth-century practice may have been to have chief pledges also perform as jurors.[15] The Upwood court roll of 1294 opens with entries to the effect that six men called to be jurors did not respond. An explanation for this refusal appears later in the court record. The four of these men who were from the Le Moigne fee had large numbers (13, 9, 10, 8) in tithing who would not come to the view of frankpledge. The chief pledges were fined accordingly, 6s.8d., 3s.6d., an undisclosed amount, and 2s. Later in the record it is noted that John Curteys, one of the other six chief pledges referred to above and who represented a small submanor with one tithing, had four men not in tithing. Of the sixth man who refused to be a juror and who represented another small submanor with only one tithing there is no further mention in the court record.

Over the following year matters continued to deteriorate. The four men of the Le Moigne fee or submanor again refused to be jurors. The court of 1295 further records with respect to these four that Walter, son of Adam Reeve, and his tithing, and Augustine de War-boys and his tithing all refused to come to court. Each group was fined a substantial 3s.4d. for contempt. This year brought matters to a climax, and an agreement was reached between Ramsey and Le Moigne sometime during 1296.

The agreement, which came into effect in the November court of 1297, was entered in the 1297 court record. By this agreement Lord William Le Moigne assumed responsibility for his men being in tithing. In return Le Moigne paid annually thereafter 5s. at the annual frankpledge court session.[16] It took some time for administrative wrinkles to be worked out. Lists of those not in tithing in the Le Moigne manor (as well as the two small one-tithing manors of Clervaux and Deen) were entered in Upwood courts until 1302, with indications that the fines should go to Le Moigne. The fact that there were 29 not in tithing in these three small non-Ramsey manors in 1297, 27 in 1299, and 15 in 1302 shows that the agreement was not an attractive proposition for Le Moigne. Nor was there an attractive financial reward. The 1297 record of this agreement specifies that fines should be reasonable, and for 13 men not in tithing in 1297 Le Moigne is recorded as receiving only 18d. in fines. Le Moigne apparently recognized that in this populous era those customary tenants who served as chief pledges were less and less willing to carry the legal burden of the landless.

Very likely the chief pledges at Upwood who could not account for members in their tithings were unable to do so for the simple reason that many or all of these were no longer in the village. For all manors it was the responsibility of the chief pledge to keep track of those in tithing who had wandered beyond the manor. But why do so when villagers managed these matters themselves under the *capitagium* system? So court rolls rarely mentioned the unlicensed, beyond the one exception of Warboys, where large numbers were listed beyond the manor without licence during and after the 1290s.[17] In the following lists the second column indicates the number licensed to be abroad, and the third column has the number of unlicensed individuals who have left.

| | VILLAGERS WHO HAVE LEFT | | | VILLAGERS WHO HAVE LEFT | |
	With licence	Without licence		With licence	Without licence
WARBOYS			WISTOW		
1290	1	2	1278	–	1
1292	3	4	1279	–	1
1294 (2)	10	23	1291	–	1
1299	7	12	1294	1	–
1301	–	7	1294	–	2
1301	7	–	1297	–	1
1306	1	–	1299	1	–
1306	10	7	1301	–	1
1306	4	1	1307	1	3
1313	22	3	1313	2	1
1316	2	2	1316	–	1
1320	1	1	1318	1	1
1322	2	2	1326	3	1
1325	1	1	1333	3	–
1326	8	1	1333	2	–
1331	9	2	1339	4	1
1333	–	1			
1333	8	–	ABBOTS RIPTON		
1334	11	–	1274	1	–
1339	7	1	1295	–	2
1353	1	1	1296	–	4
1371	2	–	1299	–	3
1372	1	–	1301	–	2
1390	1	–	1318	–	–

	VILLAGERS WHO HAVE LEFT			VILLAGERS WHO HAVE LEFT	
	With licence	*Without licence*		*With licence*	*Without licence*
ABBOTS RIPTON *(cont.)*			**UPWOOD**		
1321	–	–	1279	–	2
1332	3	–	1295	–	4
1340	8	–	1297	2	4
1343	9	–	1299	1	3
1356	5	–	1302	1	1
			1307	3	1
BROUGHTON			1308	4	–
1288	–	1	1311	–	2
1294	1	2	1313	4	–
1294	–	4	1318	1	1
1297	–	3	1320	–	1
1299	–	–	1328	–	2
1306	2	–	1332	3	–
1316	–	2	1333	3	–
1318	–	2	1334	4	–
1329	2	–	1339	5	–
1331	1	–	1340	7	–
1333	2	–	1353	2	3
1337	3	1	1390	1	–
1339	3	–	1391	1	–
1340	7	–			
1390	1	–			

Significantly, it is at Warboys that the first detailed statement can be found of how the chief pledges were relieved of their burden of reporting at the view of frankpledge. No doubt many of the steps in this evolution escape the historian. One can only perceive that in the first extant court roll for Warboys (1290) there is a picture of confusion, since twelve men are listed as chief pledges and jurors and then a further twelve men are listed as (having refused?) being chief pledges. In the next extant roll (1292) the landless and their chief pledge are relieved of their burden of appearing at the view of frankpledge by the neat expedient of having payment of the tithing penny assumed to cover the responsibility of being in tithing. That is to say, at Warboys the traditional *capitagium* payment of 13s.4d. was given an extended meaning. The 1292 entry states that the *capitagium* is given to the lord lest all the landless in tithing should have to appear (*De capitagio dant domino ne omnes anelepimanni existenti in decenna non venirent xiiis. iiiid. domino*). This rather elliptical clause is covered thereafter at Warboys and in our other villages[18] by the abbreviated form: *Dat capitagio ne vocentur.*

References to chief pledges are rarely to be found in court rolls from this time. Only at Warboys do we find a problem from time to time with the de Higney family, who do not appear to have been customary tenants of Ramsey. In 1301 a John de Higney did not have eleven in his tithing, and in 1326 a Hugh de Higney did not have three in his tithing. It cannot be determined whether difficulties with the de Higney family explain the large numbers of unlicensed individuals remaining abroad from Warboys. In any case, the two references to de Higneys as chief pledges underline how completely the new system had succeeded.

As would be the case again one hundred years later, this ennui of manorial records encouraged for a time the continued recording of meaningless entries. The two courts following 1292 give long lists of those beyond the manor without licence, adding rather lamely that they should be seized should they reappear. But at Warboys as elsewhere, these entries virtually cease from this time. The lord was no longer interested in those who had nothing to add to the "bottom line" of the court roll. Meanwhile, to the chagrin of the historian, the chief pledges would keep their business to themselves.

Chief pledges were in all cases customary tenants, so we can return now from the digression with the knowledge that the customary tenants had for decades been collecting the head tax by their own methods and had subsumed responsibility for the tithing system under the same mechanism. Scores of individuals leaving Warboys and other manors, and no doubt the scores who entered these manors, were not villeins. They were the landless mobile population who by sheer numbers seem to have broken the lord's direct interest in the personnel of the tithing system. This shifting of obligations will have its later parallel in the various "parish" systems of support for the poor. Customary tenants had the power simply to evict landless immigrants who would not keep the rules by staying in tithing and employed this power to evict even those with some *pied-à-terre* in the village.[19]

In addition to the landless just described, the lords of Ramsey had villeins who left their manors with or without licence. These were sons and daughters of customary tenants; as we have noted earlier in this chapter, they had received some start in life in some form of wealth given by the customary tenant parent. Hence the legal charge was that they had left with the lord's chattels,[20] since the lord claimed ultimate ownership of customary land and related wealth. Not many children of main customary tenants left without licence. The cause was not the coercive power of the lord to pursue his fleeing villeins:

despite the existence of this power in common-law theory,[21] the lord did not have the power to pursue anyone beyond the manor, and the sheriff would not assist.[22] Nor did the lord have the opportunity to coerce the customary-tenant parent, since the son had already acquired his independent responsible role in tithing.

There may have been an attempt at Upwood in the 1320s to employ the lord's administration to control such unlicensed movements. For example, over 1328–29 the reeve and Richard Holy, who was likely the beadle, were charged with failure to arrest seven people off the lord's demesne. But there is no evidence of success by this approach, even with the one man who was in neighbouring Ramsey. In consequence, the names of the unlicensed wanderers were simply dropped from succeeding court rolls. Generally, the order "to arrest should he return" remained longer on the record of the culprits whose whereabouts were known. But such orders were no more effective. All other things being equal, the lord had simply to write off the movement of these villeins and their chattels out of his jurisdiction. For this reason data for villeins abroad with chattels show a decline from the beginning of the fourteenth century comparable to data for those without chattels, and may be grouped together.[23]

Other things were not entirely equal, however, since those with customary status in the manor enjoyed a stronger pledging support system. Much of our evidence for those with chattels who left the lord's demesne without licence comes from an apparently casual or careless use of the pledging system. Bartholomew Sperver (a falconer) of Warboys was typical of many not coming from larger customary tenements. Sperver was licensed to be abroad in 1301 and again in 1306. By 1309 he was not reappearing at the view, as he had agreed, so he was ordered to be put out of tithing and no one was to receive him. The books were cleared that same year by putting four out of another tithing and two more out of Sperver's tithing, all for the same reason. When Bartholomew Sperver returned we do not know. He had returned to pick up more chattels a decade later, for in 1320 an order was given again that he be arrested for staying abroad without licence and taking chattels with him.

More substantial families might have sons leaving with chattels because of the maverick disposition of an individual or because the family as a whole seemed disposed to law-breaking. Fathers of careless or recalcitrant sons sometimes displayed more patience than the tithing system. With sons who wandered about, as with daughters who got pregnant outside of marriage, well-established families sought to impose good family morality. Two examples will be given in illustration of these points.

In the series of extant Warboys court rolls, which begins in 1290, a John Isabel was also juror in 1294 but then disappears from view. A Henry Isabel was one of those younger men who refused when asked to be a chief pledge in 1290. By 1294 Henry, who was likely a son of John, was a juror. Henry Isabel's fortune may have waned, for henceforth he appears only as a pledge. In 1301 he was fined for cursing the twelve jurors in the presence of the steward and in the same year was fined for selling reeds to men of Broughton. By 1313 we are told that Henry's son Richard had left Warboys and married in Holywell, so he should be arrested if he returned. Henry apparently went surety for his son, but in 1316 Henry was fined threepence for the non-appearance of Richard. Again in 1320 Henry was fined for the non-appearance of Richard. The aging man may well have missed his son's assistance, for he was fined twice in 1320 for failure to do carrying and harvest work. Richard was not in Warboys again in 1322, the year his father died. A formal order was recorded that Richard should find another pledge. But he did not, and, following orders for a few years to arrest should he appear, Richard's name gradually disappeared from the village of Warboys. In 1331 an order was issued to seize Agnes Isabel, who had married without licence, apparently outside the vill. The last entry was the fining of Matilda, wife of William Isabel, for brewing infractions in 1347. William Isabel was noted to be a son of Henry when he was cited for debt in 1326. But William then disappeared among the poorer people of the town and is not heard from again. The once proud Isabel family does not make the tax lists of 1327 and 1332 and disappears from Warboys' history.

Our next example is from the Kaunt (Caunt) family, which seem to have appeared in the late thirteenth century and maintained an active presence in Warboys for two generations. The Kaunt family are unusual inasmuch as their property holdings were small, certainly not enough to appear in lay subsidies or land transactions, and yet they sought to retain a status in the town. Apparently they were tradespeople. Lawrence Kaunt first appears in 1290 as pledge for a daughter pregnant outside marriage by a member of another family with a trade name Spenser and with much the same history. In 1292 a Henry Kaunt was fined for having withdrawn from the lord's fee and found a pledge to remain. By 1294 Henry had two pledges (William Kaunt and John Lucas) that he would stay on the lord's fee. Later in the 1294 court roll it is recorded that Henry Kaunt had two people to pledge that he would remain a resident and do customary services from the messuage he held from the lord. Later in the same year Henry signified his presence by trespassing on a neighbour.

By 1299 another recalcitrant Kaunt appears: we are given the unusual detail that a Nicholas Kaunt is useless and disobeys his chief pledge, words that are usually a prelude to eviction. Further detail in the court of that year notes that Nicholas had trespassed in the lord's wood and been cited for an infraction in the court of Warboys. In the October 1301 court Lawrence Kaunt pledged for Nicholas, since the latter had refused to be available for autumn work but rather had stayed in Cambridgeshire all autumn.[24]

Lawrence Kaunt himself was no model of conformity, since in the same year he was fined twice for digging reeds to the damage of others and for selling reeds to the men of Broughton. This pattern continued when in 1306 Nicholas and Lawrence were fined individually for damaging the marsh by digging turf and for selling turves. They pledged one another. Nicholas apparently had his own house by now, since one of his neighbours killed some of his chickens. But by the autumn court Lawrence had to pledge for Nicholas again when the latter was fined for trespassing in the lord's woods. Andrew, who may have been a son of Nicholas, got into the family spirit the same year for taking things from the woodward's house, and Nicholas pledged for the boy. Owing to gaps in the records, we lose sight of the family until January 1313, when Nicholas is fined for adultery with a woman from outside the village (*extranea*). Later in the record he is fined for receiving Matilda, daughter of William Pilche, who had gleaned wrongly. Our last entry for Nicholas occurs in 1316, when he trespassed on his neighbour's fields with his "beasts."

Old Lawrence was in business as a pledge for the last time when Henry Kaunt surfaced again in 1320 because someone had raised the hue and cry on Henry for an unspecified reason. A Juliana Kaunt was fined in 1320 and again in 1321 for giving birth to a child while unmarried. The name of Richard Kaunt appears in 1322 as trespassing in the lord's woods and again in 1333 as wrongly handling reeds. With such increasingly scattered references the name Kaunt disappears from Warboys records. The last mention is of a Nicholas who failed to appear in court to pursue his plea on some unnamed charge. As a counterbalance to the impression that villagers sought to flee from the oppression of the lord, the Kaunt family provide an example of people seeking by fair means or foul to retain a place in the village. At times a chief pledge must have heartily wished the family would leave Warboys, but some member always came forward to pledge.

The normal traditional pattern would be for substantial customary tenants to employ the licensing system for non-inheriting sons. In the first extant court roll of Warboys (1290), Martin and Richard Bonde were pledges for Luke Bonde to be abroad. Martin Bonde was a prosperous villager with several people brewing in his home and exercising the office of ale-taster as well as capital pledge over a number of years. Luke Bonde's departure would be motivated by his personal ambition rather than poverty. Luke was reported to be in Weston in 1294, and he continued to be among those licensed to be away until his death in 1301.

It is difficult to feel confident that the information we have fully indicates the scope of licensing in the late thirteenth and early four-teenth centuries when we do not have extant entry-fine rolls.[25] Some attention has been given above to the parent's purchasing property, even beyond the manor, very likely for non-inheriting children. A great variety of arrangements was possible,[26] some of which are given below. But the nagging problem remains that so many of these arrangements were entered for one year only, with no evidence in subsequent court rolls for their termination or acceptance as a *fait accompli*:

WARBOYS, 1294: And they say that Ralph Fyne has a half virgate in Caldecote and yet to the great damage of the lord's property he lives in Warboys, and in addition he has sold a grange. Therefore all his land is taken into the lord's hands.

WISTOW, 1313: Thomas son of Michael the Palmer came to Ramsey and fined with the lord to stay on free land in Wistow, and to deliver two capons every year at Easter; Michael the Palmere is his pledge. And by the same pledge he promises to come to the view of the frankpledge. And he will begin to deliver the capons at Easter of next year.

UPWOOD, 1308: And they say that John the son of Simon Bannok lives married beyond the lord's fee at Walton where he has brought his chattels. Afterwards this same John comes and fines for the payment of one capon to be delivered to the lord every year at Easter while he lives beyond the fee. His pledge is his father.

BROUGHTON, 1297: Andrew Outy is the pledge of Simon son of Ralph de Hirst of Broughton to take that half virgate that John Cok held on the Green of St Ives, or to satisfy the lord that he may withdraw from his fee.

Whatever the full picture might have been around 1300, it is abun-dantly clear by the second quarter of the fourteenth century that the licensing system had been accepted as normal procedure for those who were not chief heirs and who had opted to leave the home manor. Evidence is largely for more important families. Since these landless sons were already on their own and in tithing, fathers were not necessarily, nor indeed in most instances sought as the pledge for the person leaving. So far as the lord was concerned, this had become another item of revenue. In court rolls, yearly licence payments to be abroad (usually two capons)[27] were neatly entered at the end of the record along with other frankpledge items such as fees for bakers and butchers.

The historian of Broughton[28] has conducted a thorough analysis of this point, so no great elaboration is required here. It was established that 19 (40 per cent) of non-inheriting sons from 47 families were able to acquire an independent status in Broughton. For 17 families (36 per cent) with more than one son only the main heir established an independent household. The remaining 11 families (24 per cent) had one or more sons establish themselves abroad. By contrast, it was rare for lesser families to establish even a small foothold for second sons in their village, and Britton[29] deduces that they left to secure a living. Whether they left or remained, there is no evidence that they had the capital to make it worthwhile to be licensed to be abroad.

The smithy trade offered an outlet for sons of substantial families. The blacksmith seems to have moved about according to references from the late thirteenth and early fourteenth centuries. Licensed to be abroad from Warboys, for example, were Richard, son of Henry Faber, at Ramsey (1292–94), Benedict Faber, at Somersham (1316–39), and Hugh Faber, at Hilton (1325–39). For the second quarter of the century a Benedict, son of Thomas Faber, Stephen Pilgrim, and Robert Alot, each paying eight horseshoes as a licence fee, indicate the continuing prominence of that occupation.

But whether as smiths or not, those from Warboys, as for Broughton, came almost entirely from wealthier families: Alot, Clericus, Harsine, Margrete, Noble, Pilgrim, Seman, Wennington. The numbers of those licensed to be abroad increased rapidly during the 1340s for these five villages. By this time the system was clearly being employed entirely for the convenience of the wealthier customary tenants. Further indicative of the routine accounting procedure noted above, by this time too the courts rarely noted the current place of residence of the licensed émigré.

In chapter 1 we found that maintenance of well-endowed customary tenants was essential to the prosperity of the manorial economy. But could the capital and profits of such holdings be redirected to the benefit of the tenant's family? No villager could expect to exert his family priorities within the manorial organization unless he could employ profits from his holdings for the benefit of his family. Chapter 2 has traced some actions by which the customary tenant expressed his family priorities within the framework of the manorial economy. Main tenants assumed more responsibility through the tithing system for the landless and through the wider pledging system for stabilizing arrangements involving their landless sons who wished to seek their fortunes beyond the manor. In return, tenants were assured of more stable cost structures through fixed payments of the head tax and for the licence to be abroad. Again, the regular petty fee would be the lord's piece of the cake.[30]

These developments in the economic history of estate management do not in themselves signify any changes in attitudes or law with respect to lord and customary-tenant relationships. Nor do they necessarily indicate an improvement in the tenant's economic capacity to look after his family. Greater control of one's destiny is not in itself a guarantee of economic improvement. Prior to some of these changes, the customary tenant could be doing very well for himself according to the local lay-subsidy data summarized at the beginning of this chapter. Mobility was part of this picture. The clerk entered into the court record of Upwood for 1279 the charge that John, son of Adam, had been abroad with his chattels for four years and had become *"valde potens."* His capital pledge, Nicholas the reeve of Raveley, was given the routine order to have him in tithing but was not fined. John, son of Adam, was likely from a wealthy administrative family of the vill.

Over the second quarter of the fourteenth century the increased licensing of sons of customary tenants to be abroad may indicate that customary tenants were finding it increasingly necessary to seek opportunities abroad. These sons had some capital but they were often second sons and did not have enough capital to enter substantial lands in their home villages or abroad, so they do not come under the purview of this volume. It is hoped that a complementary study, bringing into focus the regional movement, will throw some light on this category of Ramsey villagers.

3 Allocation of Customary Labour

It is the purpose of this chapter to demonstrate how labour, the third factor in the classical triumvirate responsible for the wealth of nations, was also adapted to their economic well-being by customary tenants. Again, since we have to depend so heavily upon manorial sources rather than direct evidence from the villagers themselves, the policies of the lord are more immediately available than the policies of customary tenants. But the role of tenant management in influencing the supply and demand for labour emerges clearly throughout our period.

For a proper perspective upon labour policies of customary tenants we must begin with the fact that these tenants were perfectly capable of managing the whole manorial complex. Indeed, at two of Ramsey's estates, Ellington and Hemingford Abbots, customary tenants leased the manor from the lord by the time of the earliest account rolls of these manors in the thirteenth century and throughout the fourteenth. As usual the local people kept their business affairs to themselves, and we do not know any more about their internal management operations than how they actually collected the *capitagium* around 1300 and the lay subsidies from the 1330s. But we do know that these customary tenants themselves allocated labour services required for the continued cultivation of the demesne in these villages.

In none of the manors under study here was the demesne leased to tenants. Nevertheless, the system offered opportunities to competent tenants. Early local lay-subsidy lists indicate that reeves had thrived in this office in the thirteenth century. At Wistow, John, son of Adam Prepositus, had over £4 of surplus in 1290 as well as having one son and one daughter with surplus. At Great Raveley, Philip Prepositus had a surplus of £11.15s.10d. and Henry Prepositus £6.9s.10d. At Upwood the two sons of Nicholas Prepositus, Simon and William, had surpluses of some £6 and £12 respectively. The very fact that these families had assumed the surname Prepositus, changed to le Reve in the early fourteenth century, suggests that the office had become quasi-hereditary for such families. Something of how this role could be assumed can be discerned for Thomas Raven at Warboys from the second decade of the fourteenth century and in the same village for William Pakerel over the 1330s and 1340s.[1] By contrast, as manorial accounting began to encounter difficulties over the second half of the fourteenth century, reeves could not collect the moneys for which they were held accountable at the foot of the account-roll revenue section.[2] The office became correspondingly undesirable and frequently passed from one hand to another almost year by year.[3]

While functioning as officials and in particular as reeves and bea-dles, customary tenants were excused the work service they owed for their virgates or half virgates. Such tenants could profit by apply-ing their extra labour resources to short-term leased properties in the manner described in the previous chapter. Confirmation of this will be found in the complete tenant lists that appear later in the four-teenth century. We find in these lists a consistent picture of officials adding to their holdings during their term of office.[4]

For wealthier tenants there was also the option of a traditional arrangement for paying money rent during the whole year, and often in practice for several years, in lieu of work services. This commuta-tion system, designated *ad censum*, is noted in the mid-thirteenth-century extents,[5] although no properties were noted as *ad censum* in the extant mid-century account rolls. There is every reason to believe that the annual *ad censum* rate was simply the total of all work owed throughout the year evaluated at the seasonal rate. That is to say, when full data become available, in the fourteenth century, the total value of these works is around the most common *ad censum* rate of 15s.

Evidence will show that seasonal commutation rates appear to have varied from manor to manor in the thirteenth century. Greater uniformity was introduced from the early fourteenth century. But we do not know why the virgate *ad censum* rates varied at Upwood and Wistow, where virgate rates were what might be expected from semi-virgates, and in fact such rates were doubled after the Black Death.

No doubt variations are to be explained by the considerable work still expected from these tenements. The rate for cotlands at Wistow was also doubled after the mid-fourteenth century. The relation of the *ad censum* to works owed is actually described for some years at Upwood. In 1313 two cotlands owing two works per week were *ad censum* for 1s.6d.; in the same year three cotlands owing three works were let at 2s. In 1319 three cotlands owing three works were let at 1s.6d. and two cotlands owing four works at 3s. During 1324 one cotland owing two works per week was let at 3s. Clearly some allowances were made after the famine period. The whole picture is suggestive of some bargaining process. Some virgates had some work service, especially to be seen for Warboys after 1348, but by and large, account rolls leave us in ignorance about such details before the Black Death. Certainly the great variations from manor to manor in numbers of properties with commuted services seen in the lists below cannot be explained by *ad censum* data alone.

The two villages of Abbots Ripton and Warboys indicate that villagers simply leased fewer lands *ad censum* during more difficult economic times. At first, tenants of Warboys paid the highest *ad censum* rate (20s.) to be found in any of our manors, but during the second decade of the fourteenth century they responded by not taking any properties *ad censum* at traditional rates. Rather, the *ad censum* properties were severely discounted over several decades, much in the same manner as entry fines. Warboys people found the same *ad censum* arrangement more attractive after 1348. In a new compromise agreement from 1354, the money rent payment was only one-half the amount paid around 1300, while the tenants agreed to pay foddercorn, heusire, and carrying services.[6]

LANDS *AD CENSUM*

ABBOTS RIPTON @ 15s.*

1298	8v
1308	8v
1317	1v
1324	3v
1341	¾v
1364	10v
1369	9½v
1375	9¼v
1384	7¾v

1387	6¼v
1389	7v
1394	6¾v
1395	6½v

BROUGHTON @ 14s.8d.**

1307	4v
1311	4v
1312	4v
1314	3v

* This rate continued for the next century.
** This rate continued throughout the century.

1319 4v

1324 3v

1326 4½v

1342 2v

1344 2v

1346 1¾v

1378 7v

1380 5½v

1386 5¾v

UPWOOD

1297 1v. 6s.8d.*

1303 1v

1306 4v
  1 cot at 1s.6d.

1312 2v
  3 cot at 2s.6d.

1313 2v
  2 cot at 1s.6d.
  3 cot at 2s.

1319 1v
  2 cot at 3s.
  3 cot at 1s.6d.

1324 4½v
  1 cot at 3s.

1343 4v
  2 cot of 2a each at 3s.

1347 2½v
  3 cot of 1a at 18d.

1357 2½v at 16s.
  2v at 15s.
  2½ cot(2a) at 6s.
  3 cot(1a) at 3s.

1371 4v at 13s.4d.
  4 cot(1a) at 3s.

1385 3½v at 13s.4d.
  3 cot(2a) at 6s.8d.

WISTOW

1297 4½v at 6s.8d.**
  2 cot at 1s.2d. ob.
  +?

1307 5v

1311 5¾v
  ½ cot at 12d.

1316 5v
  1½ cot at 3s.

1324 5¼v
  6½ cot at 2s.

1335 5½v
  3 cot at 2s.

[ ] 4v
  4 cot at 2s.

1351 3v at 13s.4d.

1352 5¾v
  ¾ v at 5s.
  8½ cot at 4s.

1368 7¼v
  9 cot at 4s.

1379 6¾v
  6 cot at 4s.

1388 6¾v
  5 cot at 4s.
  1 cot (2a) at 6s.8d.
  1 cot (2a) at 4s.
  1 cot (2a) at 6s.
  1 cot (2a) at 7s.
  1 cot (2a) at 3s.
  4 cot (1a) at 3s.
  1 cot (1a) at 2s.

* All virgates were at 6s.8d. until 1357.
** All virgates were at 6s.8d. until 1351 and thereafter at 13s.4d.

WARBOYS *ad c.* are paid for 3 terms only

1301 6v *ad c.* at 20s.; 6½ crofts for 6s.8d.

1306 6v *ad c.* at 20s.; 6 crofts at 10d. + 2 × ½ crofts at 8d.

1318–19 1½v *ad c.* for 3s.2d.; 5 crofts at 10d. + 2 × ½ crofts at 8d.

1324 2½v *ad c.* for 7s.6d.; 5 crofts at 10d. + 2½ crofts at 8d.

1325   o; 1 croft at 10d. + 2½ crofts at 8d.

1330   ½v of akermanland for 3s.; 2 crofts at 10d. + 2 × ½ crofts at 8d.

1335   ½v of mondaymanland for 3s.; 2 crofts at 10d. + 2 × ½ crofts at 8d.

1336   ½v of mondaymanland for 3s.; 2 crofts at 10d. + 2 × ½ croft at 8d.

1342   ½v *ad c.* at 10s.; 2 × ½ crofts at 8d.

1354   8½v *ad c.* at 10s. for all op. + 2 akermanland *ad c.* at 10s.

1359   6v at 10s. + maltmanland at 5s. + 1 akermanland at 5s. + 2 mondaymanland + 2 akermanland at 12s. + 2 mondaymanland at 5s.

The less wealthy landholders would not have the cash for such hefty transfers. So it is not surprising that when names of tenants begin to become available, one finds lands were held *ad censum* by the wealthier villagers. At the same time, such villagers did not enter *ad censum* agreement in order to free their own holdings from work service. They tended to retain their larger holdings *ad opera* and to employ the *ad censum* arrangements to add to their properties. In extant tenant lists[7] all villages abound with evidence for virgaters *ad opus* also holding one-half or one-quarter virgate *ad censum*. In short, what appears in the *opera* accounts as so many virgates *ad censum* actually means that several wealthier villagers shared one virgate *ad censum* among themselves. Again, at every turn we become aware that the formal arrangements of the accounting system were being adapted to their own purpose by villagers.

In addition to commutation for officials and putting lands *ad censum*, individual units of work could be sold back to the villager at various times of the year according to seasonal rates. This was an old arrangement going back at least to our earliest references in the mid-thirteenth century. According to the extents there was some variation in rates (in pennies) from manor to manor:

MANOR	WINTER	SUMMER	AUTUMN
Warboys[8]	½	1	1½
Abbots Ripton[9]	¾	1	2
Broughton[10]	1	1	2

Revenues from the sale of individual works were entered in account rolls as *opera vendita*. There is no entry under this title in the six extant account rolls for Upwood and Wistow ca 1250. Only when the account-roll series begin in the 1290s does sale of work become a regular item, relatively few in number over the 1290s but increasing considerably after 1300. From the end of the thirteenth century, too, commutation rates became fixed at levels that would remain the same throughout the fourteenth century. By this time there had been reductions in the commutation rates for winter work at Broughton and summer work at Warboys from the mid-thirteenth-century rates given above. Post-autumn rates were also introduced at a level below autumn rates (in pennies):

MANOR	WINTER	SUMMER	AUTUMN	POST-AUTUMN
Abbots Ripton		¾	1	2
Broughton	½	1	2	
Upwood	½	¾	1½	1
Warboys	½	¾		
Wistow	½	¾	1½	1

The economic rationale behind the sale of works is obvious enough. From the point of view of estate management, profits would be sought from the sale of work services not required for operation of the demesne. The fact that there was no anticipated demand for a certain number of *opera* would mean that an *ad censum* agreement could be reached prior to the beginning of the accounting year (Michaelmas). At the same time, the sale of *opera* in varying amounts during the year could be a more *ad hoc* affair, depending upon the many variations in labour demand following upon weather conditions, cyclical changes in preparations for cropping, success of the harvest, and so forth.

What was an obvious rationale for demesne management did not necessarily apply to the purchase of work. To begin with, the sale of smaller clusters of *opera* was no more at the whim of the lord than the yearly *ad censum* arrangement. Work would not readily be purchased by smallholders who had enough labour left over from their own property requirements to do work service for the lord. *Prima facie*, one might expect that *opera* were purchased by the more wealthy tenants, that is, those with money for the purchase and with greater labour-supply requirements. That larger landholders purchased their work service for money does indeed seem to be the case. And significantly, the fact that no references have been found of fines for refusing to purchase *opera* argues to the demand for labour supply by customary tenants as exceeding the supply available by repurchase.

The fortuitous recent discovery of a fragment[11] from the Public Record Office collection of the records for Warboys gives us a unique account of the actual personal disposition of *opera* sales. Attached to the account roll for the year 1298–99 (Michaelmas to Michaelmas) is the following list of thirty names with payments:

Albyn Segeley	2s. 2d.q.
Henry Isabel	2s. 2d.q.
William Pakerel	2s. 1d.
William, son of Richard	2s.½d.
Richard le Noble	2s. 2d.
Robert Smart	2s. 2d.
Simon Margaret	2s. 2d.
William Pearson	13½d.
Godfrey Halyday	13d.
Nicholas, son of Walter	2s. 2d.
Robert Agace	2s. 2d.
Godfrey, son of Cecilia	2s. 2d.
Agnes Rolf	1s.10d.
John Lenot	1s.
Simon Roger	13d.
Dionysius le Botiller	13d.
William Berenger	13d.
Laurence Pikerel	2s. 2d.
William le Longe	13d.
Robert Bronning	13d.
William Harsine	13d.
Albyn Prepositus	1s. 8d.
John Segeley	13d.
Richard, son of Robert	13d.
Richard Pilgrim	13d.
Simon, son of John	8½d.
Robert, son of Richard Harsine	2s. 2d.
John Martyn	nil
Ralph Scut	5d.
Nicholas Plumbe	debet

SUM: 43s.4d. Item 9d. from which the beadle owes 18d.

Payments were clearly grouped about two levels of 2s.2d. (paid by ten) and 13d. (or one-half the previous amount) paid by ten individuals. Two payments (William Pakerel and William, son of Richard) were slightly below the 2s.2d. level. A marginal note (debet 1d.) explains why John Lenot was one penny shy of the 13d. quota, and an addition in the margin may explain why William Person (also called Vicory), newcomer and rapidly accumulating wealth, was above 13d. Agnes Rolf may also have been allowed 1s.8d. since she was a widow at a transitional stage. Ralph Scut was a smallholder but also overseer of turfing. Simon, son of John, is not easily traceable in records. As we have seen in chapter 1, Nicholas Plumbe had died that year, and apparently the beadle's list had not yet been adjusted to this fact. For some reason John Martyn was dropped from the payment list. When we get some notion of all the considerations that went into the system, we can sympathize with the beadle's falling short in his account.

There are plenty of indications that the larger payment was made by virgaters. Albyn Segeley was a virgater whose son took over the virgate in 1307. Richard le Noble was associated with a virgate that his son took over in 1318. The Pakerels, Harsines, Smarts, and Margarets continued to be virgaters for decades to come. No doubt the 13d. figure had become identified with the half virgate, though at this time evidence points only to several (Lenot, Berenger, Bronning, Pilgrim, Richard, son of Roger) in this category.

But why these thirty names chosen from a total number of virgaters and semi-virgaters some three times that number? One factor determining the choice is clear. Even from an incomplete series of account and court rolls, at least twenty of these names can be found as jurors and reeves. In short, sale of *opera* was a preferential treatment that complemented the cancellation of work services for the performance of one office or another. The other factor is less immediately apparent but may have been even more pivotal. When information is available about these individuals, they do not present evidence for a large family-support system. For neighbouring Wistow, M.P. Hogan has found that such smaller family groups were disappearing rapidly from the historical scene.[12] As we saw in chapter 1, some of the names on the list above (Agace, Long) were to disappear from Warboys too. We have noted in the previous chapter that the Isabel and Noble families were trying to keep their sons at home. And we know that Nicholas Plumbe had no heirs. It is well within the logic of a system that cancelled work service when the customary tenant was ill,[13] thereby allowing other labour resources of the tenant to work the tenement, to cancel some labour services owed when the labour resources of the tenants were depleted for other reasons.

The revenue for the account roll of 1298–99 complements the fragment we have been discussing. That is, the account roll indicates that *opera* sold to these individuals for this amount of money were composed of 800 works sold at a halfpenny and 138 works sold at halfpenny farthing. Very likely the total *opera* owed for this year was the same amount before deductions as some thirty years later, when the first extant *opera* account survives for Warboys.[14] In this case the 938 works would be slightly more than 10 per cent of the total owed.

Sale of works at Abbots Ripton, Broughton, Upwood, and Wistow usually fluctuated well below 20 per cent,[15] although for the first extant *opera* accounts the figures were somewhat higher (Broughton 1314: 20 per cent; Upwood 1324: 23 per cent; Abbots Ripton 1324: 17 per cent). This fluctuation above or about 10 per cent may indicate what the manorial organization considered a safe margin for the operation of the demesne. No *opera* accounts survive for Warboys for the first half of the century, and thereafter the sale pattern differed greatly from the other four villages.[16]

For the customary tenant enabled to repurchase his own work services in this manner, the benefit was significant. The 800 winter works and 138 summer works can be calculated as approximately 35 winter and 6 summer works for a virgate. In turn, *opera* owed from a virgate year after year comes to 177 or 178 works.[17] The 41 *opera* repurchased by a tenant would then be slightly more than 22 per cent of his yearly quota. *Opera* sales indicated in the revenues section of account rolls in the late thirteenth century (in 1297 for Upwood, Warboys, Wistow) show sales only during the winter season. This was an obvious convenience for the lord, since winter was the season of low demand. Whether this had been the normal pattern in the thirteenth century cannot be determined, owing to a paucity of evidence. But this was not the situation in the fourteenth century.

From early in the fourteenth century the actual percentage of works sold in the winter does not vary greatly from the percentages sold in other seasons.[18] The preferential-purchase option revealed above from the Warboys fragment would seem to explain the spread of sales throughout the year. If a customary tenant was found with a title to repurchase his labour, such a title would exist throughout the year, since it was an ongoing labour shortage. Decision would then be made again prior to the Michaelmas beginning the year. In short, such arrangements did not cater to *ad hoc* seasonal adjustment most beneficial to the operation of the demesne. In the final analysis the sale of *opera* had the same rationale for the tenant as the *ad censum* and *ad officium* commutations.

A fourth alternative open to customary tenants who required their own *opera* services was simply the refusal of work. Such refusal to work virtually never occurred during the winter and pre-harvest summer periods. In short, tenants were apparently content with the *opera* supply available during these seasons. But during the hard-pressed harvest season it could be otherwise. Since these refusals were not always actions repeated by the same individuals, it cannot be deduced that these were people who had been refused the opportunity to repurchase more work. Rather, there is an *ad hoc* pattern about refusals to work. At the same time there are some interesting general features reflected by this fourth option.

Refusal to work may have been as much an attitude towards work services under certain conditions as a response to a more difficult economic environment. There were significant refusals by freemen in the 1290s. At Broughton, Ralph Norreys refused to work twice in 1290, once in 1291, and once in 1294. Another freeman from the same village, John de Broughton, refused to work twice in 1294, twice in 1297, and later, once in 1307 and once in 1316. Some twenty other customary tenants refused to work, though usually only once, over the 1290s at Broughton. At Upwood, William, son of John de Raveley, totally refused for two years to perform work service by the claim he was a freeman. At Upwood, as in all other villages, refusals are few and scattered when viewed in terms of single customary tenants.

With increasing numbers of refusals as the fourteenth century progressed, this pattern emerges more clearly. That is to say, refusals to work are bunched about certain individuals who are wealthy, sometimes freemen, not regularly involved as jurors, but who may have been prominent long-standing reeves. An example of the latter was William Pakerel, reeve during the 1320s at Warboys, who refused to work three times in 1320, twice in 1322, and once in 1326. Other examples from Warboys of customary tenants rarely or not at all involved as jurors who refused work from time to time (indicated within parentheses) are as follows:

Robert Berenger: 1320 (3), 1325 (1), 1326 (2), 1331 (1), 1333 (1), 1334 (1), 1337 (1), 1339 (1), 1343 (1), 1347 (1)
Simon Dike: 1325 (1), 1331 (2), 1333 (1), 1334 (2), 1337 (1), 1343 (1), 1347 (2)
John Harsine: 1333 (1), 1337 (1), 1339 (1), 1347 (1), 1353 (2)
William Lone: 1343 (2), 1347 (2), 1353 (3)
William Vicory: 1333 (2), 1337 (2), 1339 (4), 1343 (1), 1347 (2)

One exception at Warboys was Robert Smart, who was often a juror, yet this virgater not only bound corn badly with several others in 1326 but was the only one cited for ploughing poorly that year. In 1331 Robert Smart was cited with several others for refusal to thresh, but he was also the only one fined that year for not assisting with ditches. Every village had wealthy tenants following the Warboys pattern. At Broughton, among some twenty individuals cited for work failures in 1308, John Balde is charged for three failures, Ralph Prepositus for two, and Thomas Waleboy for two. Henry, son of John, is charged with five failures to work, among these being the keeping back of one man from both the first and second special autumn boon work service (*precaria*). At Upwood, John King appeared regularly among those failing to perform works over the late 1330s and early 1340s, beginning with the entry of 1334, where he was charged with disturbing (*perturbavit*) others during their work. At Abbots Ripton in 1334 William Thedwar refused to mow or to come to thresh and continued to refuse often over succeeding years.

Another attitude is betrayed by a group refusal to work. For Warboys, where ten of the first fifteen surviving court rolls have no references to failures in work performance and references that do occur are very individual, the post-famine period brought a change. The court roll of January 1320 records the names of twenty-two individuals fined at threepence each for refusing to carry oats from the "new place" (*novum locum*) to Ramsey: Robert, son of Albyn de Caldecote, Henry Isabel, William Pakerel, Robert, son of Simon Lone, Richard, son of Godfrey le Noble, Robert Smart, Robert Margaret, William Persun, Nicholas, son of Walter, Richard Segeley, Simon Faber, Robert Egace, William Rolf, John de Ellsworth, Robert Berenger, Benedict Pakerel, Robert Bronning, William le Nunne, Ralph Fyne, Robert Aleyn, Simon le Noble, Simon Pakerel. The court roll of November 1320 lists the names of twenty individuals fined at threepence for not coming to reap: Henry Isabel, William Pakerel, Robert, son of Simon Lone, Robert Margarete, Godfrey Harsine, William Rolf, Robert Berenger (twice), Benedict Pakerel, Simon le Couhirde, Hawysia Catoun, Thomas Puttock, John Bercarius. Seven of these are repeats. All are listed here to illustrate that they came from the main families, that is, the largest landholders of the village.

Collective refusals to work noted above have not included the few references to those who were not major tenants. At Warboys in 1306, four women (Grace Pakerel, Alice Sculle, Matilda Attewode, and Beatrice Kaye) were fined sixpence each for refusing to work in the autumn. The entry suggests but does not make clear whether this refusal continued over the whole six weeks or some of the autumn season. Among the six men of Warboys fined sixpence each for not threshing properly the sheaves given to them in 1333, three were lesser tenants (John Gosse, Stephen le Smyth, John Schut), while the other three (John Nicholas, John Palmer, Hugh Beneyt) appear with subsidies in the lists of the previous year. Aside from the large group refusals to work at Upwood in 1340 were three lesser tenants who refused to carry peas.

Since we are not privy to the villagers' discussions, it is only indirectly – that is, through the occasional greater detail of entries – that we can see more clearly the calculated competition for labour resources. As has been exemplified above (e.g. Warboys 1337), from time to time it is simply reported that an insufficient number of workers were sent. In other instances (Upwood 1295 and 1297) it is specified that one or two men were not sent. The villager's decision to give priority to his own work requirements comes out more clearly at Broughton in 1311, when three major tenants were charged with distraining two men from attending the autumn special work (*precaria*). Perhaps the men had looked forward to the special meal that the lord was to provide for this extra service. The more domestic side of the tenant's labour control was revealed at Upwood in 1307, when two tenants kept their wives from working. And again at Upwood in 1311, the wealthy Godfrey Godes would not permit his son Thomas to go to work for the lord.

Although we cannot recapture the drama[19] that must often have accompanied refusal to work, the following lists do indicate something of the variety of refusals. Except where bad work is indicated, the following shortened entries do not repeat the usual form "did not come to work, harvests, etc., when called." For economy of space, references to single refusals are only illustrated for Wistow, although other villages had much the same pattern. "Work" signifies unspecified labour-service refusal. Penalties are given in brackets. What a hassle it must have been to assess differing penalties for the same work!

SOME SCHEDULES OF WORK REFUSALS[20]

WARBOYS

1320 22 carrying (at 3d.); 12 harvest (at 3d.)

1322 4 work (1 at 6d., 3 at 3d.); 2 carrying (at 3d.)

1325 6 thresh (4 at 6d., 2 at 3d.)

1326 4 carrying (3 at 6d., 1 at 3d.); 9 bound grain badly (at 3d.)

1331 8 thresh (at 6d.); 6 carrying (at 3d.)

1333 6 thresh badly (at 6d.); 8 thresh (at 6d.); 4 work (1 at 6d., 3 at 3d.); 9 work (at 3d.); 4 late to work (at 2d.)

1334 2 work (at 3d.); 7 carrying (1 at 12d., 6 at 6d.)

1337 15 carrying (at 6d.); 5 insufficient workers (at 6d.)

1339 16 thresh (5 at 6d., 11 at 3d.); 3 reap (2 at 6d., 1 at 3d.); 4 carrying (3 at 6d., 1 at 3d.)

1343 5 work (1 at 6d., 4 at 3d.); 4 work (at 3d.); 2 work (at 3d.)

1347 16 work (at 3d.); 6 carrying (at 6d.); 11 thresh (at 3d.); 5 ploughed badly (at 3d.)

1350 5 work (at 3d.); 2 harvested badly (at 3d.); 3 bound grain badly (at 3d.); 2 work (at 3d.)

1353 10 late to work (at 4d.); 20 work (most at 3d.); 3 work (2 at 6d., 1 at 3d.); 4 late to work (at 3d.); 14 reap (6 at 6d., 7 at 3d., 1 at 2d.)

UPWOOD

1295　4 carrying (2 at 2d., 1 at 6d., 1 condoned)

1297　6 did not send 2 workers (5 at 3d., 1 at 6d.); 3 did not send 1 worker (at 3d.)

1299　11 work (5 at 6d., 5 at 3d., 1 condoned); 2 insufficient workers (at 6d.)

1302　1 kept 2 men from work (at 6d.); and ploughed badly (at 6d.)

1307　2 kept wives from work (at 3d.); 4 ploughed badly (at 6d.); 3 work (at 3d.); 9 late to reap (at 3d.)

1308　2 ploughed badly (at 6d.)

1311　3 bound peas badly (at 6d.); 3 ploughed badly (2 at 6d., 1 at 3d.); 4 harvested badly (at 3d.); 2 insufficient workers at harvest (1 at 3d., 1 at 6d.)

1318　4 fen work (at 3d.); 4 thresh (at 3d.); 5 work (at 3d.)

1320　6 carrying (at 12d.); 9 cut fen (at 3d.); 3 harvest (at 3d.)

1322　0

1325　7 ploughed badly (at 6d.); 3 insufficient workers to thresh (at 3d.); 2 carrying (at 3d.)

1326　0

1329　4 summer work (at 3d.)

1331　2 post-autumn work (at 3d.)

1333　2 carrying (at 3d.); 1 insufficient worker to ditch (at 6d.)

1339　6 harvested badly (at 3d.); 3 late to work (at 3d.); 2 ploughed badly (at 6d.); 5 ditching (at 3d.)

1340　3 harvest work (at 3d.); 5 work (4 at 6d., 1 at 3d.); 9 ploughed badly (at 6d.); 4 insufficient workers (at 3d.); 10 harvested badly (at 3d.); 11?

1344　3 ploughed badly (at 6d.); 2 harvested badly (at 6d.); 3 work (at 3d.)

1347　8 harvest work (at 3d.); 16 hedged badly (3 at 6d., 3 at 2d., 10 at 3d.); 3 reap (at 2d.)

1349　16 work (at 3s.); 29 work (at 3d.)

1350　7 withdrew famuli (at 40d.); 8 work (7 at 3d., 1 at 6d.); 3 work (2 at 6d., 1 at 3d.)

1353　1 carrying (at 6d.); 2 plough work (at 3d.); 2 work (at 2d.); 5 reap (at 2d.); 13 clean weir (at 2d.)

WISTOW

1279　14 harvested badly (7 at 6d., 7 condoned)

1291　0

1292　1 lacking 8 men at boon (3s.); 2 harvested badly (?); 1 2 men short (?)

1294　1 1 man short (at 6d.); 3 ploughed badly (at 6d.)

1297　2 carrying (at 3d.)

1299　0

1301　1 work (?); 1 bad work (at 3d.); 3 boon work (at 12d.)

1307　4 ploughed badly (at 6d.); 1 harvest (at 6d.)

[1308]　10 late for harvesting (at 3d.); 9 harvest (at 6d.); 1 harvested badly (at 3d.); 3 collected grain badly (at 3d.); 2 late for harvest (at 3d.);

2 harvested badly (at 6d.); 1 servants late for harrowing (at 6d.); 1 collected grain badly (6d.); 6 ploughed badly (at 6d.)

1309   0

1313   1 ploughed badly (at 6d.); 1 harvest (6d. for two days); 5 bound grain badly (at 3d.); 14 work (at 3d.); 1½ day only (at 3d.)

1316   4 late reaping (at 3d.); 3 ploughed badly (at 6d.); 4 harrowing (at 3d.); 11 reaping (at 3d.); 1 reaped badly (at 3d.); 3 ploughed badly (at 3d.)

1318   1 late to work (at 3d.); 13 carrying (at 3d.); 3 harvested badly (2 at 6d., 1 at 3d.); 4 ploughed badly (at 3d.); 5 carrying (at 3d.); 2 spread manure badly (at 3d.)

1320   14 winnow (at 3d.); 10 work (at 3d.); 3 gathered grain badly (at 3d.); 5 gathered grain badly (at 3d.); 2 ploughed badly (at 3d.); 10 harrowing (at 3d.)

1322   2 harvest (at 3d.); 1 refused all work (at 40d.)

1325   4 ploughed badly (at 6d.); 2 carrying (at 6d.); 2 ploughed badly (at 6d.)

1326   5 ploughed badly (at 6d.); 9 carry in fen (at 6d.); 2 ploughed badly (at 6d.)

1329   7 carrying (at 3d.); 1 winnow (at 4d.)

1331   3 ploughed badly (?); 6 late to work (?)

1333   3 ploughed badly (at 6d.); 1 ploughed badly (at 6d.); 1 insufficient men (at 3d.)

1334   2 work disturbance (at 6d.); 2 work (at 3d.)

1339   4 gathered grain badly (at 6d.); 9 ploughed badly (at 6d.); 4 insufficient workers (at 6d.)

1344   5 work (at 3d.); 8 work (at 3d.); 11 winnow (at 3d.)

1347   8 late to work (at 3d.); 4 reap (at 3d.); 5 work (1 at 6d., 5 at 3d.)

Fines imposed for failure to perform work services were certainly not large enough to be prohibitive for main tenants. Fines for carrying would cover the cost of draught animals and carts as well as human labour, and tended correspondingly to be higher.[21] However, the large-scale refusal to carry at Warboys only brought a penalty of threepence for each individual, though in the next recorded year the penalty for not carrying was sixpence. The usual fine for non-performance of other works was threepence. When it is recalled that autumn works were commuted at twopence per work, this appears to be a nominal figure, disciplinary but not punitive. When Richard ad Fontem of Wistow refused to do any work in 1322, he was fined forty pence, certainly a sum much less than the total commuted value of services he owed for one virgate! However, as with all such exceptional cases, we are not told whether some special conditions moderated the arrangements.

It is frustrating that the records do not allow us the information to pursue the matter further. Entries merely cite failure to perform such and such a work. But was it for a whole day, part of a day, or for several days? The cryptic Latin entry could as well refer to the whole autumn season as to one day. A court roll for Warboys in 1353 finally gives us some satisfaction. In this court the clerk enters the failures to work in autumn ("default in autumn" without further specification) in the same manner as were traditionally entered defaults in ale brewing. That is, there was a standard fine, and this is multiplied by the number of occurrences (appearing in parentheses below). If this may be taken as the underlying "system," then the threepence fine would seem to have been the normal penalty for refusing one work:

John Hichesson	(3) 9d.	Thomas Semar	(2) 6d.
John Pilgrim	(3) 9d.	William Higeneye	(1) 3d.
Richard Alot	(1) 3d.	Thomas Raven	(1) 3d.
Richard Semar	(2) 6d.	Richard Mold	(4)12d.
Robert Berenger	(3) 9d.	John Flemyng	(3) 9d.
John, son of Godfrey	(1) 3d.	Juliana Wilk	(2) 6d.
John Lenot	(3) 9d.	William Semar	(1) 3d.
John Harsene	(2) 6d.	John Bronnyng	(4) 6d.
William Brid	(3) 9d.	John, son of Godfrey	(4) 6d.
William Love	(3) 9d.	Robert Beronger	(3) 4d.

But the last three entries show a more benign assessment! And did the Black Death influence the arrangements?

From the evidence given above it appears that the lord was not interested in punitive action or aggressive imposition of his authority. What must now be seen as a familiar pattern applies to the policy of fines for dereliction of work. These were main tenants, and their contribution to the manorial economy must not be undermined. Work could be avoided with an expectation of the cost. The system could be administered by a bailiff, reeves, and other officials as part of their operational jurisdiction.

This fourth option open to some customary tenants for the maintenance of their own supply of labour was distinct from the three options discussed above. Unlike those who repurchased their own labour, those who frequently refused services to the lord did not have any special title to consideration. Rather, those refusing in this manner were simply the wealthiest customary tenants in the village, who could afford to pay the price charged for refusal to work. However, those main tenants who were only found refusing work services when it was in the company of others were reflecting a very different reality. Such group refusals were a category of group action, and that properly should be viewed along with those large-scale trespasses that have been discussed elsewhere.[22] More than any other evidence, those group reactions provide an indication of the sensitive mentality lying behind what the tenants considered to be "contractual agreements" with the lords of Ramsey.

In the final analysis, then, our conclusion about the role of labour in the administration of these five estates must be the same as the conclusion concerning capital in chapters 1 and 2. The lords of Ramsey and their advisers considered tenants to be of paramount importance. All sorts of adjustments would be made in order to guarantee the continued servicing of the customary tenement. The demesne could be rented out entirely or in part, and labour of varying skills could be hired for the operation of the demesne. Customary services could be commuted in several ways. But the customary tenement must be kept operable.

Again, we must stress that the manorial administration was only being rational by these administrative arrangements. In view of the great amount of mobility seen in chapter 1, the stability of the vast majority of these wealthy tenants is remarkable. By fixing firm foreseeable limits to the labour demand of the demesne, the lord was not yielding to pressure but wisely guaranteeing a commitment to his manors.

Why we have failed to perceive this problem properly involves another fascinating case-study in historiography that cannot detain us here. The long lists of detailed labour services for land units of various sizes to be found in Ramsey Abbey extents appealed to the sensibilities of a nineteenth-century English-speaking world striving to overcome the horrors of labour conditions in the early Industrial Revolution and exercised by a civil war fought over slavery. Not surprisingly, labour services to the lord became the emotional centrepiece for over one hundred years of historiography. The sentiment became entrenched in the discipline of economic history that burgeoned from the end of the century to such a degree that no adequate attention was given to the more fundamental question: what percentage of his annual labour resources was required of the customary tenant? A full analysis of this question lies beyond the scope of this study. But the direction of the answer is clear. A simple literal calculation[23] indicates that only some 10 per cent of the labour resources of the tenant were owed to demesne services. The collapse of the manorial economy would turn upon the depletion of total labour resources in the village.

PART TWO

Transformation within the Manor

4 Capital Conquers

i CONTINUITIES AND FURTHER
EVOLUTION

The impact of the Black Death and the recurrence of similar epidem-
ics upon manorial estates is a well-rehearsed topic and will not be
reiterated here.[1] Of interest to this study is the fact that the policies
traced over the previous three chapters were not in any way "corrected," much less reversed, following the new series of crises. Rather,
these policies appear to have been accepted as normal adjustment
practices. Perhaps this is not surprising for the short run, especially
by the 1360s, when chronic indebtedness first appears on the account
rolls and manorial administrators were engaged in yearly scrambles
to recover rents owed on the accounts for which they were held
responsible. Rents in kind were commuted for lump-sum payments,
usually at substantial losses of 50 to 75 per cent. Debts were amor-
tized, but usually without significant success. Whether from thinner
sowing or poor cultivation, crop yields dropped sharply.[2] There was
no foolish destruction of the capital base of the tenants' economy. In
fact, these policies of restraint with respect to the tenants would
continue late into the century despite fundamental erosions in the
traditional manorial economy.

Some of the continuation over the first two decades after 1348 can
be briefly indicated. In the three villages of Broughton, Upwood, and
Wistow customary tenants held much the same amount of land for
annual money rents (*ad censum*). Refusal to work at various times

also continued in much the same fashion, as did the range of fines for such refusal. Some traditional adjustment policies were carried even further. Entry fines virtually disappeared at this time, and there is no tangible evidence from either account rolls or court rolls of efforts to control the movements of villeins beyond their home manors.

Despite some major adjustments in the supply and demand for labour on the market, the "convenience" of the practice of sale of work services described in chapter 3 would continue as an independent option. This may be seen in Table 3. The sale price of *opera* does not seem to have changed after 1348.[3]

PERCENTAGE OF AVAILABLE *OPERA* SOLD

ABBOTS RIPTON		BROUGHTON (for two seasons)		UPWOOD		WISTOW		WARBOYS	
1324	17	1314	20, 19	1324	23	1335	6	1335	42
1342	29	1342	15, 16	1343	17	1351	10	1342	44
1364	15	1378	12, 6	1347	11	1389	13	1344	40
1384	10	1380	24, 13	1357	19	1393	13	1346	34
1387	16	1386	15, 12	1371	29	1394	14	1347	40
1389	8	1392	9, 10	1385	17			1348	40
1391	9			1386	15			1353	39
1394	16			1392	17			1354	35
1395	20			1398	24			1359	36
				1403	39			1360	29
				1406	20			1362	34
				1408	37			1363	26
				1412	54			1366	22
								1371	29
								1373	26
								1374	25
								1375	17
								1377	23
								1378	22
								1379	24
								1393	26
								1404	43
								1407	47

Major adjustments in the supply of labour available from customary tenants occurred in the first decade or so after the Black Death. The following synoptic view of this adjustment may be seen from figures for the largest amount owed in one year of a decade over a series of four decades.[4]

OPERA OWED

	ABBOTS RIPTON	BROUGHTON	UPWOOD	WARBOYS	WISTOW
1340s	7242	3555	5733	3688	4859 (1335–36)
1360s	4350	?	4042 (1357–58)	2173	3626
1370s	5030	2868	3270	1370	3428
1380s	5005	3114	3184	?	3463
1390s	4302	2766	3231	1236	3466

From these data, the lord appears to have established a new level of stability vis-à-vis his tenants. One can further identify the strategy behind Ramsey manorial administrations over the latter half of the fourteenth century. Properties must not fall vacant into the lord's hands. To ensure this end, the number of customary tenants would have to be maintained. In this the administration succeeded and have left us the following data for numbers of customary tenants:

ABBOTS RIPTON		BROUGHTON		UPWOOD		WARBOYS		WISTOW	
		1378	37?	1371	29	1371	82	1368	51
1375	41	1380	39	1385	32	1373	81	1388	51
1379	43	1383	37	1392	35	1374	76	1389	52
1384	46	1392	35			1375	82	1393	46
1387	36					1377	81	1394	47
1389	42					1378	82		
1390	41					1379	80		
1394	40								

Total tenant numbers tended to increase considerably during the last quarter of the century. Whether the economic significance of this phenomenon was important will be challenged in the following sections of this chapter. At both Abbots Ripton and Broughton these total figures were not of any permanent significance, whereas in the other three villages numbers were larger and more permanent. Total numbers of tenants were as follows:

ABBOTS RIPTON		BROUGHTON		UPWOOD		WARBOYS		WISTOW	
		1378	44	1385	68	1371	92	1368	65
1384	52	1380	44	1392	57	1373	93	1388	65
1387	41	1392	40			1374	94	1389	65
1389	45					1375	93	1393	61
1394	43					1377	94		
						1378	97		
						1379	99		

There was also a corps of continuing families for decades after 1348. Customary tenants were inherited by the tenants in these Ramsey Abbey villages, and the inheriting individual received his land from the lord's hands for life.[5] Such a system still prevailed throughout the later fourteenth century. Indeed, extant data allow considerable measurement of the "lifetime" of each tenure. For example, at Upwood[6] and Warboys,[7] 20 (60 per cent) and 40 (50 per cent) of customary tenants in these respective villages held the same land for more than twenty-five years in the late fourteenth century. Something of the administrative significance of the identification of property and family can be seen for Broughton. The student of this village has shown that in 1380 and again in 1409 former tenants as far back as the pre–Black Death period were identified in rent rolls.[8]

Over the 1370s and 1380s Ramsey administration attempted to streamline the manorial system in order to take advantage of commercial opportunities.[9] The evidence for increased sowing by acre[10] is in line with the so-called advanced economy to be found in Norfolk.[11] A series of good harvests rewarded Ramsey for these efforts. But it was also a period of low prices[12] and increasing capital costs on the demesne.[13] On the whole, this brief experiment became a prelude to an even greater emphasis on cash rents by the lord. At the same time, the main customary tenants do not appear to have lost ground from the new experiment with direct farming despite a short-term decline in the percentage of works sold and a levelling off and occasional slight decrease in the number of tenements let at money rent. Indeed, it was over the last quarter of the fourteenth century that conditions by which customary tenements were held began to shift to more permanent rent arrangements (*ad arrentatum*). So we must turn now to the story of the customary tenant.

ii   TRANSFORMATION OF THE CUSTOMARY TENANT HOLDINGS

It is amazing how little the seemingly stable or controlled administrative picture tells us about actual economic conditions among customary tenants. The most fundamental reality was the degree to which renewed attacks of the plague undermined the traditional customary-tenant population of these villages. Substantial families simply disappeared more rapidly than at any other time since the late fourteenth century. The Black Death had an uneven impact upon village families. For each of the five villages under study here some large families of the period before 1348 as well as smaller families were entirely wiped out when the disease first struck. Equally significant for the post–Black Death period, some large families were so decimated and weakened that these gradually died out.[14] In the following summation, the number of identifiable members for the two generations prior to the Black Death is in brackets. At Wistow, only two members of the once numerous Bonde (7) family survived to the 1370s, five of the Catelyne (8) to the 1380s; one of the Clerk (8), one of Marchaunt (9), one of Martyn (9), three of Palmer (12), one of Paris (8), two of Raveley (5), three of Richard (9), and two of Roger (10) survived to the last quarter of the century.[15] At Upwood, two survived for a time for the Austyn family (3), two for the Carter (10), one for the Cowherd (10), three for Holy (5), one for Wold (3), two for Snape (5), two for Thacher (5), and one for West (5).[16] At Broughton, two survived for a generation from the Abbot family (4), three from the Attedam (5), one from the Attehill (4), one from the Brigge (5), three from the Crane (11), four from the Catelyne (8), two from the Randolf (10).[17]

Were labour services the unique consideration, one might have expected the response to this population devastation to come by greater subdivision of properties – that is to say, labour services might be better guaranteed by increasing the number of smaller labour-bearing tenements in order to gain maximum commitment from the many smaller and declining family units. In fact the movement would be towards the combination of holdings rather than a thinner spread. Evidence below shows that the advent of a wide variety of tenurial options ensured that those with capital dictated the future scene.

In the mid-thirteenth-century extents and no doubt over the following hundred years, the great majority of the tenants could be grouped under the virgate or semi-virgate holding. At Abbots Ripton 10 tenants held one virgate each and 61 one-half virgate each; at Broughton 7 and 43; at Upwood 17 and 10; at Warboys 13 and 30; at Wistow 9 and 35. Within two decades after 1348, this long perduring spread had been radically transformed. As the complete picture of names and holdings first becomes available in records, the following information emerges:

WISTOW (1368): 1 virgate, 8 individuals; ¾ virgate, 5 individuals; ½ virgate, 12 individuals; ¼ virgate, 4 individuals; 1 cotland, 5 individuals; 1 hideman-land, 2 individuals; ½ virgate + ¼ virgate, 1 individual; 1 virgate + ¼ virgate, 3 individuals; ½ virgate + 1 cotland, 3 individuals; ¼ virgate + ½ cotland, 1 individual; ½ virgate + ½ cotland, 2 individuals; ½ virgate + 1 hidemanland, 1 individual; ¼ virgate + 1 hidemanland, 2 individuals; ¾ virgate + 1 cotland, 1 individual; ½ virgate + 1 cotland + 1 cotland, 1 individual.

UPWOOD (1371): 1 virgate, 5 individuals; ½ virgate, 3 individuals; ¼ virgate, 2 individuals; 1 virgate + ½ virgate, 5 individuals; 1 virgate + ¼ virgate, 2 individuals; ½ virgate + ¼ virgate, 1 individual; ½ virgate + ½ virgate + 1 cotland, 1 individual; ½ virgate + 1 cotland, 1 individual; ½ virgate + ½ virgate + ¼ virgate, 1 individual; 1 virgate + ½ virgate + 1 cotland, 1 individual; 1 cotland + 1 cotland, 2 individuals; 1 cotland, 2 individuals; ½ cotland, 1 individual.

WARBOYS (1371): 1 virgate, 7 individuals; 1 and ½ virgate, 3 individuals; 1 and ¼ virgate, 4 individuals; ½ virgate, 9 individuals; ¼ virgate, 7 individuals; ¾ virgate, 3 individuals; ½ virgate + ¼ virgate, 2 individuals; ¼ virgate + ¼ virgate, 1 individual; ½ maltmanland, 4 individuals; 2 dikemanland, 2 individuals; 1 dikemanland, 3 individuals; 1 mondaymanland, 13 individuals; ¾ virgate + 1 mondaymanland, 1 individual; ½ virgate + 2 mondaymanland, 1 individual; 1 akermanland, 2 individuals; ½ akermanland, 1 individual; ½ virgate + 1 maltmanland, 1 individual; ½ virgate + 2 and ½ mondaymanland, 1 individual; 1 akermanland + ½ virgate, 1 individual; ½ virgate + 1 mondaymanland, 3 individuals; ¼ virgate + 1 maltmanland, 1 individual; ½ virgate + 1 dikemanland, 1 individual; ½ virgate + ½ akermanland, 1 individual; ¼ virgate + 1 mondaymanland, 3 individuals; ¼ virgate + 1 dikemanland, 1 individual; 1 mondaymanland + headland, 1 individual; 3 mondaymanlands + ½ akermanland, 1 individual; 1 dikemanland + ½ maltmanland + 1 mondaymanland + ½ akermanland, 1 individual; ½ maltmanland + 1 mondaymanland + 1 maltmanland, 1 individual.

ABBOTS RIPTON (1375): 1 virgate, 13 individuals; ¾ virgate, 1 individual; ½ virgate, 3 individuals; ¼ virgate, 1 individual; 1 virgate + ½ virgate, 7 individuals; 1 virgate + ¼ virgate, 1 individual; 1 virgate + ½ virgate + land, 1 individual; ½ virgate + ½ virgate, 3 individuals; ½ virgate + ¼ virgate, 2 individuals; 1 virgate + ½ virgate + ½ virgate, 1 individual; 2 and ¼ virgate + ½ virgate, 1 individual; ¼ virgate + land, 1 individual; 1 cotland, 2 individuals; 1 cotland + 1 cotland + ½ virgate, 1 individual; land, 1 individual.

BROUGHTON (1378): 1 virgate, 7 individuals; ½ virgate, 10 individuals; ¼ virgate, 8 individuals; ⅛ virgate, 2 individuals; ½ virgate + ½ virgate, 1 individual; 1 virgate + 1 virgate, 1 individual; 1 virgate + ½ virgate, 1 individual; 1 virgate + ¼ virgate, 10 individuals; 1 and ¼ virgate + ½ virgate, 1 individual; ¾ virgate + ½ virgate, 1 individual; ¼ virgate + ½ virgate, 1 individual; ¼ virgate + 1 cotland, 1 individual; 1 cotland, 2 individuals.

These detailed lists of landholdings are given here in order to dramatize the difference between villein tenure as seen in manorial records of payments by service or money rent and the actual landholding structure among villagers. The various customary units continued to be employed, as these had been for centuries, but were more often than not employed in a wide array of combinations. Among the most common customary units, the virgate or semi-virgate, there was only about a 10 per cent chance that two villagers would hold properties of the same size. The norm for these vills was an individual arrangement between the villager and the lord's official.

Another perspective on these transformations can be obtained by looking solely at the variety of options chosen by individuals rather than the size of holdings. Given here is the accumulated total of tenurial arrangements by 121 tenants at Warboys and 92 at Wistow over roughly the last quarter of the fourteenth century. Since we are dealing with larger tenants, these figures do not include rentals of small pieces of demesne. These variations in tenurial structure dramatize particularly how the work-service arrangement had declined in importance.

	Total of tenants
WARBOYS VARIATIONS	
ad opus	53
ad opus + *ad arrentatum*	21
ad opus and beadle	2
ad arrentatum	27
ad opus + *ad arrentatum* and akermanland	1
ad opus + *ad arrentatum* + *ad censum*	1
ad opus and reeve	3
ad opus + *ad censum* and reeve	1
ad censum and beadle	1
ad arrentatum and bailiff	1
ad censum	2
ad opus + *ad arrentatum* and office	2
ad opus + *ad censum*	6
	121

	Total of tenants
WISTOW VARIATIONS	
ad opus	29
ad opus + *ad censum*	12
ad opus + *ad arrentatum*	5
ad censum	16
ad censum + demesne	1
ad censum and akermanland	2
ad opus + *ad censum* and demesne	3

ad opus + *ad censum* and beadle	2
ad opus + *ad censum* and akermanland	2
ad opus + *ad censum* and reeve	1
ad opus + *ad arrentatum* and beadle	1
ad opus and akermanland	1
ad censum and bailiff	1
ad arrentatum	8
ad arrentatum + *ad censum*	3
ad censum + *ad arrentatum* + *ad opus* and reeve	4
ad censum + *ad arrentatum* + *ad opus* and akermanland	1
	92

iii   THE ROLE OF WEALTHIER TENANTS IN THE TENURIAL TRANSFORMATION

These variations in the amount of holdings and the type of tenurial arrangement can be given more meaning when seen as the actions of the traditional core group of villagers. Wealthy customary tenants, whether free or villein, were in a position to take advantage of new opportunities. These opportunities arose primarily on the two levels of traditional service tenements and more recently commuted service holdings. Lands owing work service were literally taken for a price. This price was the addition of land owing money rent rather than services.

This was a different pattern from that found at the end of the thirteenth century. Official tasks were no longer a clear path to wealth, since these official tasks now involved sharing the burdens of a depressed manorial economy. Efforts were made to spread the burden more widely by changing reeves, beadles, and haywards from year to year.[18] There is plenty of evidence that wealthier officials were able to have cancelled the debts they had been unable to collect while in office. Was this because they and their peers had the means to occupy indebted properties rather than leave the latter vacant? Records unfortunately do not make us privy to such detail in personal bargaining arrangements. But the results are certainly suggestive of the direction the bargaining had taken.

There were of course immense variations from manor to manor and individual to individual. Broughton had the most stable scene over the latter half of the fourteenth century, thereby making general patterns more observable. Of the sixteen customary tenants with one virgate or more, all but one had additional property with commuted services. Again, there would be much bargaining that does not come through our records. But some priorities in demesne management can be clearly seen. For service as ploughman (*akermanus*) William Bigge as well as John Neel received one-half virgate and another one-half virgate *ad censum*; Thomas Couper received one-half virgate along with a virgate and one-quarter *ad censum*; Ivo atte Cros received one-half virgate and another three-quarters of a virgate *ad censum*, as did Richard Gernoun and William Lomb, while Thomas Athewold received one virgate *ad censum* with the one-half virgate as ploughman.

More important skills brought better arrangements. William Leighton performed as both beadle and reeve over 1378–79 for one and one-quarter virgate, as did Simon Fisher over 1380–81. John Shepherd performed as reeve and ploughman over 1392–93 for one and one-quarter virgate. William Boteler represents another type of compromise. Over 1383–84 William performed the services of reeve and had one-quarter virgate *ad censum*. But by the next account roll (1392) William had one and one-quarter virgate *ad censum*. As we shall see for villages where records are more numerous over the late 1390s and into the fifteenth century, the demesne administration ceded more and more virgates to commutation. Broughton was also more restrained at this time in letting lands for the long-term commutation (*ad arrentatum*). Only the two wealthy tenants, John Catoun and Simon Shepherd, each held one-quarter virgate in this manner from the 1370s to the 1390s.

It would be misleading to assume that official tasks plus beneficial commutation provided an inevitable path to prosperity. Abbots Ripton supplies useful records in this regard. There we find the same combination of virgates *ad opus* along with one-half (in two instances one-quarter) virgates *ad censum*: Attechirche (junior and senior), Bettes, Haulond, Huberd, Henry, Hiche, Howe, Juell, John Martyn, Outy, Prikke, Stevens, West. The same pattern reappears with other families over the 1380s: Colle, Littlejohn, Sabyn, Thedwar, Wattes, White. But the very good series of records for Abbots Ripton over the 1380s and early 1390s also reveals that most of these families did not improve their condition. No doubt they suffered along with the lord from the poorer harvest. They might come to hold most or all of their properties for the annual money rent and an official task, as did the tenants Bettes (½v *ad censum* and 1v as ploughman), Howe (½v *ad censum* and ½v as beadle), and Prikke (½v *ad censum* and ½v as ploughman). But they all remained within the traditional system, and none was able to obtain more lands for money rent over the longer term, especially the long-term money lease (*ad arrentatum*).

In this village ten tenants did improve their condition over this time. Two of these, Juell and Nicol, seem to have pulled themselves up by their own bootstraps despite the manorial system. John Juell had ½v *ad censum* and ½v as hayward in the late 1370s, 1v *ad opus* and ½v *ad censum* in 1384, by 1389 1v *ad censum* and ½v as ploughman, over the next year ½v *ad censum*, ½v as beadle, and ½v as hayward, and he was holding 1½v in 1394 by the same conditions as in 1389. John Nicol was able to take more advantage of the *ad censum* arrangements: 1v *ad opus* from 1370 to 1391 along with ¾v *ad censum* by 1387 and ½v as ploughman, but by the 1390s he had 1¼v *ad censum*, and over 1394–95 was listed as holding 1½v *ad censum* and ½v as ploughman. In short, these two individuals had the resources to pay substantial money rent every year. Such a capacity was indeed typical of this group of ten, although the remaining eight exercised the same role by long-term leases.

As might be expected for those with more resources, these wealthy people with long-term money leases had a more varied tenurial pattern than their less wealthy neighbours. William Jurdon had 2¼v at long-term lease over 1375–76, along with ½v at short term. Over the next decade he held all 2¾v for the long-term lease. By the 1390s William was replaced by Robert Jurdon, but significantly Robert could only hold the 2¾v for long term by sharing with John Hulot (1v) and John Shepherd (¼v). Thereafter, over the early 1390s, Robert could only maintain ½v for the long-term lease and held 1v for work service. Philip Ladde first appeared in 1379 with 1v at long-term lease, ½v at short term, and ½v as ploughman. Philip maintained this ratio over the 1380s with 1v long-term rent and 1v at work service.

There were six more or less contemporaneous Martyn families, so their holdings are not readily distinguishable. John Martyn junior does not seem to have improved his work-service and short-term rental-property ratios. Clearly of a different family, William Martyn of Wennington first appears with 1v at long-term rent in 1375, added ½v for short-term rent by 1380, and over the 1380s held 1v at long-term rent and 1v for work services. A William Martyn of Ripton first appears in 1390 holding 1v for long-term rent and 1v for work services; over the following year he held 1½v for work services and extended his long-term rental holdings to 1v and 1 cotland. John Robbes junior followed much the same pattern.

Andrew Outy and Nicholas Huberd show interesting patterns of official responsibilities and success. Huberd was apparently less wealthy, with ½v at yearly rent along with ½v as ploughman in 1375 and again ten years later, while he had 1v for work services over 1379–80. But by 1387 he had 1v for long-term rent and ½v for work services. After his stint as reeve in 1390–91 he increased his holding, though at the cost of more services, holding in 1394 ½v for long-term rent, ½v as beadle, and 1v for work services. Andrew Outy, by contrast, appears first (1379–80) with 1v at work services and ½v at money rent; five years later his 1½v were held in equal rents for short-term rent, as beadle and as hayward; over the last three years of this decade he held 2½v (1v for work, 1v for long-term rent, ½v for short-term rent); by the mid-1390s he held 2¾v (1v for work and 1¾ for long-term rent).

It seems logical to ask whether less wealthy tenants could not better survive by working more closely together. Evidence for this is sparse. Thomas Nene and Littlejohn shared one-half virgate over 1379–80 by working as ploughmen. At Wistow in 1381 four couples shared the work owed for one-half virgates: Henry Hiche with Richard Hobbe, John Gouler with Emma Randolf, John Grigge with Ralph Sabyn, John de Welles with William Taillour. But these seem to have been emergency or failed situations, since at least four of the five (Nene, Randolf, Grigge, and Welles) disappear from tenant lists after this one year. Apparently additional labour was not enough. Customary tenants did not seem to have adequate resources to revive a practice that was so common at the time of the mid-thirteenth-century extents.

As indicated briefly above, tenant failure did provide obvious opportunities for those with resources. In 1389 the wealthy Robert Jurdon of Abbots Ripton first appears in the tenant list as holding one virgate at long-term lease with John Hulot. Hulot had disappeared by the next year, and Jurdon held the whole virgate by himself. In 1389 Robert Jurdon also held one-quarter virgate with John Schepherd, and Schepherd, who also only entered the tenant list in 1389, held this property by himself for the following years. The wealthy William Boteler of Broughton held one-half virgate with Beatrice Cateline in 1381 and seems to have added this to his holdings when Beatrice disappears as tenant after that year. Significantly, the wealthy John Catoun and Simon Fisher of Broughton continued to hold one-half virgate together for at least a decade around this time. In the same fashion William Colleville first appears in the tenant list of Warboys over 1393–94 as teamed up with the wealthy John Hikkesson of Upwood for one and one-quarter virgates. Both prospered, but it is impossible to follow this arrangement, if indeed it continued.

Such co-operation among wealthier tenants was not new. From the beginning of the fourteenth century at Abbots Ripton, and at all our villages by the 1340s, it had become the practice to lease portions of the demesne to individuals identified only as "customaries" in the account rolls. This was of course evidence for increasing village control over labour resources. That the practice continued after 1348 is but another example of the force of established manorial practices. At Broughton, four substantial demesne (fields?), one of 11 acres and three around 25 acres, continued to be farmed from 1346 to 1378. Although one cannot be absolutely certain of the identification, two or three of these same fields appear to have been leased into the 1390s. There had been an overall increase in demesne acres farmed, from 87 in 1346 to 112 in 1492. Parallel increases were to be found for other villages: Warboys 39 (1342), 60 (1359), 133 (1373), 152 (1379), 119 (1404); Wistow 53 (1346), 116 (1379), 124 (1388), 139 (1423).[19]

From late in the third quarter of the century customary tenants began to be named, and the names of those leasing portions of the demesne also began to be identified. It comes as no surprise to find that those leasing substantial portions of these demesne fields in association with others of their wealth status were substantial customary tenants. More revealing and corroborative of sparse indications available about this practice, as noted in chapter 2, is the discovery that so many of those leasing demesne were from outside the village. The field system of Wistow has recently been reconstructed in detail,[20] and accordingly our illustrations of the above points will be taken from that village.

In the Wistow account rolls for 1368 it was stated that 36 acres, 2½ rods of the demesne at Kingslonde had been leased to someone (name indecipherable) and his associates for twenty years, this being the second year of the lease. Twenty years later accounts refer to this land as leased to customaries of Upwood. The rationale for this lease in terms of field management was clear enough, since Kingslonde was next to Upwood in Rooks Grove Field. By the 1380s the account rolls begin to give the names of these associates and the amount of rent each paid towards the lease, so that the approximate acreage held by each customary tenant can be calculated. By relating to the tenant lists of Upwood, it is easy to ascertain that these were indeed substantial tenants of the latter vill, each holding as follows in Kingslonde: Richard Albyn (4½ acres), William Attestede (5½ acres), Walter Baker (4½ acres), John Bigge (4½ acres), Thomas Newman (4½ acres), John Siwelle (4½ acres), Thomas Smyth (5½ acres), and John Wyse (4½ acres).

In 1363 William Aubyn (or Hawkyn) of Upwood and associates leased 34½ acres for forty years in le Brache – that is, in the more modern Breach in Milne Hill Field. We know when names appear in 1381 that this lease, lying next to Broughton in part, attracted the wealthy William de Leighton of Broughton and the half-virgater John Randolf. Their relative portions were: William Aubyn (3½ acres), John London (5 acres), John Mice (5 acres), Emma Miller (4½ acres),

William de Leighton (5 acres), William Prikke of Abbots Ripton (3 acres), John Randolf (4 acres), John de Wennington of Warboys (4½ acres).

Not all fields were rented to customaries from one or another of the five villages. Lying northeast of Burywood Field, next to the hamlet of Bury, was a field called Stokking with two parts containing in total 53 acres. This field was leased to the "men of Bury" in 1341. Over the 1360s and 1370s it is stated that four men of Bury held 20 demesne acres in Stokking; the Almoner of Ramsey Abbey held the remaining 33 (1369) or 34 (1379) acres over the same period. By 1388 a wealthy outsider, William Lache, held 28 acres, one perch of Stokking. By the early 1390s this land was in the lord's hands, and then it was leased for life to another wealthy outsider, John Augustyn, over 1393–94.

Another pattern can be seen from 1364, when William de Broughton (of Broughton) and William Newman (of Upwood) leased 9½ acres for ten years at Bishopwong (likely the later Bishopholm in Buryhood Field). By 1379 the rector of Wistow along with two other men of the vill, Richard of Ely[21] and Richard Sabyn,[22] were holding this land for life. Two other local men, Stephen Aylmar and Robert Rede, were added as tenants in the 1380s, but by the 1390s the original three names were alone listed as tenants of the unit. This tendency for more local people to get involved in the leasing of smaller units of land by the 1380s can also be illustrated for another field. At Lowe Field in 1381, a 6-acre land was leased, to John Bronnote (½ acre), John Attegate (½ acre), Richard de Ely (½ acre, 2 rods), William Waryn (1 acre), Andrew Smyth (2 rods), John Eliot with John Bronnote (½ acre), Richard de Ely with William Sabyn (1 acre), and Richard Shepherd (1 acre).

Units of this size were the ordinary operational arable properties according to descriptions to be found in charters.[23] There were also listed as leased from the demesne at Wistow some seventeen separate holdings of these smaller units. Several can be seen changing hands three or four times over the 1380s and 1390s. The increase in the number of these smaller units of demesne coming on the market over the last quarter of the fourteenth century can also be seen for Broughton: 1378 (7), 1380 (12), 1392 (16).[24] On the whole these were new names to the tenant lists and seem to have been landless local people such as petty tradesmen or perhaps outsiders within convenient distance. At Abbots Ripton, for example, a Thomas Atehill from Hartford held a small "land" over 1375–76; John Broun obtained a cottage and a parcel of land for life in 1384; Thomas Fuller acquired one acre in 1387; a John Marewyk held two acres over 1387–89; John

Thacher (of London?) entered two acres for life in 1394; Robert Vernon entered a tenement owing three shillings annually in the same year, and John Webester obtained three acres for life in 1387. Many of these people held no other property in these five villages and in fact shared some of these small holdings. It is the appearance of the smallholders that explains much of the increase in the total number of tenants over the late fourteenth century. The good harvests of the 1370s and 1380s would have attracted such smallholders and would explain the temporary family association with land for many of these people.

This leasing of small units of demesne arable to an ever-widening circle of individuals seems to have been a desperate effort to attract more tenants. The leases were for money rent, and it is noteworthy that those customary tenants of moderate wealth who were struggling from year to year to maintain their economic status by some combination of work service holdings, short-term money leases, and official tasks did not have the resources to take advantage of these opportunities. Nor did these bits and pieces of property attract the attention of those more substantial tenants who were more interested in their capacity to control significant portions of the demesne. With the virtual collapse of the demesne economy in the early fifteenth century, there would be a change of focus in peasant property arrangements. For example, at Warboys beginning in the first quarter of the fifteenth century, and increasing during the second quarter, several families centred their estate-building about small units of property: Broun, Boys, Bonde, Berenger, Catoun, Hunter, Owndill, Sharp, Shepherd, and White.[25] In order to assess this development more fully we must now turn our attention to the role of families.

One final point must be raised before closing this chapter: Why could customary tenants succeed where the lord had failed? It was pointed out long ago[26] that the high level of consumption demand severely limited the amount of capital available for productive investment by the lord. Above all, profits from compensatory investment from time to time in animals rather than grain did not produce a level of profits adequate to the lord's requirements. But for customary tenants animal husbandry had become a regular part of their economy.[27] The market picture for peasant livestock might be difficult to deduce.[28] But the reproductive process for animals favoured the smaller scale, less dependent upon major cycles of reinvestment.

5 Family Priorities

i   THE ROLE OF THE FAMILY IN CAPITAL
    MAINTENANCE

Co-operation could also be internal to the family. It has already been
noted in chapter 1 and elsewhere[1] that survival was not a special
privilege of the more wealthy. While many families dwindled and
disappeared, it must not be expected that the future of these villages
lay entirely in the hands of the more substantial local tenants whose
ranks were supplemented by the entry of well-endowed outsiders.
Demographic luck kept in business a good number of traditional
families who were not necessarily the most wealthy in the village.
Despite the long-term decline in population over the late fourteenth
and throughout most of the fifteenth centuries, some families survived in goodly numbers.

In Table 5.1 accompanying, data abstracted from Appendix iv has
been set down in such a way as not only to illustrate something of
the distribution of land among tenants but also to demonstrate the
importance of families in the various patterns of landholding. For
each of the five villages, the period that possessed the fullest amount
of account-roll data has been selected. Although this period varied
somewhat from village to village, with the longest period for a single
village being thirty-two years in the case of Upwood, the general
time-span covered by Table 5.1 is 1368–1423. The total 579 tenants
whose holdings were recorded in the account rolls during this period
have been grouped according to village, the size of their tenements,[2]

Table 5.1
Land Tenure and Families

Village	Under 10 acres		10–29 acres		30 acres or more		Totals	
	Individual	Family	Individual	Family	Individual	Family	Individual	Family
Abbots Ripton 1375–95	11	4	17	28	10	22	38 (41%)	54 (59%)
Broughton 1378–93	9	8	7	8	12	30	28 (38%)	46 (62%)
Upwood 1392–1423	17	25	6	20	9	28	32 (30%)	73 (70%)
Warboys 1393–1422	28	50	15	53	5	26	48 (27%)	129 (73%)
Wistow 1368–95	27	25	20	25	6	28	53 (40%)	78 (60%)
Overall statistic	92 (45%)	112 (55%)	65 (33%)	134 (67%)	42 (24%)	134 (76%)	199 (34%)	380 (66%)
	204 (35%)		199 (34%)		176 (31%)		579 (100%)	

and whether or not they appear in the account rolls with other members of their families. For example, in the case of John Atte-churche senior of Abbots Ripton, he has been included, albeit only as a number, in the column headed "10–29 acres" and under the subheading "Family." He was placed here because he held a virgate (20 acres) of land in Abbots Ripton and because he was not the only member of the Attechurche family to hold land in the village between 1375 and 1395. However, John Bele of the same village, who also has been included under "10–29 acres" (he too held 20 acres), appears under the heading "Individual," since he was the only member of the Bele family listed as a tenant during the period. All the tenants in the five villages have been categorized in a similar manner under the appropriate columns, and separate totals for each village, as well as the overall total for the five, have been provided.

Table 5.1 clearly illustrates the primacy of family involvement in the land markets of these villages. The overall statistics, which show that 380 (66 per cent) of the total 579 tenants appear in the account rolls with one or more members of their families[3] who were also tenants, while only 199 (34 per cent) of that total appear alone, are representative of the five villages. Although Warboys, at 73 per cent, seems to have had the highest level of family involvement and Abbots Ripton, at 59 per cent, the lowest, neither was far removed from the overall average of 66 per cent. Thus there seems to have been a consistently high level of family participation in landholding throughout the five villages.

If one examines the level of family involvement even more closely, especially by relating it to the various sizes of properties held, a significant pattern soon emerges. As one moves from left to right in Table 5.1 – that is, from tenants holding smaller properties to those holding larger properties – the ratio between tenants appearing alone and those appearing with other members of their families changes dramatically in favour of family involvement.[4] In other words, the level of family involvement in landholding seems to vary directly with the amount of property held. This pattern is clearly visible in the overall statistics for the five villages, for whereas 55 per cent of the tenants with less than 10 acres exhibit family involvement, this percentage climbs to 67 per cent in the case of tenants with 10–29 acres and then rises to 76 per cent with respect to tenants holding 30 acres or more. Thus, as one moves up the tenurial ladder in these villages, the degree of family involvement in land noticeably intensifies.

The central thrust of family-management policy was towards the preservation and betterment of all members of the family. Some traditional customs of these villages have been treated elsewhere,[5] but it will be useful to supplement our understanding by the exceptional information provided by the Court Book.[6] This fifteenth-century record offers information about the intra-family transfer of property, details not to be found in account rolls and court rolls. Although most of this information is about the more wealthy families, it is not exclusively so, and in any case, for our purposes it reveals something of the role of capital in promoting greater family involvement among wealthier tenants.

The Court Book offers evidence on at least four different ways in which young men who were denied a share of the family tenement were still able to gain control of property in their native villages, property that was to serve as the nucleus for their own family tenements. Of these various means, the most common seems to have been the apparent independent acquisition of land by the younger son. For example, in the village of Warboys, John Berenger junior, who was the younger son of John Berenger (alias Wryghte), seems to have been able to acquire land on his own, for it is recorded in the Court Book that in 1411 he gave the lord a capon as the entry fine to a monday-manland formerly held by John Heryng, for which he was to pay an annual rent of 4s. Furthermore, according to the account rolls of Warboys, he was also able to take up another 15 acres in the village in 1421. This property allowed John to establish his own family, for the Court Book indicates that he had two daughters, Agnes and Joan. John's older brother William likely worked with his father or leased land, since he did not acquire land as early as John. He had to wait until 1425 to receive 15 acres from his father and another thirteen years before he took over another 15 acres, plus a house and a croft, in partnership with his father.

Another example of a younger son who was able to provide himself with his own family tenement is Thomas Outy of Wistow. Although Thomas's older brother, John, received their father's 45 acres, as indicated by the account rolls of the village, and was able to go on to accumulate a great deal more land than Thomas, the younger brother was still able to acquire enough land to marry and support a family. By 1414 the account rolls of the village show that Thomas held about 23 acres of land, and a Court Book entry for 1416 offers some evidence of how Thomas was able to augment his income beyond that which he was able to derive from his land. In 1416 Thomas paid Ramsey Abbey 12d. as a licence fee to serve as the village blacksmith. This activity very likely provided him with the extra capital with which to take over 8 acres from his older brother in 1424, for which he paid an entry fine of 12d. and an annual rent of 4s.

While the Court Book offers clear evidence that Thomas was able to establish his own family in the village, members of his particular branch of the Outy family do not seem to have been interested in remaining in Wistow. Thomas's wife, Anna, gave him two sons, John and Robert, but neither of these young men decided to stay on in the village. In a Court Book entry for 1444 John is said to have been living outside the Ramsey estates, and his brother, Robert, is said to have been living in Hartford (Hunts.) in 1448. Since both these individuals paid an annual fine to the Abbey for living beyond the Ramsey properties, it is likely that they had some intention of moving back to Wistow and thus were concerned with keeping their affairs in order in the village. In any case, whether or not Thomas's sons chose to live beyond the village permanently does not alter the fact that Thomas himself had been able to establish his own family in Wistow, even though he had not received a share of his father's land.

A final example of a non-inheriting son who was able to establish himself in his native village may be taken from Broughton. John Crowche, the younger son of Robert Crowche, seems to have been able to provide himself with a tenement despite the fact that all his father's land passed to his elder brother, Thomas, in 1416. In 1420 John paid a nominal entry fine of 6 capons and gained access to a tenement formerly held by Thomas Botiller, which contained about 40 acres of land. Although John was not able to accumulate as much land as his older brother, whom the account rolls of 1449–58 show to have been holding almost 70 acres, John did possess a sizeable tenement. Furthermore, he was able to support a wife and family as well as to participate extensively in village politics.

These three examples of younger sons taking up land, apparently independently, in their native villages are typical of the extant evidence on this method of land acquisition. In all cases these younger sons appear to be establishing themselves on land that had no obvious connection with their parents' lands. Exactly how they were able to acquire the capital with which to take up these lands raises some interesting questions. To be sure, the entry fines were often only nominal, but these young men still would have needed a certain amount of capital to get themselves started as farmers: implements, seeds, livestock, and other provisions would have to be purchased; also, they had to pay their annual rents and perhaps make repairs to their tenements, since dilapidation was a fairly common occurrence on a good many holdings. Only in the case of Thomas Outy of Wistow is there any clue about how he was able to accumulate capital, but even in this instance the first mention of him as a blacksmith occurs two years after he acquired his first holding.

Since it is impossible to determine the economic arrangements behind the Court Book entries indicating that non-inheriting sons were able to acquire land of their own, one can only hypothesize how such young men were able to accumulate sufficient capital to take up their lands and begin to work them. It would seem likely, especially in view of the complete lack of evidence that younger sons had any independent sources of income prior to acquiring land, that they received financial assistance from their parents as they had some one hundred years earlier (see chapter 2). Non-inheriting children were entitled to a share of their parents' moveable property, and since they could receive that share prior to their parents' deaths, this would be the means by which younger sons acquired sufficient capital to take up land and to work it.

Although there may be little difference between providing a younger son with land directly and providing him with the capital to acquire his own property, when viewed from the perspective of the independence, or lack of same, exhibited by such a young man, there is a very great difference in method from the perspective of the property management of the families concerned. This difference becomes apparent as soon as we examine just how land was transferred directly to a younger son. For example, in the village of Broughton, Thomas Pulter junior, the younger son of Thomas senior, was able to receive land from his father even though the bulk of the family tenement had passed to his older brother Richard. In the same year that Richard took over about 48 acres from his father, 1443, Thomas was also provided with some land. He received a messuage and 8 acres from his father, which seems to have provided him and his wife, Katherine, with the beginnings of their own tenement. Three years later Thomas junior acquired a holding from Thomas Crowche that contained about 45 acres of land. Although it cannot be determined whether Thomas's successful management of the small tenement he received from his father in 1443 enabled him to accumulate the capital with which to take over the larger holding, it is certainly clear that the possession of this small tenement at least gave Thomas an entry into the village land market and allowed him to marry.

Although Thomas Pulter junior received his land in the same year as his older brother, this was not always the case in such direct transfer of property. In the village of Wistow, for example, Thomas Aylmar received a small tenement containing about 20 acres from his father, Robert, in 1447. This was seventeen years after Robert had provided his eldest son, John, with a house and modest tenement, which seems to have enabled John to marry Alice Plumbe of Warboys in 1430. In order to provide for himself and his younger son after transferring a messuage and 15 acres to John, Robert acquired another messuage and about 15 acres in 1430. It was from this holding that Thomas received his land in 1447.

These two examples from Broughton and Wistow offer considerable insight into why few families chose to provide their younger sons with land directly. Unless they had a great deal of land, as in the case of the Pulters in Broughton, the prevailing system of impartible inheritance based upon primogeniture made it very difficult to transfer any land directly to a younger son. The eldest son must first be provided for, and this usually left his younger brothers with none of their father's land. Even in cases in which a younger son was provided with land directly from his father, as in the Aylmar family, the land seems to have had to be acquired specifically for that purpose and followed the main conveyance to the elder brother.

Although the prevailing system of land inheritance posed very serious problems for those who wished to provide a younger son with land directly, the reasons a few families resorted to this method go somewhat beyond the dictates of inheritance customs. This is suggested by the fact that even fathers with a good deal of land did not very often choose to transfer land to their youngest sons. For example, in the case of the Outy family in Wistow, which has already been mentioned, although Thomas senior possessed at least 45 acres of land, he did not see fit to transfer any of it to his younger son, Thomas. Instead, Thomas junior acquired his own land, very likely with the assistance of his father.

The fact that two families with roughly the same size holdings, namely the family of Thomas Pulter senior in Broughton and that of Thomas Outy senior of Wistow, should choose two very different methods of providing younger sons with land indicates that there was more than inheritance customs or the size of the family tenements involved in the decision-making process that resulted in provisions being made for younger sons. In part it would seem that in order for a father to provide a younger son with a tenement directly, he was required to take up an extra tenement, which included a messuage. In other words, he would have to do either as Thomas Pulter senior did, who seems to have carried an extra tenement with messuage for some time, or as Robert Aylmar did, who took up a second tenement in the same year that he transferred his former tenement to his eldest son. The demands that carrying an extra holding, as the Pulters did, would make on the property-managing skills of a family, not to mention the drain on its labour resources, seem to have discouraged most families from pursuing this course; even fewer were willing to start virtually anew as Robert Aylmar did. Thus, inheritance customs or the size of family tenements only partially explain why some younger sons received land directly and others were provided with the capital to acquire it on their own. In the final analysis it was the economic priorities of each family that determined just how younger sons were to be provided for, if at all.

Some idea of the complexity of the process by which younger sons acquired land, and the degree to which this process depended upon the very personal and unique circumstances of each family, may be gained from examining some examples of the third method by which younger sons came to take up land. In this case land was transferred to a non-inheriting son by a member of the family other than a parent. The Cabe family in Broughton offers an especially interesting example of this type of conveyance. John Cabe senior let the family tenement, which contained about 40 acres, pass to his eldest son Richard in 1405. As in a good many "yeoman" families the next eldest son, who by custom was not to receive any of his parents' land, was able to acquire land in the village. Although the extant sources make it difficult to know exactly how much land John junior was able to take up, it was considerable, for in 1423 he transferred a messuage and

40 acres to his younger brother, William. Thus, although John Cabe senior did not transfer land directly to anyone other than his eldest son, his second son seems not only to have been provided with enough capital to establish his own branch of the family but also to see to it that his younger brother was able to acquire a family tenement of his own.

Another example of such a direct conveyance of land to a younger son may also be taken from the village of Broughton. In 1420 John Justice passed all his lands, about 65 acres, to his eldest son, William. However, a younger son, Edward, was not to go without land in the village simply because of this conveyance. In 1423 Edward was able to acquire a messuage and 32 acres that had formerly been held by Thomas de Broughton. This acquisition, which was likely made possible by capital received from his parents and which represented his share of their moveable property, was not the only land Edward took up in 1423. In that same year he also received 16 acres from a certain Alice Justice. Alice was the widow of a certain William Justice, who was the brother of Edward's grandfather, also called Edward. This rather complex genealogical picture simply means that Edward received land from his great-aunt (by marriage) in 1423. We cannot know much about the negotiations involved in this transfer, but since Alice was living in Upwood in 1423 and had married into an entirely different family, the Payns, it is likely that the Justice family was concerned about keeping Alice's lands within their family.

This example thus offers one further piece of evidence of the various and complex means by which non-inheriting sons were provided with land. Edward Justice's acquisition of a family tenement involved not only the first method discussed in these pages but also the third. Furthermore, when he took up land formerly held by Alice Justice, the conveyance not only crossed more than one generation of the family; it also involved residents of two different villages.

There remains one more method by which families, each in light of its own particular circumstances, determined how and when younger sons were to be provided with land. This fourth method is somewhat similar to the second and third, by which younger sons received land directly from their fathers or from other members of their families, but it differs in that the sons did not receive land exclusively but rather held in partnership with other members of their families.

An example of this type of partnership may be seen in the Juell family in Abbots Ripton. Agnes Juell, the widow of Robert Juell, had two sons, John and Thomas. Thomas, who seems to have been the elder of the two, received a messuage and 10 acres from Agnes in

1442. In the same year Agnes and John Juell together assumed a messuage and 10 acres that had recently been held by Robert. In effect, it would seem that contrary to the custom of impartible inheritance, Robert's two messuages and 20 acres were split between his wife and two sons, with one half going to his eldest son and the other, which may perhaps be regarded as Agnes's dower right, being held in partnership by the mother and younger son.

In Wistow the Willessons offer an example of a family in which a younger son held land in partnership not only with his father but also with his brother. Richard Willesson had two sons, Thomas and John. The evidence in the village court rolls and the Court Book would seem to indicate that John was the younger of the two, but this does not seem to have been a great disadvantage to him with respect to taking up land. In 1427 he and his older brother acquired about 8 acres of land, but it was the holdings he took up two years later in partnership with his father and brother that allowed him to establish himself in the village. In 1429 John and Thomas joined their father in farming all the lands and tenements in Little Raveley, a small hamlet within the township of Wistow. Although John never acquired as much land as his older brother, he was able to marry and to join with his brother in leasing pasture land in 1450 and in acquiring a small holding of about 8 acres in 1454.

The various means by which younger sons came to acquire land not only illustrates something of the intricacies of land management at the family level; it also illustrates the extent to which there was room for flexibility and independent action within a system of impartible land inheritance based upon primogeniture.

Although the tenurial provisions made for younger sons are one of the most noteworthy features of the relationship between families and their land, they are by no means the only type of land dealings that took place within "yeoman" families. There were, of course, the customary transfers of family tenements to eldest sons, and some of these have been mentioned incidentally in discussing non-inheriting sons. However, the Court Book offers many examples of land dealings among family members that had no direct connection with the transfer of land to sons but rather represented a shifting of holdings within families, or joint acquisitions. In such circumstances, the term "family" must be understood to embrace the notion of kin group, and within such a context the idea of the family tenement, of course, takes on a much wider frame of reference.

There seem to have been two general levels upon which land dealings involving family members took place. On the first it was the next of kin, primarily brothers, who took part in land transactions with each other. As one might expect from the foregoing discussion, the variety and complexity of the reasons behind such transactions were often considerable. One of the most common reasons was the acquisition of land. This has already been seen in the case of the Willesson family in Wistow, in which John and Thomas not only joined their father in farming all the lands and tenements in Little Raveley but also went together in acquiring land. While their early acquisitions in 1427 and the farming lease for Little Raveley must be regarded as a means by which sons were provided for, their later acquisitions in 1450 and 1454 should be considered simply as joint property ventures. Similarly, in Upwood in 1411 two brothers, John and William Aleyn, took up a messuage and croft along with 15 acres in the open fields. This joint assumption of property seems to have benefited John in particular, for he went on to take up another 45 acres in the years between 1411 and 1443.

Aside from joining together for the purpose of accumulating land, brothers sometimes entered into transactions with each other in order to reorganize their own particular holdings. For example, in 1425 John Crowche of Broughton transferred about 40 acres to his older brother, Thomas. Since Thomas had already received his father's tenement, the logic of this conveyance would not make much sense unless one knew that in the same year John took up 30 acres and two lots of unspecified size from John Schepperd. Furthermore, one should also know that besides taking land from his brother, Thomas also gave up 38 acres to a certain John Pooll in order to acquire his brother's holding. Although one cannot discover the exact reasons for such a major reorganization of holdings by the Crowche brothers, it was clearly a dramatic step in property management and seems to have benefited both parties, for in the years after 1425 John and Thomas each went on to accumulate more holdings.

Land exchanges between brothers for the purpose of reorganizing their holdings do not always seem to have been directed towards further land accumulation in their native villages. For example, in 1425 John Cabe junior of Broughton transferred 24 acres and a lot to his younger brother, William, and William's wife Cristina. In return John received 50 acres from William. Such an exchange does not on the surface appear to have been in William's favour, but since one does not know if any moveable property, particularly money, changed hands, it would be presumptuous to assume that William had been swindled by his older brother. In fact, if one follows William's activities in the village court rolls, his reasons for taking part in such an exchange may seem a little clearer. By 1432 William was no longer a resident of Broughton. In that year he is said to be first in Upwood and then in Wennington, a hamlet within the township of Abbots Ripton. According to the Court Book, William acquired a messuage and 30 acres in Abbots Ripton, but he gave that land up prior to 1444. In 1446 the court roll of Broughton reports that William had moved to Wistow, and the account rolls of that village indicate that he had taken up a messuage and a rather diverse set of holdings there. It is very likely that William's land deal with his brother in 1425 was closely related to his subsequent departure from the village, for it not only represents an attempt to limit his tenurial commitments in Broughton; it may also have provided him with the capital to acquire land in Abbots Ripton. Thus, the land exchange between William and John Cabe may be seen as one stage in the complex set of preparations that could sometimes be involved in peasant mobility and regional property holding.

The second level upon which familial land dealings occurred did not involve the next of kin but rather more distant relatives, particularly in-laws. An example of such a land conveyance may be taken from a family that has already been mentioned with respect to land acquisitions by younger sons. It will be recalled that in 1423 Edward Justice of Broughton took up land formerly held by his great-aunt (by marriage) Alice, a widow who had remarried and was living in Upwood. This interesting land transaction, which helped to establish Edward in the village, was not the only dealing the Justice family had with Alice. In 1441 Edward's oldest brother, William, along with his wife Agnes, took over a messuage and 16 acres from Alice. Although this acquisition differed from Edward's earlier one in that it was not related to the establishment of a younger son, it very likely expressed a similar concern with keeping Alice's holdings in the family. In this regard the Justice family was successful, for the conveyance to William and his wife was the last of Alice's Broughton holdings.

The most common types of land conveyance between in-laws involved sons-in-law and fathers-in-law. For example, seven years after John Walgate junior of Wistow married Anna Willesson in 1439, he took over about 8 acres in Little Raveley from his father-in-law, Richard Willesson. As far as one may determine from the extant sources, this acquisition seems to have been closely related to an attempt by John Walgate to reorganize some of his own holdings, for in the same year that he acquired 8 acres from Richard, he gave up a cottage and 8 acres to William Outy junior. From the perspective of Richard Willesson, his conveyance to John was part of a move to limit his holdings, probably because of his advanced years.

Sometimes the land conveyances between fathers-in-law and sons-in-law were in very small units and thus reminiscent of land exchanges before the Black Death. For example, five years after William Clerk of Broughton married William Justice's daughter, Joan, in 1423, he acquired an acre, a rod, and 3 selions from his father-in-law. Although this was a small amount of land, roughly equivalent to 4 acres, it must have been very desirable land, for William paid an entry fine of 5s., more than some of his contemporaries paid for an entire virgate (32 acres).

While conveyances involving fathers- and sons-in-law usually saw the land being taken up by the sons-in-law, this was not always the case. For example, nine years after John Outy junior of Wistow took the hand of Agnes Gouler in marriage in 1399, he transferred a small tenement containing 15 acres to his father-in-law, John Gouler. This particular tenement had been taken up by John Outy senior in 1407, the year before he conveyed it to his father-in-law, and it very likely had been acquired for that purpose. It is not possible to know precisely why this land was transferred to John Gouler, but it may well have been related to the fact that when Agnes and John were married, they gained the reversion right to most of John Gouler's holdings. It would appear that by 1408 John Gouler was nearing retirement, and this land received from his son-in-law was intended to provide for him in his old age. Thus, land conveyance within families could be in the interests of the elderly as well as the young.

By no means did all the lands that changed hands during the first half of the fifteenth century come on to the market as a result of the demographic changes that took place during the half-century prior to 1400. There seem to have been a good many land exchanges designed to reorganize tenements, and there were many cases of straight accumulation and speculation involving lands that did not belong to families decimated by the plague. Such land dealings did not, however, mean that there was a weakening connection between the family and its land. Often, it can be seen that there was a "core" tenement within each family, and it did not circulate in the land market. This land, which was often held by the husband and wife together, was usually passed on intact to the eldest son. For example, in the village of Warboys, Thomas Newman senior held a considerable amount of land between 1393 and 1439, and he was involved in many land transactions during that period. Although over 70 acres passed through Thomas's hands during those years, the lands that his son, Thomas junior, received from him had been in the family for between fifteen and forty-nine years. They represented a series of holdings that, once acquired by Thomas senior, did not move beyond the family. Thus, despite the older Thomas's active participation in the village land market, the connection between the Newman family and its core tenement was a strong one.

Among those families that surveyed and prospered in the post-plague era, it is difficult to see any evidence of a weakening in the connection between family and the holding, as has been found for some other places in England. Indeed, the statistics in Table 5.1, which in part represent the extent to which yeoman families were able to support independent branches within a single village, should offer ample evidence that there was a very close, and often increasing link between families and village land. This close link has been demonstrated not only with respect to the provisions made for non-inheriting sons but also with respect to intra-family land dealings. Although the connections between families and their holdings in the post-plague era were perhaps more complex than before, they were certainly no less vital.

ii   MARRIAGE AND PROPERTY

The dominant thrust of family capital and property concentration is dramatically corroborated when one turns again to the fifteenth-century Ramsey Court Book for marriage data.[7] Unlike the data contained in manorial account rolls from the first half of the four-teenth century, which generally identify the bride and indicate the size of the marriage fine, the Court Book provides very important additional material, including the name of the groom, his place of residence, and his personal legal status. This type of information thus presents us with an invaluable opportunity for economic and social analysis.

Before analysing this material in any detail, however, certain fea-tures of the marriage entries in the Court Book must be discussed. The simple fact that there are only 104 marriages recorded in the Court Book for the five villages indicates that not all marriages were recorded in the central register. Only seven other marriages have been found in village court rolls and account rolls for the period between 1398 and 1458.[8] Since the Court Book encompasses seventy-two years, its 104 marriages represent an average marriage rate of only 1.44 per year. When this marriage rate is spread over five villages, this means that there was, on average, less than one marriage each year. Such an unrealistically low marriage rate clearly indicates that the data contained in the Court Book are selective.

In terms of social and economic status, which has been determined through the analysis of three major sets of documents, namely village court rolls, account rolls, and the Court Book itself, it is clear that the women named in the marriage listings of the Court Book were from families that represented the upper levels of village society. To say that these marriages were concluded among the higher social strata of the village does not mean that they were a homogeneous group, all holding the same amount of land. While at the lower end of the scale families such as the Hiches seem never to have controlled much more than 30 or 40 acres[9] at one time, there were at the upper end families such as the Cabes, who numbered their acreage not in tens but in hundreds. Despite such a wide discrepancy in the total amounts of land held by such families, they nevertheless exhibited a clear pattern of behaviour, especially in terms of village administration, typical of a class of families that, in studies of late thirteenth- and early fourteenth-century villages, have been described as main families[10] and are described more appropriately as yeomanry during our period.

It should now be possible to discuss in detail the truly unique aspects of these marriage entries. The Court Book gives the name of the groom in 96 (92 per cent) of the 104 marriage entries. This kind of information offers an exceptional opportunity to gain some insight into the relationships between marriage and the socio-economic hierarchies within our five communities, and in so doing helps to illustrate the central importance of the family in any attempt to understand the overall structure of peasant society.

A few examples will show the type of information at hand. In 1439 Anna Willesson of Little Raveley, a small hamlet within the township of Wistow, married John Walgate junior, also of Little Raveley. The court rolls of Wistow show the Willessons to have been an extremely active family, with Anna's father, Richard, and her two brothers, Thomas and John, performing a wide variety of administrative duties throughout the first half of the fifteenth century. The Willessons' activities in local politics were more than matched by their participation in the economic life of the community, for Anna's father and two brothers were, according to the Court Book, the farmers of all the lands and tenements in Little Raveley. Although the Court Book does not indicate the acreage involved, it must have been substantial, since the Willessons paid £10 a year for the right to farm those lands. Clearly the Willessons were of yeoman status, but what of John Walgate?

It would be difficult to find a family more involved in local matters than the Willessons, and, not too surprisingly, John Walgate could not be described as their social and economic peer. However, the extant evidence does indicate that while he was not as successful as

Table 5.2
Marriage Patterns*

Types of Marriage	Abbots Ripton	Broughton	Upwood	Warboys	Wistow	Totals
Among yeomanry within one village	7 (47%)	8 (36%)	3 (27%)	12 (32%)	14 (54%)	44 (39%)
Exogamy among the yeomanry	2 (13%)	9 (41%)	3 (27%)	9 (24%)	8 (31%)	31 (28%)
No data on husbands	5 (33%)	5 (23%)	4 (37%)	13 (34%)	3 (11%)	30 (27%)
Apparently below yeomanry	1 (7%)	– (–)	1 (9%)	4 (10%)	1 (4%)	7 (6%)
Totals	15	22	11	38	26	112

*Bracketed figures indicate the percentages of the total within each column.

the Willessons, he nevertheless was a member of the same class. Before his marriage to Anna he had already held the offices of juror, ale-taster, and autumn reeve. Moreover, the Court Book shows that he was holding about 60 acres of land in Wistow by about 1441. Thus, although John was not as prosperous as the Willessons, he was certainly well within the social and economic limits that have been set here for yeomanry.

This marriage is typical of the largest single group within the 112 marriages that have been examined. What makes it typical is not that the Willessons and Walgates were from different levels within the yeomanry but rather that the marriage of Anna and John represented the intermarriage of two yeoman families from the same village. Such marriages, of which there were 44, constitute 39 per cent of our total sample. As Table 5.2 indicates, even though this type of marriage was not necessarily the most predominant category in each of our villages, there was a definite tendency towards intermarriage within this group. When we examine the second-largest category of marriages, it soon becomes clear that such a pattern was much more than a mere tendency.

When Alice Plumbe of Warboys married John Aylmar in 1430, she left her native village and took up residence in John's village, Wistow. This example of exogamy is typical of a great many of the marriages recorded in the Court Book, a fact that has important implications with respect to the topic of peasant society from a regional perspective. However, at this point the most significant feature of this type of marriage involves the social and economic status of Alice and John rather than the exogamous nature of their union. Alice was from a Warboys family that was clearly part of the yeomanry. Her father, Richard, held about 45 acres in Warboys and participated extensively in local politics.

John Aylmar, for his part, held about 30 acres at the time of his marriage to Alice, and although he does not seem to have held any offices prior to 1430, he was deeply involved in the administrative affairs of Wistow between 1434 and 1458, serving as a reeve, beadle, juror, ale-taster, church reeve, and rent collector. Clearly John Aylmar too was a member of the same group.

Marriages such as this between Alice Plumbe and John Aylmar, which united members of yeoman families from two different communities, represent the second largest category among the 112 marriages examined here. They constitute 31 (28 per cent) of the total marriages, with the village of Broughton particularly prominent in this regard. When this figure of 28 per cent is combined with the previous one on marriage among the yeomanry within single villages (i.e., 39 per cent), we find that 67 per cent of all our marriages were cases of intermarriage among this class. With over two-thirds of the recorded marriages being of this type, it should be obvious that the frequency with which yeoman families intermarried was indicative of a general rule rather than some vague tendency. If we detach from the total number of marriages the 30 cases in which it is impossible to assess the status of the husband, the results are more dramatic. Instead of representing only 67 per cent of the total sample, the 75 cases of intermarriage among the yeomanry would amount to 91 per cent of the reduced total of 82 marriages. Thus, the extent to which intermarriage among this one class was the rule in northeast Huntingdonshire becomes even more apparent.[11]

The priority accorded to social status and property in marriage is revealed in other significant ways. Among the 112 marriages listed in the Court Book, 17 (15 per cent) were between freemen and unfree women. If we omit those recorded marriages in which there is little or no information available on husbands, then 15 (18 per cent) of 82 were "mixed," to employ Maitland's expression. With close to a fifth of this group thus representing marriages between freemen and villeins, it is clear that mixed marriages were by no means isolated incidents.

It has already been shown that class considerations were of great importance in the vast majority of marriages recorded in the Court Book, so one must ask just how the 15 freemen in our sample fitted into the social and economic life of their villages. In terms of landholding, 12 were clearly of yeoman status, with 8 of that number participating in village administration. John Grene of Abbots Ripton, for example, held about 35 acres of land in that village and served as a juror on five different occasions between 1402 and 1423. Similarly, Richard Broun of Wistow, who held about 45 acres in that village, held a jurorship on three occasions between 1402 and 1424 as well as serving as an ale-taster and autumn reeve. Theoretically, such official activities were relegated to those of villein status, but in fact these 8 freemen seem to have assumed these offices as a matter of course.

Of those 12 freemen who held about 30 acres or more, 4 do not seem to have assumed any local offices. However, in 3 of the 4 cases there is literally no information on these men in any of the court rolls of the five villages under examination in this study. It is thus quite likely that all 3 resided in other communities. John Gouler, however, who held about 40 acres in Wistow, definitely seems to have resided there. Although Thomas Gouler, perhaps John's brother, served as a juror, there is no evidence in the surviving court rolls of Wistow to suggest that John ever held any village offices.

One individual, John Forgon, who married Agnes Heryng of Upwood in 1415, was a juror in that village on four different occasions between 1452 and 1458, and also served as the sheep warden (*custos bidentium*). John Forgon is fascinating because there is no indication that he held any land in the village. This is the only case of an individual holding a local office and yet having no apparent stake in the village land market. Of course, since both the Court Book and the account rolls generally deal only with customary land and demesne land, it is possible, indeed likely, that John's land was all freehold. Unfortunately, this contention cannot be proved by means of extant sources. However, if this freeman's property was entirely freehold, it is more interesting to note his repeated assumption of offices that have traditionally been associated with villeinage.

Two individuals, John Attewode and John Nedham, both of Warboys, seem to have been below yeoman status. The former seems never to have held more than 10 acres, the latter no more than 15 acres. On one occasion, in 1405, John Nedham served as a juror. Both these individuals seem to have been minor characters in the social and economic life of Warboys, and though they may have held somewhat more land through acquisitions in the freehold market, this seems very unlikely in the case of John Nedham, who had his labour-service fines condoned in 1407–08 because he was destitute. In such circumstances John's legal freedom must have offered little consolation. However, although these two individuals do not seem to have succeeded in rising into the ranks of the yeomanry on their own, their marriages to women whose families, although unfree, were of yeoman status, may well have improved their social standing in the community.

Of the dozen freemen who, in terms of the extent of their land-holding, seem to have been of yeoman status, only one, John Outy junior, who married Agnes Gouler of Wistow in 1400, appears to have been what one might call a member of the upper level of the yeomanry. By 1411 John had acquired about 100 acres of land in Wistow as well as another 14 acres in the village of Heightmongrove. The other eleven individuals of yeoman status range from those who, with respect to the size of their holdings, were barely yeoman, such as William Wodeward junior of Abbots Ripton and John in the Wold of Broughton, each of whom held only about 30 acres, to those of middling rank, such as Richard Baroun and Robert Ely of Wistow, who held 45 acres each. If it were possible to offer a satisfactory assessment of the freehold market, we might find, of course, that the holdings of all these men were greater, but on the basis of extant evidence, both in terms of land and social activities, these freemen seem to have been quite unexceptional, especially when compared to some of the more prosperous villein families.

Further insights into the socio-economic position of these freemen may be forthcoming if we examine the status of their brides. Since class seems to have played a large part in the marriages recorded in the Court Book, the status of the bride's family in each case should help us to some idea of the relative positions of these freemen. After analysing the amounts of land held by the fathers of the brides in question, as well as assessing their respective roles in the administration of village affairs, one has the distinct impression that they were on the same general level as the freemen. Of the 17 brides, their fathers' holdings were in the general range of 30 to 50 acres in 15 instances. In other words, they ranged from those in the lower level of the yeomanry to those of intermediate position. Of this group, 9 held less than 40 acres. Only one individual, Thomas Outy of Wistow, who was the father of two brides in our sample, held more than 50 acres. He had been able to acquire something in excess of 80 acres prior to 1400; however, during the first two decades of the fifteenth century he seems never to have possessed more than 30 acres.

In the field of village administration, 12 of the 17 brides had fathers who were involved in village politics. Of these, only 3 could be said to have been deeply involved in such local affairs. They were William Aspelond of Broughton, who held a jurorship on sixteen different occasions between 1386 and 1406, as well as serving as reeve and constable; Nicholas Martyn of Wistow, who was a juror ten times between 1390 and 1410; and Richard Heryng of Upwood, who was

Table 5.3
Scale of Fines

Fine	Wistow	Abbots Ripton	Warboys	Upwood	Broughton	Totals
3d.	2					2
6d.			1(1)*	1		2(1)
10d.			1			1
1s.	1		4			5
1s.4d.					1	1
1s.6d.	2	1	2	1	1	7
1s.8d.			3			3 .
2s.				1	1	2
3s.4d.	5(1)	2	4	1	1	13(1)
4s.	1(1)		1(1)			2(2)
5s.	1		2			3
6s.7d.					1	1
6s.8d.	6(1)	3(1)	5(4)	2	2(1)	18(7)
10s.	2(1)	2(1)	1	1(1)	1	7(3)
13s.4d.	1(1)	2	1		4(1)	8(2)
20s.			2			2
Totals	21(5)	10(2)	27(6)	7(1)	12(2)	77(16)

* Figures in parentheses indicate the number of "mixed marriages" at each level of fines and
among the totals.

a juror a dozen times between 1400 and 1425 and also served as constable, ale-taster, autumn reeve, and beadle. The fathers of five of the brides took no part in local politics in so far as extant records indicate such activities.

The impression that the freemen named in our marriage fines were within a range that, in social and economic terms, could be described as low to middling is increased when one analyses the size of fines paid in such marriages. In Table 5.3, the scale of fines is presented for the 77 marriages in which the size of the merchet has been clearly set down in the Court Book. The great majority of these fines, 60 (78 per cent) of 77, were in the range from 3d. to 6s.8d., with the latter amount being the most common. Only 17 (22 per cent) of the total rose above 6s.8d. Of the 16 fines recorded with respect to our "mixed marriages," 11 (69 per cent) were on the lower level, with only 5 (31 per cent) rising above 6s.8d. Although the average fine paid in these mixed marriages, at 7s.2d., was slightly higher than that in the 61 marriages that do not seem to have been mixed, the average being 5s.4d., only 5 (29 per cent) of the 16 fines that rose above 6s.8d. involved such marriages.

If one may judge from the size of the fines, the lord of Ramsey does not seem to have taken any unusual action in the case of such marriages, despite the fact that in legal theory he was incurring some loss. Indeed, it would seem that the lord did not really care too much whom his servile women married, for there are some cases in which a fine was collected and the woman was given the right to marry anyone she and her family chose. One-half mark or one mark were not insignificant amounts of money. But they represent fixed fine ranges rather than calculations based upon the specific sizes of properties. Here again we do not move in any close relationship with the large holdings of substantial landowners.

The scale of fines indicated in Table 5.3 does serve to reinforce the impression gained throughout this section that economic status was what really mattered. Some further detail can be offered on this point. The marriage of John Grene to Alice Martyn in the village of Abbots Ripton in 1407 is typical of a half dozen cases in which it is clear that a freeman derived considerable material benefit from his marriage to a villein. In the very same year that he took Alice's hand, John also took two messuages, one and three-quarters virgates, and one cotland from his father-in-law, Thomas Martyn. This land transaction was very likely part and parcel of the dowry that had been worked out between the Martyns and the Grenes, and it would appear that this property, amounting to about 40 acres, cost John Grene only the rather modest entry fee of 2s. In some instances marriage agreements did not always result in the groom's taking immediate possession of land from his in-laws. For example, when Robert Ely of Wistow married Margaret Love in 1400, he did not receive a messuage and customary virgate from his father-in-law, John Love, only the reversion right to property. Presumably, he did not take actual possession of the land until after John's death or retirement, but for that right he nevertheless was willing to pay an entry fine of 3s.4d. Of the 15 marriages of which we possess some extant information concerning the grooms, 6 (40 per cent) involved land acquisitions similar to those of John Grene and Robert Ely. In the nine remaining cases, in which there is no surviving evidence of land dealings that seem to be linked to marriage, any profits to the grooms arising out of marriage agreements may have been in movable property and therefore were not subject to entry fines, which were then recorded in the Court Book. At any rate, it is clear that economic advantage played an important role in bringing about a good many of these mixed marriages.

6 Mobility and the Regional Economy

i MIGRATORY PATTERNS

From all major village social classes and by every channel of social and economic activity, migration accelerated rapidly from the end of the fourteenth century. The court-roll and account-roll register of licensed and unlicensed persons leaving the five villages adds up to more than 292 individuals by the middle of the fifteenth century. As the following Analysis of Villagers Emigrating from Their Home Village indicates, this emigration spread to more than eighty-two places near and far.[1] Emigration was concentrated in towns, as London (13), or regionally, as with Ramsey (30), Huntingdon (12), St Ives (10), and Godmanchester (6). Less significant clusters beyond the county such as Ely (5), King's Lynn (7), Sutton (7), and Wrestling-worth (8) generally indicate market towns. On the whole, however, more important in terms of the total identifiable migrant people than these exceptional points of concentration is the fact that market towns predominate over rural villages as the *terminus ad quem* of the emigrant (Alconbury, Ashton, Cambridge, Lavenham, Oundle, Peterborough, King's Walden, Wisbech, and Yaxley, to name but a few). This phenomenon is further emphasized by the movement of migrant workers described below. At the same time, migration to rural villages was largely to be found within a few miles' distance of the emigrant's home village.

ANALYSIS OF VILLAGERS EMIGRATING FROM THEIR HOME VILLAGES

VILLAGES OF ORIGIN*	VILLAGES EMIGRATED TO	
Upwood (1); Wistow (3)	Abbots Ripton	4
Upwood (3); Abbots Ripton (1)	Alconbury	4
Wistow (5)	Ashton	5
Wistow (2); Abbots Ripton (1); Broughton (1)	Biggin (Ramsey)	4
Wistow (1)	Brampton	1
Abbots Ripton (1); Warboys (1)	Brigstock	2
Wistow (2); Abbots Ripton (1)	Brington	3
Abbots Ripton (1)	Buckworth	1
Wistow (2)	Bury	2
Abbots Ripton (1)	Buryheath	1
Upwood (3)	Bury St Edmunds	3
Broughton (2); Wistow (1)	Bythorne	3
Upwood (1)	Caldecote	1
Warboys (1)	Cambridge	1
Wistow (2)	Chatteris	2
Broughton (5); Warboys (2)	Colne	7
Wistow (1); Upwood (1)	Covington	2
Wistow (1)	Cumberton	1
Abbots Ripton (1)	Chardel?	1
Warboys (2)	Earith	2
Broughton (1)	Edmonton	1
Broughton (2); Upwood (2); Warboys (1)	Ely	5
Upwood (1)	Exyning, next to Burwell	1
Wistow (1); Warboys (5)	Godmanchester	6
Abbots Ripton (1)	Gransden Lt	1
Abbots Ripton (2)	Graveley	2
Wistow (4); Warboys (1)	Hartford	5
Wistow (5)	Hemingford Grey	5
Warboys (2)	Hemingford Abbots	2
Warboys (2)	Hemingford (Grey or Abbots)	2
Wistow (1)	Hemmington	1
Broughton (1)	Hoddesdon	1
Broughton (1)	Holywell	1
Broughton (1)	Hoo, near Kimbolton	1
Wistow (2)	Houghton	2
Broughton (6); Wistow (3); Upwood (1); Warboys (2)	Huntingdon	12

* The figures in brackets indicate how many individuals left the village.

VILLAGES OF ORIGIN	VILLAGES EMIGRATED TO	
Warboys (1)	Kent	1
Upwood (6); Warboys (1)	King's Lynn	7
Wistow (2); Abbots Ripton (3); Upwood (1); Warboys (3)	King's Ripton	9
Broughton (1)	Lakenheath	1
Warboys (3)	Lavenham	3
Upwood (2)	Lawshall	2
Abbots Ripton (4); Upwood (1); Wistow (2); Warboys (6)	London	13
Abbots Ripton (1)	Lowick	1
Warboys (4)	Oakington	4
Warboys (1)	Old Hurst	1
Abbots Ripton (2); Warboys (1)	Oundle	3
Upwood (1); Wistow (1)	Over	3
Broughton (1); Wistow (1); Warboys (1)	Peterborough	3
Warboys (2)	Pidley	2
Warboys (1)	Potton	1
Broughton (15); Abbots Ripton (2); Warboys (4); Upwood (5); Wistow (9)	Ramsey	30
Broughton (1); Wistow (1)	Raveley Lt	2
Upwood (2)	Reach (Creache)	2
Upwood (1); Wistow (3); Abbots Ripton (1); Warboys (5)	St Ives	10
Abbots Ripton (2)	Shillington	2
Warboys (4)	Slepe	4
Upwood (2)	Soham	2
Warboys (3)	Stamford	3
Upwood (1); Wistow (3); Abbots Ripton (1); Warboys (2)	Stukeley Lt	7
Abbots Ripton (1); Wistow (6)	Sutton	7
Abbots Ripton (1)	Swaffham	1
Upwood (1)	Tenyngton?	1
Wistow (1)	Toseland	1
Warboys (2)	Tynwell	2
Warboys (2)	Upton	2
Abbots Ripton (1); Broughton (1); Wistow (3); Warboys (1)	Upwood	6
Broughton (2)	Walden King's	2
Broughton (1)	Wakefield	1
Abbots Ripton (2); Upwood (1); Warboys (1)	Walton	4

VILLAGES OF ORIGIN	VILLAGES EMIGRATED TO	
Abbots Ripton (1); Broughton (3); Wistow (7)	Warboys	11
Broughton (1); Abbots Ripton (1); Wistow (1)	Wennington	3
Abbots Ripton (1)	Weston	1
Upwood (2); Warboys (2)	Whittlesey	4
Warboys (1)	Willingham	1
Wistow (3)	Winwick	3
Upwood (3); Warboys (1)	Wisbech	4
Broughton (3); Upwood (1); Warboys (1)	Wistow	5
Warboys (2)	Woodhurst	2
Wistow (1)	Woolley	1
Abbots Ripton (4); Broughton (2); Wistow (1); Warboys (1)	Wrestlingworth	8
Broughton (1)	Yaxley	1

Abbots Ripton   53 went outside vill; 3 travelled to more than one village; 13 villagers destination not known.

Broughton   46 went outside vill; 12 travelled to more than one village; 6 villagers destination not known.

Upwood   40 went outside vill; 8 travelled to more than one village; 2 villagers destination not known.

Warboys[2]   87 went outside vill; 10 travelled to more than one village; 5 villagers destination not known.

Wistow   68 went outside vill; 12 travelled to more than one village; 6 villagers destination not known.

Maps 1 to 4 are intended to demonstrate the geographical scope of this emigration from four east Hunts villages in the early fifteenth century, without regard to concentration. Those moving to more than one location are treated separately below.

A more detailed assessment can be made of labour mobility after 1400 than is possible for the population one hundred years earlier. It may be suggested that the 42 individuals from the five villages who could not be traced represent more casual labour who moved from season to season and lost touch even with their relatives of northeast Hunts. The 45 individuals whose movements can be traced may be followed in Maps 5 to 7. These were migrants only in the sense that they moved on to more than one place and, remaining in one location for more than a season, were able to be identified with some place.

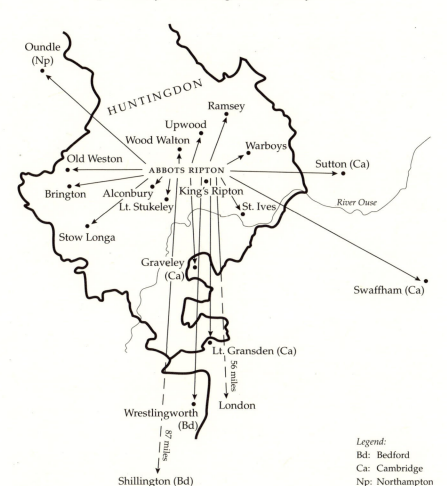

Map 1
Migration from Abbots Ripton, 1400–58

More than 90 per cent of these moved around within the county; many married and may be taken as further expression of regional involvement. Of those moving beyond the county, nearly all followed the common paths to towns (such as King's Lynn). Many of these were no doubt specialized tradesmen, such as John Justice junior from Broughton, who was a carpenter at Hoddeson (Herts) in 1450 and five years later was practising the same trade at Edmonton (Middlesex).

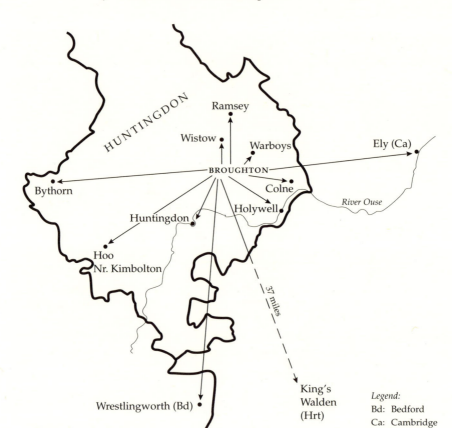

Map 2
Migration from Broughton, 1400–55

ii   A CHANGING LAND MARKET

In view of the scope of decisions about the deployment of land and labour that we have seen open to villagers, it is not surprising to find villagers reacting not only as drastically as their lord to economic conditions at the end of the fourteenth century, but prior to the lord. The lord of Ramsey expressed his disillusionment by withdrawing what remained of his direct interest in local agrarian production by farming the demesne. Villagers expressed their disillusionment and their alertness to new opportunities, as we have seen in the previous section, by rejecting their age-old ties to the land, their blood-right to customary tenements. Our records abound with references to the turnover of traditional tenements as well as

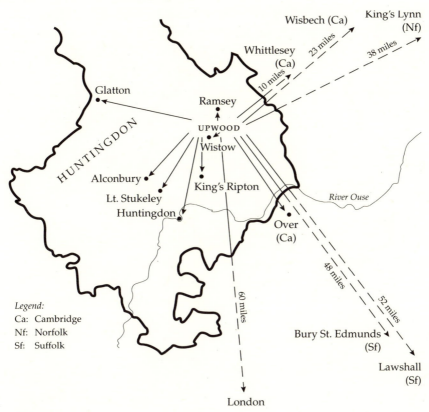

Map 3
Migration from Upwood, 1400–58

the migration of whole families and also individuals from their home villages. To understand why the villagers reacted so decisively it will be useful to look again at how conditions had changed within our five villages. These brief observations are supplementary to the description of the "haves" in chapter 5. The "have nots" could not fail to become disaffected, especially by the increasing role of aliens in the local land market, with the corresponding loss of competitive advantage to local people.

The tendency of historians to treat the dissolution of the demesne economy as explicable by the fiat of the lord has precluded, until recently, much in-depth probing of this fundamental economic reorganization. The fact that the whole demesne was finally rented out at various times throughout the manorial regions of England, as indeed of Ramsey estates, and even among these five villages,[3] does indeed indicate the precise moments of administrative decisions. But

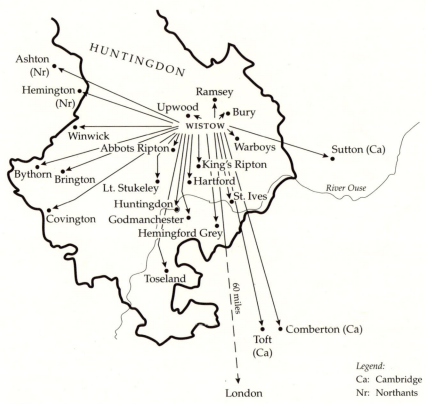

Map 4
Migration from Wistow, 1400–58

such decisions in themselves do no more to explain the economic forces at work than do bankruptcy statements of the modern firm.

This is not to say that the treatment of economic collapse at any time, even in the rural economy of late medieval England, is a simple matter. The many elements of the rural economy were so closely interwoven that cause-and-effect chain reactions are difficult to isolate. For example, many smaller tenants must have gradually lost occasions for additional revenues as the size of the demesne attenuated. But collapse there was, and it first appears around 1400 in the failure of land demand. In short, there was a coincidence with the exodus of villeins. In surviving records the most sensitive indicator of this collapse is the rapid accumulation of indebtedness by manorial officials for uncollected rents.[4]

Failure of the traditional demand for land in the manorial context did not mean that there was a collapse in the demand for land. Most

Map 5
Movement to more than one vill from Wistow, 1400–58

of the arable of these Huntingdonshire villages was kept under cultivation. Excluding Abbots Ripton, for which there are no account rolls in the early fifteenth century, it can be generally stated that only small pieces of demesne fell back into the lord's hands, and customary tenements were not long deserted. Customary units of 1 virgate (2), ½ virgate, and ½ cotland fell into the lord's hands at Wistow for a brief time in the 1390s. At Upwood[5] customary units came increasingly into the lord's hands only after 1400, and in the same village small demesne units (1 and 7 acres and 1 acre) came into the lord's hands only in 1408. At Broughton a 2-acre demesne unit came into the lord's hands for a time in 1381; excluding a 30-acre field that seems to have reverted to demesne, by 1393 demesne units of 1 acre, 4 acres, and "1 piece" along with a customary tenement (1 virgate)

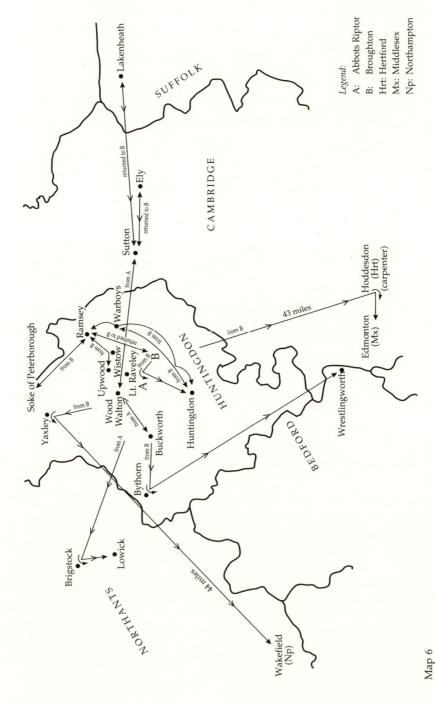

Legend:
A: Abbots Riptor
B: Broughton
Hrt: Hertford
Mx: Middlesex
Np: Northampton

Map 6
Movement to more than one vill from Abbots Ripton and Broughton, 1400–58

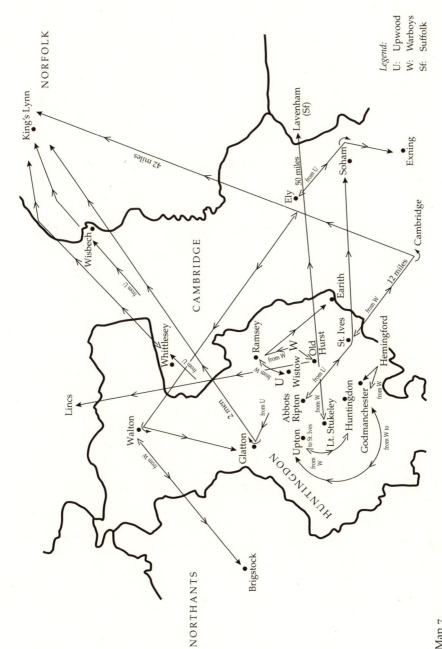

Map 7
Movement to more than one vill from Upwoods and Warboys, 1400–58

were in the lord's hands; by 1419 lands in the lord's hands were 1 acre of demesne, 1 croft, and 6 virgates of customary land.

But the capital depletion of village land-related resources must have been immense. While none of these villages became deserted, the large number of deserted villages that appear in Midland England from this time may be only a marginal indication of the dissolution of the older economy. Leases began to turn over quickly, and a deliberate policy of peasant property exploitation by the villagers themselves appeared for the first time in the history of these Hunts villages. From the 1390s account rolls began to list former tenants of various properties in order to clarify the record during this profusion of rapid changes. It is impossible to give a complete picture of this turnover, since for many years account rolls are not extant.

Demand for land remained high because there were others than native villagers hungry for Ramsey lands. Again, evidence for this demand coincides with other late fourteenth-century changes. The case of Broughton is especially well documented. During the period of attempted "normalization" after the Black Death, a Broughton rent roll[6] was drawn up listing the tenants in 1380 and the former tenants of their properties, in many instances individuals holding prior to the Black Death. Around 1400 the names of the new tenants were written over the old. About one-half dozen tenements may not have been on the market at both dates, but for the remainder, that is at least 90 properties, 56 had acquired new tenants by 1400. Only some 18 of the 56 had familiar surnames – a transition apparently more drastic than for the generation after the Black Death.[7] The same phenomenon can be recorded for Upwood in 1392. Thirteen different parcels of demesne came into different hands, in only one instance by descent from father to son. A rough measure of this market activity may be seen in the changing amounts of land held by individuals in different years (Appendix IV below).

Account rolls also began to record the provenance of many of these newcomers attracted by Ramsey lands. Nearly forty outsiders, often from some distance, took up land in these villages in the early fifteenth century. These were:

ABBOTS RIPTON: John Crosse of Barton, John Hiche of Eastthorpe, Thomas atte Hill of Hartford, Prior and Canon of Huntingdon, William de Hurst, Alexander March of Eastthorpe, William Martyn of King's Ripton, John Motwell, taylor, of Huntingdon, Thomas Smith of Shillington, George Stokle of Godmanchester, Thomas Ware of Hartford, Robert Wrighte of Huntingdon, and Richard Wrighte of Wood Walton.

BROUGHTON: Thomas Burder of Buckworth and John of Bury.

UPWOOD: The chaplain of Lt Stukeley, Richard de Freeston, Richard Greetham of Diddington, Richard Greetham of Everdon, William Hammond of Diddington, Nicholas Hendersson of Hemingford Grey, William Jonessoun of Holme, and Nicholas de Stukeley.

WARBOYS: John Bennesson senior, alias palfreyman, of Ramsey, William Broughton of Bury, William atte Hide of Bury, Richard Lancyn of Fen Stanton, John Laurence of Fen Stanton, John March of Bury, John Shepherd junior of Holywell, and William Webester of Bury.

WISTOW: Thomas Bolyon of Brampton, John Chartres of St Ives, Richard de Ely, Thomas Miller of Haddenham, William Newman of Bury, and John Pegge junior of Somersham.

Map 8, indicating the provenance of outsiders, shows that these landholders were spread fairly widely throughout Huntingdonshire, and a good number came from beyond the county. The wider economic framework of these villages is also indicated by the involvement of local villagers in lawsuits with those as far away as William Bukby of Graveley and Thomas Couper of Godmanchester.

The identification of property concentration with several members of a family, noted in the previous chapter, changed during the fifteenth century. No doubt the ongoing demographic declines were a factor here. But more central was the continuing economic attraction of the larger landholdings, thereby excluding more members of the kin group. What has been described in chapter 5 as yeoman economic status came more and more to the fore. Significantly, newcomers appear to have been of this same wealth status.

What information is extant for the 1440s and 1450s at Upwood indicates a return to concentration of properties in one branch of the family (see Aleyn, Aubes, Peny). The same phenomenon of property spread among more members of larger families in the early fifteenth century is also to be found for Warboys (Baron, Berenger, Benson, Plumbe), with a tendency to concentration again among fewer branches towards 1450. Much the same pattern may be observed for Abbots Ripton, where the traditional spread was still represented by the more than 20 of the 94 known tenants holding 1 virgate over 1375–95. Concentrations of up to 2 virgates were beginning among some dozen villages by this time, and the majority of some score smallholdings were held by new names. While no account rolls are extant for Abbots Ripton in the first half of the fifteenth century, a very detailed account roll for 1456 is available and lists more than 50 tenants, with some greater concentrations than appeared in the fourteenth century. Again, except for the families of Payne, Watts, and

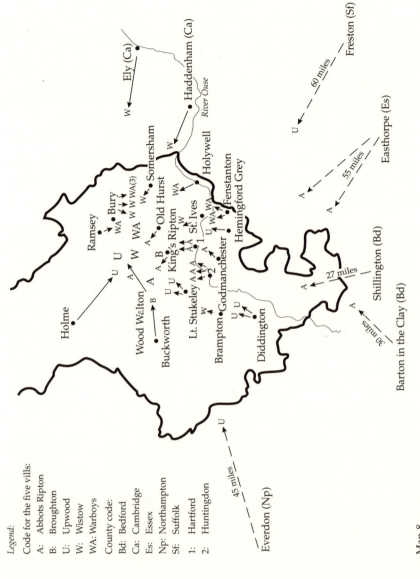

Legend:

Code for the five vills:

A: Abbots Ripton
B: Broughton
U: Upwood
W: Wistow
WA: Warboys

County code:

Bd: Bedford
Ca: Cambridge
Es: Essex
Np: Northampton
Sf: Suffolk

1: Hartford
2: Huntingdon

Map 8

Outsiders holding property within the five vills, ɔ.400–58

Weston, there is no spread of holdings among several members of families by 1456.

One further indicator of the direction of change in the land market may be seen in the gradual tendency towards holding land in more than one village. The more scattered survival of fifteenth-century records does not provide good bases for full assessment of the picture. Furthermore, by the nature of the development one should not expect extra-vill holdings to be limited to our five villages. Descriptions of tenants holding pieces of demesne field at Wistow already have demonstrated the involvement of the "men of Bury." But older families were continuing the practice, and new families became involved in the same fashion as they replaced disappearing families. While the measurable increase in the numbers of those holding property in more than one vill in the early fifteenth century had been only from 54 to 62, the following lists do show how common multi-village tenure had become.

INDIVIDUALS HOLDING LAND IN MORE THAN ONE VILLAGE AFTER 1400

Albyn, Richard	Upwood and Wistow
Asplond, John	Warboys and Wistow
Asplond, Robert (alias Ploughwrighte)	Warboys and Wistow
Asplond, Thomas (alias Ploughwrighte)	Warboys and Wistow
Asplond, William (alias Ploughwrighte)	Broughton, Warboys, and Wistow
Attegate, John	Warboys and Wistow
Baker, Walter	Upwood and Wistow
Baron (Baroun), John	Warboys and Wistow
Baron (Baroun), Richard	Upwood, Warboys, and Wistow
Baron (Baroun), Thomas	Warboys and Wistow
Benet, John	Warboys and Wistow
Bigge, John	Broughton, Upwood, and Wistow
Bole, John	Upwood and Warboys
Bottiler, William	Broughton and Warboys
Bracer, William	Upwood and Wistow
Bronnote, John	Upwood, Warboys, and Wistow
Broughton, William	Broughton, Warboys, and Wistow
Broun, Richard (of Lt Raveley)	Upwood, Warboys, and Wistow
Broun, William	Upwood and Warboys
Catoun, John	Broughton and Warboys
Catelyne, John (alias shepherd)	Warboys and Wistow

Catelyne, Richard	Upwood and Wistow
Clerk, John (parson of the church)	Broughton, Warboys, and Wistow
Cook, John	Upwood and Warboys
Couper, Adam	Broughton and Warboys
Derworth, William	Warboys and Wistow
Derworth, Joan, wife of William	Warboys and Wistow
Edward, John	Upwood and Warboys
Flemyng, William	Upwood and Warboys
Fraunceys, John	Upwood, Warboys, and Wistow
Gouler, John	Upwood and Wistow
Gouler, Thomas	Upwood and Wistow
Hering, John	Upwood and Warboys
Hering, William jr	Upwood and Wistow
Horewode, John	Upwood and Warboys
Lone, John	Upwood, Warboys, and Wistow
Martin, John	Abbots Ripton and Warboys
Martin, William	Abbots Ripton and Wistow
Miller, John	Upwood and Warboys
Newman, John	Upwood, Warboys, and Wistow
Newman, Thomas	Upwood, Warboys, and Wistow
Outy, John	Upwood and Wistow
Plumbe, John	Warboys and Wistow
Plumbe, Richard	Warboys and Wistow
Randolf, John	Broughton and Wistow
Shepherd, John	Abbots Ripton, Broughton, Warboys, and Wistow
Shepherd, Nicholas	Broughton, Warboys, and Wistow
Shepherd, Richard	Warboys and Wistow
Shepherd, William	Broughton, Warboys, and Wistow
Skinner, Richard	Upwood and Wistow
Smith, Robert	Upwood, Warboys, and Wistow
Smith, Thomas	Upwood and Wistow
Smith, William (of Wennington)	Abbots Ripton, Upwood, and Warboys
Sywell, John	Upwood and Warboys
Taylor, Robert	Warboys and Wistow
Vernoun, John	Upwood and Wistow
Vernoun, Thomas	Abbots Ripton and Upwood
Waryn, John	Warboys and Wistow
Waryn, William (of Warboys)	Warboys and Wistow
Webester, William (of Bury)	Upwood, Warboys, and Wistow
Wold, John	Broughton and Upwood
Wright, John	Broughton and Warboys

iii   THE FINAL OPTION: CUSTOMARY PEOPLE OR CUSTOMARY LAND

The increasingly exclusive quality of the local land market,[8] described in the last section, goes far to explain the exodus of so many villeins during the last decade of the fourteenth century and why this exodus became a regular feature of village life until the last quarter of the fifteenth century.[9] Clearly, onerous labour obligations were not the reason for this disaffection among former tenants. Although firm figures are impossible owing to the rapidly changing tenurial scene, well over 90 per cent of the labour services were being paid by substantial tenants at this time, tenants who were not to be counted among those leaving home villages illegally. Furthermore, many smallholders who left had been holding properties for money rent only.

But why then bother to record the names of villeins who had left illegally? Those of us who have written about this phenomenon have too readily assumed that the retention on account rolls for decades of names of villeins who had left their home manors simply signified an archaic accounting system. In the context of this study, we must conclude that such was not the case. Rather, the names of villeins were retained because they held the potential of considerable capital gains by the lord. Those leaving their native villages at this period with or without permission of the lord were not the impoverished hordes of vagrants to be found in later periods as the result of enclosures. Nor was this at all similar to migrations prior to the Black Death, discussed in chapter 2, when it had become common for members of families to leave their home villages, usually with licence from the lord, so that they remained legally members of the village manor. As we have seen in section i of this chapter, these villeins had a lively participation in the regional economy.

The lords of Ramsey and their administration were as alert in the fifteenth century to the possibility of economic profits as they had been in the heyday of the fair of St Ives in the thirteenth century. When possible, profits would be siphoned off from the growing regional economy. Such profits might be expected from three sources: those who had left Ramsey manors to pursue professional careers in larger towns or cities successfully, the ambitious new yeoman group, and those villeins whose paths were traced in section i of this chapter.

Evidence from manumissions[10] gives us the best insight into the lord's profit-seeking policies. There are only 79 cases of manumission recorded in fifteenth-century cartularies for the more than a score of manors of the abbey, and the actual manumission payments are not given for most of these cases. But a reasonably clear pattern emerges from these data. First, manumission appears to have been a prestige advantage to the new "professions" of the period. Such was a farmer of Ramsey property, although in this instance the example is not from one of our five villages. Richard Hunter of Walsoken paid £20 for manumission at the time that he farmed the hamlet of Poppenhoe in the same village.[11] William Asplond from Wistow was a citizen and brewer in London, and Everard, likely from Broughton, was a citizen and armourer in London. We do not know the amounts of their fines, only that they were paying off manumissions. Since the Asplonds and Everards had long been prominent families, such individuals might have wished to retain links with their native villages.

Secondly, the lords of Ramsey miscalculated badly when they presumed that those villeins listed in section i above might return to take up land again or would seek manumission. Those individuals and families whose names were retained decade after decade had a surer premonition of the future. Properties were stripped bare as they left. They were cutting all ties with their native surroundings. None of these sought manumissions, and the chronic failure in land demand meant that these people and their chattels were lost forever. The continuing list of migrants appended to manorial accounts does reflect the continuity of lordship. But, as with the formal lists of customary holdings described in chapter 4, the underlying economic realities were vastly changed.

Thirdly, since it was the status of the land rather than the status of the tenant that defined customary tenure, manumission would hold no attraction for most customary tenants. Certainly, those many customary tenants who were of yeoman economic status could well afford manumission prices. But the fact that there are so few manumissions underlines the lack of interest by tenants. Manumissions are insignificant in number by comparison with the 40 new tenants from outside for only five villages, listed earlier in this chapter, and the vigorous family arrangements among free and unfree surveyed in chapter 5. The lord does appear to have tempted the tenant. But those few examples of manumission of customary tenants that survive show no profit for the lord beyond his having attracted a tenant. John Mylys, the son of Robert Mylys of Upwood, who had held as much as 3 virgates around 1412, was granted manumission in 1439 for all his family. John Mylys, who now described himself as of King's Ripton, where he may have been a farmer, had a £40 fine entered only as a warranty of co-operation with the lords. More revealing still is the manumission of William Wattes, said to be holding land of the lord in Abbots Ripton, where indeed he was a modest virgater, who paid no fine and was merely bound by the warranty that he would stay on his tenement or, if he should depart, would find a suitable tenant as replacement.

This entry concerning William Wattes made a mockery of traditional villeinage, and the charade was quietly dropped, so that references to villeinage and manumissions disappear over the second half of the fifteenth century. But in any case there had been no laboured identification of villeins with customary tenants since the thirteenth century. Tenants were more interested in the fact that economic conditions favoured them in the fifteenth century. The lord was gradually forced to make more concessions in order to attract tenants. Significant, for example, was the increasing capital investment required for the repair of buildings on customary holdings. By the 1440s this had risen to as high as £14 for one year and £11.11s. the following year at Upwood.[12] Capital shortage forced the hand of the lord, as it had done two hundred years earlier. Tenure by copy was not so much a revolutionary new phenomenon as a step that had many parallels in the past. The priority of the lord over these many generations had been the maintenance of customary tenements over villeinage status.[13] By the fifteenth century this had become not just a priority but a final option. But the role of capital in the development of copyhold tenure takes us beyond our story.

7 Conclusion

Throughout this study every effort has been made to keep our investigations strictly within the compass of economic history. In the final analysis, this approach became possible because of the consistent pattern of the evidence. The result has been a striking reversal of traditional historiography, in that customary tenure becomes no longer a block to economic development but an instrument for such development. To say this does not in any way idealize the manorial system as a mode of economic organization. Rather, it elucidates another chapter in the history of the role of capital in economic development. Peasant progress occurred despite the limitations of the manorial system.

Two themes run throughout this study: the policies of the lord vis-à-vis customary tenants and the economic activity of these tenants within the framework of such policies. No attempt has been made to elaborate the policies of the lord, since the first purpose of this research has been seen as the need to isolate and trace the role of customary tenants within the various manors. None the less, in light of this research it may be useful to offer a few reflections on how a study of these policies of the lord might be advanced.

Assuredly, capital cannot play a role unless there is a political economy to allow capital to do so. Unquestionably, the lords of Ramsey retained the full legal formula of villeinage throughout the period of this study. Those texts quoting conditions of tenure to be found in chapter 1 for the early period and the closely calculated high costs of manumission along with the continual record of illegal flight discussed in chapter 6 illustrate this ongoing legal reality. The point at issue, however, is not the existence of political and/or legal power but, as in any society, how such power is exercised in relation to economic life. Increasingly, economists – Douglas C. North, for example – emphasize today that economic analysis must include institutional factors.[1] Recent studies have found the Ramsey administration functioning within a regional and international market economy during and prior to the chronological period covered by this study. The process featured in this volume, then, whereby the administration had a consistent concern for the maintenance of capital and all manner of fines were efficiency-control mechanisms rather than direct profit-taking, was not new to Ramsey. This would mean that there is every reason to believe that the lord recognized the efficiency of the peasant farmer. As has been pointed out for the lords of Ramsey, heavy jurisdictional penalties were not allowed to stand in the way of the fair and market of St Ives. Throughout this study the same practice has been found for the treatment of manorial tenants. Fines for trespass in open fields and commons of woods, marsh, and pasture, as well as fines for the dereliction of work service, were real, but not such as to jeopardize the productivity of the peasant. The extensive system of accounts and auditing would be of little value, as was so often experienced by lords after 1400, when tenements became undercapitalized and were even left vacant.

Nor should we expect to find such economic motivation unique to Ramsey. From the tin mines in Devon[2] to the salt marshes in Lincolnshire[3] and the lead mines of Derby,[4] feudal lords were aware of the need to invest in primary production. Nor would understanding of the market economy be something new to lordship. The early market and fair held by Ramsey Abbey was to be found elsewhere, at such places as Battle, Malmesbury, and Winchester. It has been observed by the historian of St Ives[5] that the same rationality exercised at Ramsey was pursued by Winchester lords over the fair of St Giles. The historian of Battle Abbey underlines parallel limitations to the lords' profits at Battle, Cambridge, and Lincoln.[6] The same would appear to be the policy at such Westminster boroughs as Staines.[7] Another practice to be found throughout this study – that is, the small jurisdictional fines – may also be found elsewhere, as at Bec and Winchester.[8] In sum, the economic role of the tenant within the manorial system is more fully appreciated as we gain in understanding of the role of lords in the commercialization process.[9]

Further attention could also be given to the fact that ancient large estate complexes had a privileged sharing in government. In short, the political economy of the lord might be expected to be comparable to the Crown in some small degree at least. Continuing studies of the commercialization of medieval rural England could usefully compare the lords' economic policies with those of the Crown. The latter enhanced the environment for economic growth through stabilization, as in minting and the assize of bread and ale, and encouraged the rational spread of markets by licensing policies. As has been seen throughout this study, the lords of Ramsey shared directly in royal authority through their privileged administration of the assize of ale and the frankpledge system. Furthermore, in both areas the lords reflected royal policy by stabilized fines and devolved control over the movement of individuals.

As we grow in awareness of the commercial importance of lordships, it becomes more necessary, however, to review again the limitations imposed upon their economic enterprise by the institutional structure of such entities, limitations that would favour the scope of peasant enterprise. Not unlike the Crown, tenants-in-chief like the lords of Ramsey Abbey and other ancient Benedictine establishments bore heavy burdens from their position in feudal society. With the rapid development of the market economy, the vague accounting system of the Anglo-Saxon and Anglo-Norman periods had to be replaced by up-to-date double accounting by the end of the twelfth century. Even more significant for old Benedictine monasteries was the division of properties at the same time between the lord and the conventual community in order to provide a guaranteed income for the latter. Administrative management of conventual community needs was placed more directly in the hands of officials responsible for specific consumer requirements, from the kitchen to the choir. Significantly, from the beginning of this reform process, money rents became a perceptible part of these allocations to officials. When these officials required more revenues, usually from the late thirteenth century, these were provided almost entirely by fixed money rents, sometimes from newly purchased properties,[10] much before money rents became so important in traditional manorial accounts.

The revenues of the lords themselves were pushed in the same direction from the late thirteenth century with the introduction of the heavy Edwardian taxation.[11] For many lords, lay as well as ecclesiastic, heavy building programs in the fourteenth century provided a similar drain upon the supply of liquid capital. Under such pressures, fixed money rents, capital available in foreseeable amounts that would make financial arrangement possible, became the order of the day.

This long process of consumer organization by feudal lords, in this instance by the bipartite conventual community and the lord abbot, was not an exercise in aristocratic dissipation. It was accompanied by increasing professionalization of accounting services, both through improved record-keeping and through the use of the expertise of professionals such as auditors and lawyers.[12] But it was a centuries-long process, so that it inevitably removed the lord's management further and further, and increasingly during the fourteenth century, from the direct economic development of the countryside. There is no reason to believe that by the fourteenth century the lords of Ramsey had lost that economic acumen so visible one hundred years earlier when they, along with other lords, constructed the "capitalist" program that so fascinated M.M. Postan and other economic historians earlier in this century. Indeed, the lords had the acumen to recognize that the economic performance of their manors was strengthened by the very entrepreneurial scope given to their tenants.

While limitations on capitalist entrepreneurs in the welfare states of the twentieth century throw more comparative light upon the entrepreneurial role of larger monastic establishments than was conceivable to economists working within nineteenth-century models, the older model is still perpetuated by the expression "direct farming," which has taken on something of the permanence of an economic principle. A hint at the historical inadequacy of the expression was brought out by emphasis on direct farming as a brief experiment.[13] A corrective challenge to the notion of the experiment as brief offered some clarification.[14] But the latter point ought to be taken further. Some degree of direct farming remained as an option to the lord.[15] For Ramsey we have seen how new experiments in direct farming would occur after the Black Death and again into the 1380s. Such experiments were consonant with more highly developed market systems – that is, the purpose of the experiment was to exploit new price and market opportunities rather than to exploit the tenant. The continuing development of the peasant economy at Ramsey ran concurrently with new direct farming experiments.

What may appear to be unique to the lord rather than the Crown is the role of what has been traditionally called "custom," in particular the customary rights and obligations of tenants, the relatively fixed commutation prices for labour obligations, and fines for various delicts and trespasses. In traditional historiography the term "custom" does not adequately spell out the full economic reality at work in these contexts. As anthropologists have discovered, custom may be as flexible as more formal legal systems. In this study custom indicates the more positive policies promoting peasant economic viability. Adjustments downward in the size of customary land-entry fines offer the most tangible evidence of this flexibility, by contrast with more uniform entry fines of the late thirteenth century. But over the long run, of greater importance was the policy of establishing relatively small fixed fines for virtually every form of trespass and commutation. This framework made it possible for customary tenants to introduce flexibilities according to the immediate needs of their own enterprise. Much of the exercise of these options is hidden from our eyes by the generic references to trespass, except when an aggressive individual makes a point of accumulating fines over a wide range of trespasses. Paradoxically, in the light of the conventional wisdom about the debilitating effects of the burden of labour services, the various steps open to exercising the options of commutation or refusal to work best illustrate how the allocations of his labour services could be flexibly adapted by the customary tenant. In short, the peasant enjoyed a framework of controlled expectations such as would encourage his participation in local markets.

Along with the notion that the lord had inadequate economic know-how, traditional historiography has too readily assumed that the manorial peasant could not be efficient by the very nature of his economic environment. This notion, too, is gradually being undermined, especially with recent studies of productivity.[16] A few references have been made to the peasants' economic potential in chapter 1. But the many facets of this question would require a volume in themselves. For example, recognition of the economic efficiency of manorial peasants is less surprising as the open-field system is acknowledged to have greater efficiency than was once thought to be the case. Donald N. McCloskey's emphasis upon this field system as providing greater risk protection[17] and Carl Dahlman's stress on transaction cost equivalences[18] are only two of many examples of this new direction among economic analysts. More efficient adaptation of power, as seen in the flexible use of the horse by peasants,[19] also adds to our knowledge of resources available to peasant production. This takes on special significance in the high-cost cultivation of heavy soils and the cultivation feasibility of the small units composing the open-field tenurial organization. At the market end of the spectrum, one has the impression that study of the local textile and brewing trades as peasant industries are still in their infancy.[20]

The various factors at play here are not something new to the economic historian. As long ago as 1963 Edward Miller could write, "Finally, the growth of both long-range and short-range commerce similarly broke down barriers and enlarged horizons."[21] Nor was the same author unaware of the fact that markets grew under what he called "the dispersal of authority" typical of medieval times. But the continuing notion that real growth in trade had to be in "the hands of the professionals"[22] and that local markets "had not been found worthy of attention"[23] has discouraged the direct investigation of economic development in the heart of feudal society. With the recognition of commercialization in the rural economy and with advanced analysis of local marketing under way, one may expect more comparisons between rural England and such well-studied continental counterparts as the Lowlands and indeed the whole area of the Hansa.

This volume might well have been called "An Introduction," to allow for the limitations of available Ramsey data. None the less, this study suggests reflections for further research upon a broader base of information. This volume has cast customary tenants in an entrepreneurial role – that is, as major actors in the economic life of the manor, responsible for agrarian productivity and presumably for marketing of such produce. Throughout the often dreary economic climate of the fourteenth and early fifteenth centuries, revenues from Ramsey estates remained strong. Such incomes coincided with a policy of capital maintenance and with a continued strong supply of aggressive and successful tenants. For the manors of Ramsey under study here, the relative size of their animal herds vis-à-vis the herds of the lord and the increasing expansion of arable through the leasing of demesne are the most ready indicators of peasant economic activities. Given this role of the tenants, investigations into capital improvements by the lord[24] might have been expected to draw a negative picture.

Despite our vastly improved knowledge about the innovative scope of peasant activities and their range of decision-making, much still remains to be done in order to obtain a proper grasp of the actual available capital resources of the English countryside by the thirteenth century. To some degree, this information may continue to elude us because the current version of the "blocked-out" customary tenant too readily assumes that the lords simply skimmed off peasant surpluses. If such was the case, where did those vast new papal and royal taxes come from? At Ramsey[25] as much as 25 to 30 per cent of the gross revenues received by the reeve were collected in one year of the late thirteenth century for such taxes (see Table 7.1). These taxes came at the time of that revolt against the penalizing of frankpledge officials that has been described in chapter 3. As we have seen, the lord shifted his demands to a fixed *capitagium* quota that the peasants were themselves to collect. The view receipts returned to normal, as we see in the 1289–90 column below. It was the lord who changed his revenue structure by purchasing new properties and arranging

Table 7.1
View of Frankpledge Receipts

	1288–89	1289–90
Abbots Ripton	£26. 9s.1d.	?
Broughton	£15.16s.	£5
King's Ripton	£23. 7s.5d.	8s.8d.
Warboys	£9.17s.5d.	18s.9d.

leases in order to enhance money rents to cover the new levels of indebtedness.[26]

Capital could become available for rural needs from townsmen. Such a use for commercial profits is a well-known phenomenon, as, for example, within the ambience of London. At Battersea and Wandsworth about 18 per cent of the tenants of Westminster Abbey held both free and customary land.[27] Burgesses of Battle Abbey also invested in the countryside, and peasants of the area held messuages in the borough of Battle.[28] Ramsey estates also provide information about town profits supporting investment in the countryside. A future study is to investigate the provenance of new customary tenants and the role of all customary tenants, free and unfree, in markets. For all Ramsey estates this becomes a regional and possibly multi-regional study of major dimensions. For the present, two examples may serve to illustrate the possibilities for this future research.

John Ballard of Broughton, who left many references in records between 1288 and 1316, may be taken as one example. Although information about his customary holdings is not extant, Ballard's customary obligations were many. His official duties included the positions of capital pledge and juror. He was personal pledge on at least fifteen occasions for a wide variety of individuals, from Ralph Norreys, a major freeholder in the area, to lesser lights such as Robert Curteys, a local butcher. His son Richard was cited for not being in tithing in 1301, and by 1314 John Ballard was required to produce a charter for the 24 acres and 1 messuage that he had purchased and delivered to Richard. John had a strong base in the market of St Ives, where he held 1 messuage and 2 rows of houses between 1293 and 1314. But he was also active on the rural scene, since we find him fined in the 1294 court of Warboys for taking turves illegally and around the same time in the court of Wistow for some vaguely defined trespass.

Those entering Ramsey estates from outside require a different pattern of research. The Cristemesse family may be taken as an example. The name appears in West Hunts in early fourteenth-century lay-subsidy rolls. Court rolls for the central market borough of Huntingdon show a Simon Cristemesse as a merchant in the early 1360s. Simon disappears from the records by the end of that decade. Shortly thereafter, that is by 1371, an Emma Cristemesse appears as an important brewer and remains involved as defendant or plaintiff in the many debt pleas typical of that trade until the end of the Huntingdon court series in August 1382. The name Cristemesse first appears in the countryside of East Hunts in relation to two cotlands at Holywell, next to our cluster of villages, in 1362. But when large amounts of property became available in that village after 1400, the Cristemesse family quickly became one of the larger landholders. Undoubtedly, profits from the Huntingdon trade were invested in order to make such land purchase possible.

Those such as John Ballard who drew capital from local commercial enterprises opted to remain in the countryside as customary tenants. In addition, we have seen in chapter 1 how a thin stream of individuals with, presumably, capital from commercial endeavours would continue to move into Ramsey estates. However, perhaps the most important conclusion of this study suggests another dimension to the question of town or country investment. Owing no doubt to the well-advanced use of money and well-developed markets, the countryside could compete with the town by providing capital for rural investment. Relatively few outsiders entered Ramsey customary lands because local tenants themselves could generate adequate capital. Whether the lord deliberately limited the numbers of outsiders seeking to invest in the customary lands of his manors we do not know. But the policies of the lord made it possible for his native customary tenants to remain in possession of their traditional family holdings and to enjoy market opportunities comparable to those of their peers in the market and fair of St Ives.

While Ramsey sources have made possible the analysis of the role of customary tenants within the manorial economy, the existence of successful customary tenants as such is not something new to the historian. Edmund King's analysis of the *Carte Nativorum*[29] may be seen as an early fourteenth-century companion study to this volume on Ramsey. The *Carte* was concerned with freehold, and there is no such record to make possible a comparable assessment of the use of freehold by customary tenants at Ramsey. But King's identification of customary tenants as economic actors is entirely familiar to the villages of Ramsey studied here. His "aristocrats" among villeins represented by the Gere and le Wro families are typical of "major tenants" in Ramsey. The capacity to pay high fines, to fine for services, and to make family arrangements without breaking up customary tenements are part of the one picture. The use of freemen when customary tenants were not available is equally relevant to the issue of working capital.

The Peterborough experience is actually more closely reflected in one of our villages, King's Ripton, owing to the ancient demesne format of that village. Anne DeWindt has isolated the various leading tenants of King's Ripton, and these are comparable in their land-marketing practices to Gere and le Wro. For example, a number of families accumulated pieces of land in the following patterns: 7 acres and 2 messuages by 13 different transactions; 12½ acres in 35 transfers; 12 to 13 acres in 5 transactions; 7½ acres, 5½ acres, and so forth.[30] In a study more focused on the land market than families, the same scholar identified 292 property transfers between 1280 and 1397 involving 253 individuals.[31] As has been noted in chapters 4 and 6 above, tenants from neighbouring villages, especially Broughton, participated in the King's Ripton land market.

Supplementary evidence about Ramsey's neighbour to the east raises some interesting questions concerning the length of time customary tenants may have had such an active part in the economic scene. In the words of Edward Miller: "Free tenants were buying and selling land amongst themselves ... and, as we shall see, with the villeins ... But clearly, at least, there was a very flourishing land-market amongst the peasantry in the estate in the early thirteenth century; ... and it was mainly (though soon not exclusively) the free and the semi-free who were paying those prices."[32] Do we find an echo of this same land market at Ramsey in the late thirteenth century? Miller's masterful analysis takes us up to the early thirteenth century only and, perhaps for this reason, has been somewhat neglected in recent studies of the land market. It is a familiar anthropological axiom that peasant cultures, including the economic practices of such cultures, are not wont to arise phoenix-like after a gap of two or three generations. In any case, it might be interesting to note that Edward Miller finds a basic "direction of economic evolution" that did not change with the shift to more tenure by will from the money rents prevalent in the twelfth century. The student of Ramsey estates must find Miller's concluding remarks to be prescient: "The incidental profits of villein land and villein status were preserved for the peasant England that was to come; the insecurity of villein status and villein tenure made a contribution to the more flexible types of rent-contract devised in the thirteenth century and put into widespread operation in the fourteenth; and ultimately the copyholder and the leaseholder, rather than the freeholder, became the typical peasant farmer of the later Middle Ages."[33]

Did the presence of freemen in some Ramsey manors provide leadership for the more independent role the villagers were to play in the frankpledge system? For a few years in the 1290s the Clairvaux, who were freemen, refused ploughing services on the plea of their freedom. But these services were clearly owed according to the mid-thirteenth-century extents, when in fact it was common for freemen to owe a variety of services. Such services appear to have continued into the fourteenth century and, if anything, may have conditioned the attraction of customary tenements for freemen. As we have seen in chapter 5, it was as customary tenants that freemen would establish themselves on larger properties, and often by marriage with villeins, in the late fourteenth and early fifteenth centuries. Over the fourteenth century one finds increasingly that village administration, especially by means of by-laws, was able to challenge tenants of any social level who might try to disrupt manorial organization. As is well known, the servants of the lords of Ramsey were brought to task for trespass along with the most humble villager. Powerful freeholders, as were the Hurst family from the village of that name, were even threatened with exclusion from the commons because of repeated infractions of the by-laws of neighbouring vills.

This phenomenon of gradual concentration of lands, especially of customary holdings, from the late fourteenth century, has been traced throughout those parts of England where partible inheritance was not in vogue: the North, Yorkshire and Lancashire, West Midlands, Home Counties, Southern Counties, Devon, and Cornwall.[34] But investigation of these concentrations as an evolution over the previous century has not to this date been widely addressed. Study of these Ramsey villages indicates that this evolution can only be properly traced through the families of the villagers. Furthermore, it has been possible to focus upon the economy of the customary tenant throughout this volume because the normal administrative references in account rolls and court rolls refer simply to the actions of customary tenants (custumarii). While the neat simplicity of these references is entirely consonant with a highly developed accounting system, legal and social realities were much more complex, as Edward Miller noted long ago in his Ely study.[35]

Unfortunately, recognition of the potential of villagers' surnames on manorial records has had to go through the same tedious process that for long excluded other important record collections from fuller use by the historian.[36] However, we have come a long way since Peter Laslett proclaimed: "Not so long before the reign of Elizabeth most Englishmen were without even surnames."[37]

Understandably, students of demography like Richard M. Smith turn their attention to sources more amenable to their methodology. For England, this has brought concentrated studies of East Anglia.[38] As a by-product of this volume it may be suggested that demographers could assist economic historians by giving more attention to the Midlands. There would seem to have been hitherto inadequate analysis of the social (family) consequences of that odd imbalance, the great number of families not replacing themselves in a primogeniture system whereas other families could have numerous surviving progeny. Secondly, overweening concern for vital-statistic absolutes could distract from analysis of the potential of the concept "homestead." It was noted in the previous chapter that the sudden appearance of numerous names for a family like the Berrengers, which had been listed as having only two names in the tenant lists, may point to the numerous nominal families of pre–Black Death records as *prima facie* possible. Coincident with this phenomenon is the lower survival rate of families with fewer nominal members, as has been noted in chapter 1.

The temper of the relationship between lord and peasant depicted in this study also contrasts with the spirit of traditional historiography. That guru of modern communication analysis, Marshall McLuhan, once quipped in an interview with a popular television weather reporter that television had discovered weather. That is to say, meteorologists appealed to the widespread attraction of death and disaster news in their portrayal of potential storms and weather disturbances. A similar appeal from the "dismal science" came one hundred years earlier. A young Danish scholar, Nils Hybel, has performed a valuable service by tracing one facet of the dismal approach, the concept of crisis as employed by students of late medieval English agrarian history from the 1860s through the 1960s. This study of Ramsey supplies supporting evidence for Hybel's conclusion that neo-classical and neo-Marxist models have stayed in place so long simply because they have not been adequately tested.[39]

The social counterpart to economic crisis is today widely designated conflict theory. Here too the more ideological tradition has sought out evidence to fit the *a priori* model. A recent example of this practice may be seen in Robert Brenner's misrepresentation of data from my study *Tenure and Mobility*.[40] Proper interpretation of peasant experience actually suggests an alternative to conflict theories. Indeed, on the whole, studies of later fourteenth-century lord and peasant, such as those noted above from the *Agrarian History of England and Wales*, have moved away from crass interpretation of the Brenner type as the lives of individual peasants are brought to the fore. As was the case with Kosminsky, happily the massive research of traditional proponents of Marxist conflict theories, especially R.H. Hilton, has been conducted with sufficient scientific rigour that the Marxist theory is not essential to their contribution to historical studies. Students now find it possible to read the many works of Hilton[41] and others of the Birmingham school[42] without reference to the *a priori* conflict system.

Another "hangover" from earlier ideological stages of conflict theory has been the use of such terms as "kulak" to refer to exploitation of peasant by peasant. Anyone still inclined to so identify the substantial manorial peasants described in this study might well be advised to recall the words of Alexandr I. Solzhenitsyn: "In Russian, a *kulak* is a miserly, dishonest rural trader who grows rich not by his own labor but through someone else's, through usury and operating as a middleman. In every locality even before the Revolution such *kulaks* could be numbered on one's fingers ... Subsequently, after 1917, by a transfer of meaning, the name *kulak* began to be applied ... to all those who in any way hired workers, ... But the inflation of this scathing word *kulak* proceeded relentlessly, and by 1933 *all strong peasants in general* were being so called – all peasants strong in management, strong in work, or even strong merely in convictions. The term *kulak* was used to smash the *strength* of the peasantry."[43]

Conflict there was, of course, as peasants tried to improve their lot. The famous case of Vale Royal[44] shows a genuine vendetta, obviously irrational economic behaviour by the lord that could not have benefited his income. Efforts to change status under the title of ancient demesne seem to have come from the aggressive behaviour of wealthier peasants. Ramsey Abbey had a clear instance of this in the legal conflict over the ancient demesne of King's Ripton.[45] It would be useful if various conflicts could be set within a chronology of economic conditions. By and large, peasants did not protest at times of dire economic disaster arising from economic conditions in themselves, such as a great famine of the early fourteenth century, but at the prospect of new economic opportunity.

It would also be useful to have surviving evidence for open and prolonged conflict collected in the context of the thousands of manors in the open-field Midlands of thirteenth- and fourteenth-century England. The normal peasant guarantee of protection for the rewards to be gained from his ambitions and extra labour was his appeal to custom.

As we have already seen in chapter 3 and may be seen more fully in Appendix II, labour too became largely a predictable rent charge for the peasant. The discipline required by the complex operation of the open fields and common was provided by by-laws. The economic conditions of customary tenants, whether free or unfree, as described in this study go far to explain why men of "the neighbouring county" and "others from the countryside" opposed rebels at Huntingdon and again at Ramsey town in June 1381.[46]

Traditional conflict theories were also supported by perceiving peasants as a class, or at least a coherent group. There have been repeated references throughout this volume to customary tenants acting as a corps or group. Such actions derived from the administrative structure of the manor rather than originating with the tenants. That is to say, tenants acted in concert when they perceived the lord to be challenging them as a group. This we have seen happening when certain work was considered to be contrary to traditional obligations and when by-laws had not yet secured control of trespass on fen and turf. Since the corps of customary tenants represented the main capital resources of the customary arrangement, the lord adopted a policy common to the whole group, as has been seen in the convenience of the sale of work.

There is no reason to believe that members of the corps, among themselves, ceded individual and family priorities to some community priority. Variations in wealth were noticeable features of lay-subsidy and entry-fine information, along with the capacity to purchase properties for families of varying sizes. Profiles of individuals and of individual families followed no common pattern.[47] Various customary tenants might pool resources in order to lease fields from the demesne. But when tenurial holdings can be related to names, such tenants would be found to differ greatly among themselves in the amount of land they held and in the variety of rental forms by which they exploited their properties. Furthermore, how much more likely that the peasant could and did exercise free economic decisions when there was so much variety in wealth among individuals! As is well known among economic historians, such individual action favoured a market economy and innovation. Owing to dependence upon manorial extents and surveys, historians have focused too closely upon the uniformity of the tenurial structure. What would be the nature of borough and urban history if the omnipresent messuage was given a similar focus in economic analysis?

The methodology possible from the sources employed for this volume leads to the measurement of success rather than failure. Did those failed tenants and lesser tenants whose names disappear from manorial records with the dwindling of service to the demesne become impoverished, or did they become employees of their successful neighbours? The question of measuring poverty would seem to require a completely different methodology and possibly a different geographical setting from this study. One such investigation for the St Ives complex is now being conducted by Ellen Moore. Certainly the classical approach through comparison of prices and wages cannot be pursued owing to the dearth of information on Ramsey estate account rolls.

Did increasingly wealthy tenants absorb the services of more family members? There is a hint of this in the study of P.M. Hogan referred to in chapter 2, suggesting a general correspondence of family success or failure with the availability or failed replacement of many adult members. Regrettably, as the fourteenth century progresses, the perduring terminology, that is the concern only for the tenant holding immediately from the lord, has made it impossible to pursue this question further. Records from other estate organizations may be more productive.

The economic success of customary tenants undoubtedly enhanced the capacity of such tenants to improve family conditions throughout the whole later period under study here. Such improvements would be relative to issues of famine and price changes. However, it would be as misleading to equate the welfare of the village with the leading customary tenants as to equate the economic rationale of the manor-village with decisions by the lord. Current investigations by Sherri Olson demonstrate that the whole of the village is much more than the sum of the major tenants. As we become more enlightened about the scope of village government, above all in the frankpledge juries, an avenue may be opened for more thorough investigation into the welfare of the whole village.

Why then peasants' progress? Certainly one cannot suggest that an era of prosperity followed upon the sad events of the fourteenth century: continual wars, famine, plague, and the remorseless continuation of disease.[48] The word "progress" is introduced here in part to give balance to the overwhelming emphasis upon regress by classical capitalist ideology and Marxist ideology. Data from the estates of Ramsey Abbey were found particularly useful for both these intellectual systems.[49]

But all these concepts, including "progress," are expressions of our modern culture, not the culture of the fourteenth century, except perhaps in so far as literary fiction may search for a mirror of our times. Economic history is still history from the perspective of the dismal science. But economic history does have criteria for economic development. It is this limited sense, the capacity of the peasant to participate in economic development, that provides a title to the use of the term "progress" to describe the experience traced in this volume.

APPENDIX I

Witnesses to Land Charters

That there should be a communication structure alerting outsiders to opportunities in local manorial land markets is no longer surprising to historians. The role of all levels of society in the administration of legal matters has been clarified for Hunts by the thorough study *Royal Justice in the Medieval English Countryside*.[1] Apparently such an involvement of peasantry was a widespread geographical phenomenon.[2] Although it is fundamental to this volume that freemen be seen as involved in customary tenant matters, perhaps a more sensitive grasp of the peasant community might recognize that in their turn villeins, or at least those holding in villeinage, were involved in the affairs of freemen. The names of witnesses to land charters provide an opportunity for illustration of such involvement.

References to land charters occur in court rolls and in extant charters themselves. Court-roll references most often occur in a desultory fashion – that is, when the individual has failed to be enfeoffed by the lords rather than regularly as entries of record. It is also impossible to determine how many charters actually existed at any period of our study. However, 34 charters do survive for the four villages of Broughton, Upwood, Warboys, and Wistow between 1285 and 1346.[3]

Unlike the *Carte Nativorum*,[4] most of these charters record conveyances between freemen, and nearly all would seem to involve freehold rather than customary lands.[5] As is the case with the *Carte Nativorum*, the size of the property is small, usually less than 10 acres.

The status of most of the witnesses can be determined from our many manorial records. In Table 1.1 the 115 different individuals who witnessed the charters have been listed, along with the names of the villages in which the land was situated, the dates of the charters, an assessment of personal legal status, and an indication of their provenance. From the data contained in this list, a second table has been prepared in which the statistics on legal status are presented in detail (see Table 1.2). The statistics contained in Table 1.2 not only give a breakdown of the percentages of free and villein or villein-tenure witnesses for the charters of each village, but also overall percentages for the 115 individuals as a group. In terms of the statistics for individual villages, Upwood, at 61 per cent, had the highest number of villeins in its group of witnesses, while Warboys, at 38 per cent, had the lowest. The overall average, at 45 per cent, was just about midway between these two not very distant extremes. Thus, almost half of the witnesses to the charters were villeins. In view of the fact that historians seem to have assumed that witnesses were always freemen, such a statistic is quite extraordinary and thus merits closer examination.

Identifying free and unfree as witnesses to these charters poses an interesting conundrum for the historian. If the witnesses were not identified by status on the charter, may it not be misleading for the historian to introduce such categories? To compensate for this problem, the identifications given in Table 1.1 have been most broadly based. The 52 individuals who have been categorized as unfree come under the traditional identifications as jurors, capital pledges, and so forth for such a status.[6] Such a general category may have included some of those who had rather recently entered customary tenements.

As for the 63 people who do not seem to have been of villein status, some can definitely be identified as freemen. For example, John de Raveley of Upwood, who witnessed two charters relating to the village in 1285, was described explicitly as a freeman in the court rolls of that village.[7] Similarly, John Unfrey of Warboys, who witnessed a charter in that village in 1303, was also called a freeman in the court rolls.[8] However, it must be said that few can be identified in this manner, since court rolls seldom give even passing attention to the issue of personal legal status.

In the vast majority of cases in which there is some evidence on the individuals in question, that is the 38 (60 per cent) of the 63 individuals who cannot be shown to have been of villein status, any indications of free status are much more indirect than in the cases of John de Raveley and John Unfrey. For example, in such cases as John de Deen, who witnessed charters in 1310, 1320, and ca 1340, and William le Moigne, who was a witness in 1318, 1328, 1336, and ca 1340, it seems obvious that they were free since both were knights.[9] Similarly, it is likely that Hugh de Croft, probably a royal justice, was also a freeman.[10] Finally, there are individuals such as John de Lechworth and John de Washingley, who were attorneys,[11] William de Washingley and Nicholas de Stukeley, who were stewards of Ramsey Abbey,[12] and extensive freeholders in the region, such as Ralph Norreys and William Mowyn of Old Hurst.[13]

Although 17 (27 per cent) of the 63 individuals who cannot be shown to have been villeins show such direct and indirect signs of being freemen, the majority of those who show no evidence of servitude also show no obvious signs of freedom. Of the 46 individuals in this group, 21 (46 per cent) have been identified by means of the manorial records, while 25 (54 per cent) could not be identified by that means. Since the burden of this study is to demonstrate that at least some of the witnesses to these Huntingdonshire charters were villeins, it would seem that, for those who cannot be shown to have been villeins, there must be a presumption of freedom. On this basis, those who show no sign of villein activity have been categorized as free.

The first hypothesis one would venture on the status of witnesses generally is that the principals involved in the charter would have chosen individuals who were not only known to them but were also respected members of the community. By choosing such respected individuals, the charter would possess greater legal credibility; and with regard to the legal credibility offered by witnesses, the procedure involved in the event of litigation surrounding the charters should be borne in mind.[14] As far as community respect is concerned, there cannot be too much doubt about the status of knights such as William le Moigne and John de Deen, nor about that of individuals such as Hugh de Croft and Nicholas de Stukeley. Similarly, it should be safe to assume that major freehold tenants in the region, such as Ralph Norreys and William Mowyn, were well-known and probably respected members of the community. But what of the villeins who also appear as witnesses? Although such people may well have been legally unfree according to the common law, they were nevertheless at the very heart of village life.

The charters also reveal that the social position of witnesses does not seem to have been confined exclusively to their places of residence. Many of the witnesses functioned beyond their own communities, as Table 1.1 indicates. In fact, of the 96 witnesses whose provenance has been indicated, as many as 67 (70 per cent) served as witnesses at least once for charters that did not involve land in the communities in which they resided. Of this group, 37 (55 per cent) were villeins. Thus, the charters not only illustrate that free and unfree or tenants of customary lands functioned together, but also that their interaction took place within a regional framework.

Table 1.1
The Witnesses

Name	Broughton	Upwood	Warboys	Wistow	Status	Provenance
Ace, Roger	–	1331	–	ca 1335	V	Ramsey
Alan, William, son of	1315	–	–	–	V	Broughton
Andrew, Geoffrey	–	–	–	1310	V	Ramsey
Aspelon, John	ca 1300	–	–	–	V	Broughton
Atehale, Thomas	–	–	1330	–	X	Woodhurst
Attedam, John	1329, 1339, 1346	–	1330	–	V	Broughton
Aula, Stephen de	–	–	1303	–	V	Warboys
Ballard, John	1315	–	–	1310	V	Broughton
Barker, John	–	–	–	1310, ca 1315	V	Ramsey
Baron, John	–	–	1334	–	V	Warboys
Baroun, John	1336	–	–	–	V	Ramsey
Baylolf, Ivo	1346	–	–	–	*	Broughton
–, Richard	ca 1290, ca 1300	–	–	–	*	Broughton
Baillolf, William	1322	–	–	–	V	Broughton
Beaumeys, Robert de	–	ca 1285	–	–	V	Ramsey
Berenger, Robert	–	–	1341, 1342	–	V	Warboys
Biker, Robert le	–	1327, 1331	–	1324	*	Ramsey
Blasine, Thomas	1339	–	–	–	*	Broughton
Boys, John de	–	–	1331	–	*	Warboys
Braciator, William	–	ca 1285, 1285	–	–	*	Ramsey
Broughton, John de	1315	–	1300, 1303, 1318	1310	V	Broughton
–, William de	ca 1290, ca 1300	–	–	–	*	Broughton
–, William de	ca 1322, 1329, 1339	–	1324, 1325, 1328, 1330, 1334	–	V	Broughton
Campronn, Hugh the	–	–	1300	–	X	–
Carter, Nicholas	–	1338	–	–	V	Ramsey
Catoun, John	–	–	1330, 1334, 1342	–	V	Warboys
Chacede, William	–	1331	1330	–	V	Ramsey
Chamberlain, Benedict	1322	–	1324, 1325, 1328(2), 1330, 1331	–	X	Woodhurst
Chartres, Roger de	1336	–	–	–	X	–
Claxton, John de	–	–	1328	–	*	Wistow

Name	Broughton	Upwood	Warboys	Wistow	Status	Provenance
Clere, Roger	–	ca 1340	ca 1340	ca 1340	V	Ramsey
Clericus, John	ca 1300	–	–	–	*	Kings Ripton
–, John	1329, 1346	–	1330	–	V	Broughton
–, Richard	ca 1300	–	1290	–	V	Broughton
–, Roger	–	1338	–	–	X	–
–, Thomas	1346	–	1324, 1325, 1328(2), 1330	–	V	Broughton
Clervaux, John de	–	1327	–	1310, 1315	F	Upwood
–, Ralph de	1322	–	–	–	X	Little Raveley
–, Ralph de	1315, 1329	–	1328	1315	V	Wistow
–, Ranulph de	–	ca 1285, 1285	1290	–	F	Little Raveley
Cocus (le Keu), Alan	–	–	–	1310	X	Raveley
–, John	1315, 1322	–	–	–	V	Broughton
Cook, Thomas	–	–	1290	–	X	Wistow
Cotes, Robert de	–	ca 1340	ca 1340	1342, ca 1340	V	Wistow
Cotenham, Hugh de	–	–	1300	–	X	–
Couherde, William	–	–	1341, 1342	–	V	Warboys
Crane, John	–	ca 1285, 1285	–	–	V	Upwood
Croft, Hugh de	–	ca 1340	ca 1340	ca 1340	F	–
Curteys, Richard	–	1338	–	–	V	Ramsey
Deen, John De	–	1340	1328, ca 1340	1310, ca 1340	F	Upwood
–, Walter de	–	–	1303	–	X	–
Ellsworth, William de	–	–	–	ca 1315	V	Height- mongrove
Eydon, Hugh de	–	–	1293, 1300	–	V	Warboys
Forester, Geoffrey	–	–	1330, 1331	–	X	Woodhurst
–, Geoffrey	–	–	1324, 1325	–	X	Pidley
–, Simon	–	ca 1285, 1285	–	–	X	Ramsey
Fulchet, John	–	–	1293	–	X	–
Gerveys, William	–	–	–	1310, ca 1315, 1315	V	Ramsey
Gernoun, John	–	–	–	1310, ca 1315	*	Wistow
Gosceline, John	ca 1300	–	1303	–	V	Broughton
–, Thomas	1329, 1346	–	–	–	*	Broughton

Name	Broughton	Upwood	Warboys	Wistow	Status	Provenance
Grendale, Alan de	–	–	1300	–	V	Warboys
–, Richard de	–	–	1318	–	*	Fenton
Grymbaud, Roger	1336	–	–	–	X	–
Gryndale, Roger de	–	–	1293	–	X	–
Hale, Robert de	–	–	1290	–	F	–
Higney, Hugh de	–	–	1324, 1325	–	V	Warboys
–, John de	–	–	1293, 1303, 1318	–	V	Warboys
–, William de	–	–	1290	–	*	Warboys
Houghton, Gilbert de	1336	–	1328, 1330	–	X	–
Hurst, Ivo de	–	–	1300	–	*	Warboys
–, Roger de	1322	–	–	–	X	Oldhurst
–, Roger de	1329, 1336	ca 1340	ca 1340	ca 1340	V	Ramsey
–, Roger de	–	–	1318, 1324, 1325, 1341, 1342	–	*	Warboys
–, Thomas de	–	–	1290	–	F	Woodhurst
Hrien, Reginald	–	–	1300	–	X	Elton
Jardyn, William	–	–	–	1324	X	–
Kendale, Walter de	–	1331, 1338	–	–	V	Ramsey
Lechworth, John de	–	1331, 1338, ca 1340	1330, ca 1340	ca 1340	F	Ramsey
Leyr, Henry	–	–	1342	–	X	Woodhurst
London, William de	ca 1290, ca 1300	–	1290, 1293	–	V	Warboys
Mayster, William le	–	1327	–	ca 1315	V	Ramsey
Milner, Nicholas le	–	–	1331	–	*	Warboys
Moigne, William le	1336	ca 1340	1318, 1328(2)	ca 1340	F	Sawtry?
–, William le	–	–	1290	–	F	Sawtry?
Morton, Richard de	–	–	1330	1324	V	Height-mongrove
Mountabon, John	–	1331	–	–	*	Ramsey
Mowyn, William	1315, 1322, 1329	–	1318, 1324, 1325, 1328(2), 1330, 1331, 1334	–	F	Old Hurst
Norreys, Ralph	ca 1290, ca 1300	–	1300, 1303	–	F	Oldhurst

Name	Broughton	Upwood	Warboys	Wistow	Status	Provenance
Norman, John	–	ca 1285, 1285	–	–	V	Ramsey
Parker, Stephen	–	1331	–	–	V	Ramsey
Parys, Andrew	–	–	–	1342	V	Wistow
–, John	–	–	–	1310, ca 1315	*	Wistow
Provost, Stephen	–	1327	–	–	V	Ramsey
Ralph, William son of	–	–	1290	–	*	Broughton
Raveley, John de	–	ca 1285, 1285	–	–	F	Upwood
–, John de	–	1327, ca 1340	1328(2)	1315, 1324, ca 1335	V	Ramsey
Rideman, Thomas le	–	–	1350	1342	X	Height- mongrove
Smyth, Walter le	–	–	–	1342	X	–
Somersham, William de	–	1338	–	–	V	Ramsey
Stivintone, James de	–	–	1290	–	X	–
Stukeley, Nicholas de	1336	–	1334	–	F	Stukeley?
Swynelond, William de	–	–	1290	–	X	–
Tannatore, John	–	–	–	1315	V	Ramsey
Temesford, John de	–	1327	–	1324, 1335	V	Ramsey
Unfrey, John	–	–	1303	1310	F	Warboys
–, William	–	–	1318	–	*	Warboys
Warboys, John de	1315	–	–	1315	V	Wistow
Warewyk, Thomas de	–	–	–	1315	X	–
Washingley, John de	–	ca 1340	ca 1340	ca 1340	F	–
–, William de	–	–	1293	–	F	–
Wistow, John de	–	–	1293	–	V	Broughton
Wodeward, Robert le	–	1327	–	1310, ca 1315	V	Ramsey
Wraw, Benedict	–	1338	–	1324, 1335, 1342	V	Ramsey
Yaxley, Robert de	–	ca 1340	ca 1340	ca 1340	F	–

Note: V = villein

F = freeman

* = data does not indicate villeinage

X = no data

Table I.2
Summary of the Status of Witnesses

Village	Number of witnesses	Villeins	Freemen	Villeinage not indicated	No data
Broughton	33	17 (52%)	4	6	6
Upwood	33	20 (61%)	9	3	1
Warboys	65	25 (38%)	15	9	16
Wistow	36	19 (53%)	8	4	5
Cumulative totals	115*	52 (45%)	17	21	25

* This figure is not a sum of the village totals (33 + 33 + 65 + 36 = 167), for some individuals served as witnesses to charters relating to more than one village. In this figure such individuals have only been counted once.

APPENDIX II

Preliminary Observations towards a Calculus of Opera Obligations

A surprising array of evidence for calculating the actual work-service obligations is at hand. For Ramsey estates, such service is predicated upon the size of the holding rather than upon all the potential labour of a settlement. Obligations vary with the season and are calculated in terms of so many days per week. Specific quotas are given for piece-work such as digging ditches. Cartularies from other estate complexes could complement those of Ramsey because of variations in detail from one lordship administration to another. Thus, for example, at Battle Abbey, the work-service day was often to be found as one-half the daylight hours.[1] But for Ramsey the most important feature is that all these specifics made possible the operational section of the manorial accounting system that is designated simply *opera*.

Opera accounts are actual synoptic lists of work units required from customary tenants. These are balanced accounts in so far as the disposition of every *opus* is accounted for. These accounts derive from the long lists of obligations owed by individual customary tenants that are drawn up in customary extents. But the actual form of the account is impersonal to the extreme in so far as it is part of a sophisticated presentation for legally trained stewards and auditors[2] who were far removed from personal interest in individual villagers. The accounts list the number of tenants, but not their names, and the number of *opera* owed by all tenants of each category of land for the two or three work seasons of the year. The section on the disposition of *opera* then indicates the number of *opera* performed, quitted, or sold in order to come to a figure equivalent to the total owed.

The *opera* account for Broughton over 1314–15, a two-season account, is given below as an example. Except where multiples of twenty were explicitly employed, the long hundred (120) was used in this account. While the autumn works were accounted for exactly, 20 more works were allocated during the previous part of the year than can be traced in the first paragraph of this account. A summary of the amounts to be found in this account are entered under the first date entry in Table II.1.

The *Opera* Account of 1314–15

Compotus operum

Idem respondet de M^DM^D.ix^c.v^{xx}.xi. operibus de .xxxi. virgatariis et dimidio a festo Sancti Michaelis usque festum Nativitatis Sancti Johannis Baptiste pro .xxxviii. septimis et duos dies non operabiles quorum quilibet facit .iii. opera per septimam. Et de. cxxxii. operibus de quatuor cotmannis ibidem per idem tempus quorum quilibet facit .i. opus per septimam. Et de .cccclv. operibus et dimidio de eisdem virgatariis a festo Sancti Johannis predicto usque ad gulam Augusti per quinque septimas et duos dies operabiles quorum quilibet facit .iii. opera per septimam ut supra. Et de .xxiiii. operibus de predictis quatuor cotmannis per idem tempus quorum quilibet facit .i. opus per septimam ut supra per diem lune.

Summa .iii.M^D.v^{xx}.ii opera et di.

De quibus allocantur preposito bedello wodewardo .iiii. akermaniis et .iii. virgatis terre ad censum per supradictum tempus .DC.v^{xx}.xviii. et di. Iterim xxv virgate terre in opere pro .xxviii. diebus festivis .D.v^{xx}. Interim .iiii. cotmanni pro ebdomeda Natale, Pascale et Pentecoste .xii. Infirmis .xlviii. In stipula falcanda et colligenda .lxix. In caruce fuganda frumento et semine quadragesimali hercianda et waterforewyng .D.iii. In blada trituranda .vii^{xx}. vii. In domibus cooperandis .lxiii. In vigilandum ad feriam Sancti Ivonis .xxiiii. In fymis colligendis .xl. In foreis et haiis facienda circa curiam .ccxxxi. In carpetria in curia .iiii^{xx}. xiiii. In spino prostrando et meremio .viii^{xx}. viii. In falcatione et levatione feni .c^{xx}. Iterim apud hydek .lx. In serculatione .iiii^{xx}. xvii. In fymis marlandis .lx. In venditione .Dcc.xxviii. inter festa sanctorum Michaelis et J. Baptiste, pretium operis obulus.

Et eque

Opera autumpna

Idem respondet de .Dccxlii. operibus de supradictis .xxxi. virgatis et dimidia a gula augusti usque Nativitatem beate Marie per .v. septimas et .iii. dies operabiles quorum quilibet facit .v. opera per septimam. Et de .xxv. operibus et dimidio de eisdem in crastino prime precarie que dur' bouzeld quilibet facit .i. opus qui est in opere. Et de .v^{xx}. ii. operibus de eisdem per predictum tempus quorum quilbet virgatarius in opere facit .iiii^{o}r. opera in autumpno preter opera predicta. Et de .xx. operibus de predictis quatuor cotmannis per idem tempus videlicet de quolibet .i. opus per septimam. Et de .v. operibus de Simone ate Dam per idem tempus videlicet quolibet die lune .i. opus. Et de .iii. operibus de Beatrice Beneit per idem tempus. Et de .cccv^{xx}.xii operibus et dimidio de supradictis virgatariis et dimidio a festo Nativitatis beate Marie usque festum Sancti Michaelis per tres septimas quorum quilibet facit .v. opera per septimam ut supra in autumpno. Et de .xii. operibus de quatuor cotmannis per idem tempus de quolibet .i. opus per septimam. Et de .iii. operibus de Simone atedam per idem tempus videlicet quolibet die lune .i. opus.

Summa operum .M^D.cciiii^{xx}.v. opera

De quibus allocantur proposito bedello .iiii. akermannis et .iii. virgatis terre ad censum per supradictum tempus .ccvi. Iterim .xxv. virgate et dimidia terre in opere pro .vii. diebus festivis .clviii. et di. Infirmis .viii. In blada metenda et colligenda .iiii^c. v^{xx}. xvii. In sicera facienda .xxii. In meya facienda .xl. In spinis prostrandis .xv. Iterim pro .v. Bethsolewes .c.vii. et di. In venditione .ccli. in autummno, pretium operis .ii.d. an' nat'.

Et eque

It can be calculated that the work-days owed by tenants of a customary virgate at Broughton village amounted to approximately one-half of the year, the actual average being 177 days (1314: 179; 1342: 174; 1378: 176; 1380: 177; 1386: 177; 1392: 177). Work-days owed at Warboys were much the same per virgate: 1335–36: 174; 1342–43: 177; 1344–45: 176; 1347–48: 177. *Opera* owed at Upwood were slightly more per virgate: 1324–25: 182; 1343–44: 183; 1347–48: 185.

All our sources indicate that the virgater was expected to hire labour. That is to say, not only are there references to this in extents, but court rolls show evidence of fines for poor work by virgaters' helpers, and *opera* accounts show busy-season obligations of eight work-days per week. More importantly, David Herlihy[3] argues (from the Broughton village study of E. Britton) that as the largest landholder of the village, the virgater generated larger households. In demographic terms it is easy to demonstrate from court rolls that over the late thirteenth and early fourteenth centuries most virgaters would seem to have more than replaced themselves. For such virgaters there would often be two young men to assist the father. However, vital statistics are impossible to come by for most estates. So, for convenience, let us assume a minimum figure of 2½ working bodies available per virgate, that is over a life-cycle, the husband as one unit and wife and one young adult as one and one-half, the latter unit being supplemented when necessary by hired labour. The virgater would then have available 910 (365 × 2.5) work-day units per year. The one-half-year labour services owed by the virgater would be, then, one-fifth of the total labour resources of this customary unit.

Structural rigidities of various sorts actually left a much larger proportion of his labour resources for the disposition of the peasant himself. For *opera* accounts that have been analysed, the work quota expected from land units of various sizes remained the same for our earliest evidence in the thirteenth century to the end of the fourteenth century – the point at which our evidence no longer becomes available because the demesne is put to farm. Changes in total amounts of *opera* owed that do occur over this period can be specifically related to decreases or increases in the number of land units listed as owing labour services. Secondly, as we have seen in chapter 3, the sale price or commutation price of labour services remained much the same throughout this period. The common valuation was a penny for a work-day throughout the year and twopence for a day in the intensive autumn harvest season.

Certain cultural features also mitigated the full demand for work. That etymological predecessor of the holiday – that is, the holyday – was most significant here. For some years the villein is found to be exempted from work for a dozen feast days of saints as well as the three weeks at Christmas, Easter, and Pentecost respectively. Not infrequently, the *opera* cancelled by the liturgical calendar amounted to some 15 per cent of all *opera* owed. This varied with the seasons. Over 1335–36 at Broughton there were 253 days allowed for feast days during the winter season (10 per cent of the season's quota), 138 for the spring season (16 per cent of the quota), and 23 for autumn (2 per cent of the quota). At Upwood there were four work seasons in 1324–25 when the total feast-day exemptions came to 582. In this case the incidence of the exemptions differed: winter: 6 per cent; summer: 7 per cent; autumn: 14 per cent; post-autumn: 14 per cent. The "sick benefits" of the time – that is, the total work service cancelled owing to illness – tended to be much less than the general liturgical absolution. Nevertheless, for the individual peasant this arrangement often amounted to work-service allowance for several weeks and would make possible his retention of the tenement.

Opera accounts list work services cancelled as a reward for special official duties (reeve, beadle, hayward) as well as services more permanently commuted (*ad censum*), sold, and relieved for holidays and sickness. In general these exemptions leave work to be performed at around 50 per cent of the total *opera* owed. In terms of the formula for the virgaters' resources suggested above, one-half of the one-fifth, or 10 per cent of such resources, would be required for labour services. The "bottom line" for actual performance percentages at Warboys was 48 per cent for 1335–36, 48 per cent for 1342–43, and 46 per cent for 1344–45. The whole structure of the considerations of these past few paragraphs are summarized in Table II.1, which charts villein work payments for Broughton.

The work-days owed and actually employed from villein tenements varied from manor to manor in the heartland of the cereal-producing open-field regions.[4] Considerably fewer *opera* were expected from land units as one enters more pastoral regions. Yet this tendency for *opera* obligations to be approximately for one man for one-half year is to be found in the southwest

Table 11.1
The Structure of Villein Work Payments

	1314–15	1342–43	1378–79	1380–81	1386–87	1392–93
Annual works due*	4,323	3,555	2,868	3,114	3,181	2,766
		(4,281)	(4,221)	(4,362)	(4,276)	(4,386)
ANNUAL WORKS ALLOCATED[†]						
Services and censa	839	(726)	(1,353)	(1,188)	(1,095)	(1,620)
percentage	19	17	32	27	26	36
Feast days	712	676	332	267	296	293
percentage	16	16	8	6	7	7
Illness	48	9	0	0	5	34
Work done	1,865	2,251	2,260	1,798	2,251	2,027
percentage	43	53	54	42	53	46
Work sold	868	636	587	1,049	630	412
percentage	20	15	12	24	15	9
Autumn works due	1,525	1,131	961	999	1,020	861
		(1,362)	(1,412)	(1,386)	(1,385)	(1,365)
AUTUMN WORKS ALLOCATED						
Services and censa	246	(231)	(451)	(387)	(365)	(504)
percentage	16	17	32	28	26	37
Feast days	179	104	104	22	23	39
percentage	12	8	7	2	2	3
Illness	8	4	4	0	27	8
Work done	802	810	770	802	805	682
percentage	53	58	55	58	59	50
Work sold	291	212	84	175	166	133
percentage	19	16	6	13	12	10

* The bracketed figures in this line include the works owed from services and *ad censum* lands
 – that is, the addition of the bracketed data of the next line – which data were not calculated
 in the summations at the end of the rolls for these years. All figures and percentages in this
 table have been rounded.
† Except for the year 1314–15, the total works accounted for every year tally almost exactly
 with the totals owed, so the totals of allocated works are not entered in this table.

of England on the more pastoral estates of Glastonbury Abbey.[5] Data from a
mid-thirteenth-century extent also demonstrate clearly corroborative evidence from the degree to which larger customary holders were not expected
to allocate the greater part of their labour resources of *opera*. That is to say,
the 5-acre tenant (close to ¼ virgate) owed almost as much labour as the large
tenant. Presumably 5 acres could supply such labour resources. In the mid-
thirteenth-century extent at Ashcot, ½ virgate owed 171 works, 5 acres 128
works; Street: 1 virgate owed 188 work units, ½ virgate 125, 5 acres 125;
Walton: 1 virgate owed 166, ½ virgate owed 171, 5 acres owed 214.

The calculations presented in this appendix have been elementary in the
extreme. Nevertheless, these data make the point that the main customary

tenant controlled enough of his labour resources that he is worthy of more advanced economic analysis. The same result could be derived by another method through the tendency for smaller land units to have as much or more labour obligations as the larger. Thus, at the Glastonbury estates of Street and Walton the ¼ virgate owed as much labour service as the larger unit. Presumably, therefore, three-quarters of the labour resources of the larger unit would be at the disposition of the virgate tenant. In this context, the tenant of the smaller unit is the genuine labour-service tenant, and indeed, in the Eastern Midlands such equivalence was often specified by the terminology for 3-, 4-, or 5-acre units (akermanland, mondaymanland, etc.).

These calculations may also give a minimal picture of the tenant's labour resources. Cicely Howell[6] cites various opinions giving the pre-plague household of persons aged five or older as around five for various places in England. This is something like twice the numbers employed in our calculations above.

In the introduction to his study *Labour and Leisure*[7] Ian Blanchard has calculated the total allocation of labour required on a fifteenth-century 2-virgate holding (64 acres) in a three-course rotation system as 264 work-days per year for each family member, whether the man or woman. Fieldwork is calculated as requiring 40 work-days from a woman and 128 work-days from the man. Comparable figures for the Ramsey village 1 virgate would be one-half, that is 132 work-days, for each of the two family members per year, with 20 and 68 fieldwork-days for the woman and man. Blanchard's suggested "dead time" of 136 days for a woman and 136 days for a man must appear preposterous from the perspective of the traditional concept of almost unremitting enforced drudgery imposed on the villein. The calculations given above for Ramsey manors would allow a comparable amount of dead time. Nevertheless, understanding dead time – that is, time relatively free from agricultural labour – still needs more study for the Midland peasant of the thirteenth and fourteenth centuries. The allocations allowed by the lord, especially for holydays as noted above, indicate the reality of such released dead time, but the totals are far from the 136 days given in the calculations summarized above.

However, modern assumptions about productive employment of labour, running on generalizations such as Gregory Clark's "low levels of work intensity due to inefficiency and under-employment,"[8] can be equally wide of the mark. Such efforts at precision quickly lead to unrealistic absolutes. That is to say, if the common formula of labour service on a virgate were commuted to some 15 shillings money rent, valuation of the remaining 90 per cent of the villein's labour resources as efficiently employable would lead to an unlikely high figure of labour worth more than £7 per year. The cultural gap between our modern era of time-and-motion measurement and medieval culture may be more comparable to the differences between industrial cultures of the Western world and indigenous cultures of the Third World. Historians may derive some consolation from the fact that it has taken scholars of the contemporary world an unconscionably long time to come to the conclusion: "The prevailing model is, we believe, that of the rational, self-interested actor who is made up of distinct preferences, feelings, traits, and abilities, and whose action is a direct function of the expression of these internal attributes. However, the indigenous psychologies developing in various parts of the world highlight some very different models of the self."[9]

APPENDIX III

The Structure of Opera Allocations

The *opera* section of the account roll has already been introduced in Appendix II. The latter appendix also contains a summary of *opera* accounts for Broughton, and allocations for Warboys may be found in the *Warboys* volume, Table xiv, pages 197–8. The purpose of Appendix III is to make available *opera* allocations for the remaining three villages of Abbots Ripton, Upwood, and Wistow.

The first line of these tables illustrates the seemingly stable accounting picture that has been discussed in chapter 4. The last line indicates the real situation – that is, the gradual decline in the total work service performed. The significance of data concerning sales has also been discussed in chapter 4. Unfortunately, data about illness are not easily interpreted. One would expect many more allowances for illness at those times when the plague revisited the countryside. However, as larger tenants became more dominant, such illnesses may have been more of a factor among their hired labour. And manorial extents do not indicate allowances for hired labour.

Opera accounts were obviously regular sections of the manorial accounts from the late thirteenth century. But extant *opera* accounts are relatively rare by contrast with the many surviving account rolls. The reason would appear to be that the *opera* account was entered as the last section of the account roll. When the latter was rolled up, *opera* accounts would be on the outside and exposed to damage and fading, as can be ascertained on several account rolls. In other instances the reeve's account rolls filled the front and dorse of the parchment and the *opera* account had to be attached on a separate piece of parchment, which was easily torn off. Some *opera* accounts have survived this precarious position.

Abbots Ripton

	Winter	Summer	Autumn	Post–Autumn	Total
1324–25					
Works due*					
42v + 8c	4070	1824	2140	444	8478
Works allocated					
1) Feast days	604	170	340	68	1182
	(15)**	(9)	(16)	(15)	(14)
2) Illness	98½	45	25+(?)	15	183½
	(2)	(2)	(1)	(3)	(2)
3) Sales	386	859	50	144	1439
	(9)	(47)	(2)	(32)	(17)
4) Customary	36				36
payments	(.01)				(.01)
Works done	***2211	***410	***1330	***147	***2098
	(54)	(22)	(62)	(33)	(25)
1342–43					
Works due					
37¼v + 8c	3765¼	1695¼	1422½	359¼	7242¼
Works allocated					
1) Feast days	372½	298	223½	37¼	931¼
	(10)	(18)	(16)	(10)	(13)
2) Illness	20½	–	34	8	62¼
	(.05)	–	(2)	(2)	(1)
3) Sales	1130	771¼	98	125	2124¼
	(30)	(45)	(7)	(35)	(29)
4) Customary	36	–	–	–	36
payments	(.01)				(.05)
Works done	2205¾	626	1067	189	4089
	(59)	(37)	(75)	(53)	(56)
1364–65					
Works due					
21½v + 4v	2038½	1075	962	274	4349½
Works allocated					
1) Feast days	129	87	129	–	345
	(6)	(8)	(13)	–	(8)
2) Illness	–	–	–	–	–
3) Sales	148	135	98	274	655
	(7)	(13)	(10)	(100)	(15)
4) Customary	21½	–	–	–	21½
payments	(.01)				(.05)

* Only for this year does this figure include the lands allotted to the reeve, beadle, 2 hay-wards, 5 ploughmen, as well as 3 virgates *ad censum*. 33½ virgates appear to have been *ad opera*.

** Figures in brackets show percentage of works due.

*** This figure gives the actual work done exclusive of officials and *ad censum*.

	Winter	Summer	Autumn	Post–Autumn	Total
Works done	1740	853	753	–	3328
	(85)	(79)	(76)		(77)
1375–76					
Works due					
24½v + 4v	2293½	1210	1245	281½	5030
Works allocated					
1) Feast days	220½	122½	196	–	539
	(10)	(10)	(16)		(11)
2) Illness	–	–	–	–	–
3) Sales	–	–	–	–	–
4) Customary	24½	–	–	–	24½
payments	(.01)				(.05)
Works done	2048½	1087½	1049	281½	4466½
	(89)	(90)	(84)	(100)	(89)
1384–85					
Works due					
24v + 4c	2375	1111½	1024	352	4862½
Works allocated					
1) Feast days	264	120	144	24	552
	(11)	(11)	(14)	(7)	(11)
2) Illness	68	37	36	10	151
	(3)	(3)	(4)	(3)	(3)
3) Sales	174	149½	40	107	470½
	(7)	(14)	(4)	(30)	(10)
4) Customary	24	–	–	–	24
payments	(.1)				(.05)
Works done	1845	805	804	211	3665
	(78)	(72)	(79)	(60)	(75)
1387–88					
Works due					
23¾v + 4c	2305	1148½	1354	198	5005½
Works allocated					
1) Feast days	166¼	142½	47½	–	356¼
	(7)	(12)	(4)		(7)
2) Illness	122	61	60	10	253
	(5)	(5)	(4)	(5)	(5)
3) Sales	213	265	172½	140	790½
	(9)	(23)	(13)	(7)	(16)
4) Customary	23¾	–	–	–	23¾
payments	(.1)				(.5)
Works done	1780	680	1074	48	3582
	(77)	(59)	(79)	(24)	(72)
1389–90					
Works due					
22½v + 4c	2240	1189½	1195	136½	4761

	Winter	Summer	Autumn	Post–Autumn	Total
Works allocated					
1) Feast days	247½	135	93	22½	498
	(11)	(11)	(8)	(17)	(10)
2) Illness	–	32½	4	–	36½
		(3)	(.03)		(1)
3) Sales	69	173	107	34	383
	(3)	(15)	(9)	(25)	(8)
4) Customary	22½	–	–	–	22½
payments	(1)				(.05)
Works done	1901	849	991	80	3821
	(85)	(71)	(83)	(58)	(80)
1391–92					
Works due					
20¼v + 4c	1952½	994½	911	279¼	4137¼
Works allocated					
1) Feast days	243	101¼	121½	20¼	486
	(12)	(10)	(13)	(7)	(12)
2) Illness	12	22½	–	–	34½
	(.06)	(2)			(.08)
3) Sales	180¼	118¾	5	84	388
	(9)	(12)	(.05)	(30)	(9)
4) Customary	20¼	–	–	–	20¼
payments	(.01)				(.05)
Works done	1497	752	784½	175	3208½
	(77)	(76)	(83)	(63)	(78)
1394–95					
Works due					
21¾v + 4c	2213	886¼	886	317	4302¼
Works allocated					
1) Feast days	261	108¾	43½	43½	456¼
	(12)	(12)	(5)	(14)	(11)
2) Illness	154	4½	–	–	158½
	(7)	(1)			(4)
3) Sales	154	208	202½	105¼	669¾
	(7)	(23)	(23)	(33)	(16)
4) Customary	21¾	–	–	–	21¾
payments	(.01)				(.05)
Works done	1622¼	565	640	*170	2997¼
	(73)	(64)	(72)	(54)	(70)
1395–96					
Works due					
21¼v + 4c	2099½	935½	951	271	4257

* These figures do not tally exactly.

	Winter	Summer	Autumn	Post–Autumn	Total
Works allocated					
1) Feast days	297½	85	85	42½	510
	(14)	(9)	(9)	(16)	(12)
2) Illness	–	3	–	–	3
		(.03)			(.07)
3) Sales	307¾	198½	193	158⅓	857¾
	(15)	(21)	(20)	(58)	(20)
4) Customary	21¼	–	–	–	21¼
payments	(.01)				(.05)
Works done	1473	649	673	70	2865
	(70)	(69)	(71)	(26)	(67)

Upwood

	Winter and Summer		Autumn	Total
CA 1300				
Works due				
22v + 18c	4400		1400	5800
Works allocated				
1) Feast days	396		–	396
	(9)			(7)
2) Illness	80		–	80
	(2)			(1)
3) Sales	–		–	–
4) Customary	103		–	103
payments	(2)			(2)
Works done	3821		1400	5221
	(87)		(100)	(90)

	Winter	Summer	Autumn	Post-Autumn	Total
1324–25					
Works due					
*28½v + 19c	3600	1571	1444	441	7056
Works allocated					
1) Feast days	219	105	196	62	582
	(6)	(7)	(14)	(14)	(8)
2) Illness	42	9	3	–	54
	(1)	(.05)	(.02)		(.07)
3) Sales	917½	341	21	337	1616½
	(25)	(22)	(1)	(76)	(23)
4) Customary	89	–	–	–	89
payments	(2)				(1)
Works done	**1526	**763	**873	**51	**3102
	(42)	(49)	(60)	(12)	(44)

* Properties allocated for official tasks – reeve, beadle, 4 ploughmen, hayward, and *ad censum* (4½v + 2c) – were included only for this year. This left 21 virgates and 10 cotlands actually owing work. The post-autumn total does not tally properly.

** This figure gives the actual work done exclusive of officials and *ad censum*.

	Winter	Summer	Autumn	Post-Autumn	Total
1343–44					
Works due					
20½v + 15c	2671½	1197	1003	321	5192½
Works allocated					
1) Feast days	259	173	150	21½	603½
	(10)	(14)	(15)	(7)	(12)
2) Illness	32	39	60	22	153
	(1)	(3)	(6)	(7)	(3)
3) Sales	604	162	39	71	876
	(23)	(14)	(4)	(22)	(17)
4) Customary	82	–	–	–	82
payments	(3)				(2)
Works done	1694½	823	754	206½	3478
	(63)	(69)	(75)	(64)	(67)
1347–48					
Works due					
22v + 15c	2724	1454	1207	348	5733
Works allocated					
1) Feast days	286	145	242	66	741
	(10)	(10)	(20)	(19)	(13)
2) Illness	31½	–	–	–	31½
	(1)				(1)
3) Sales	172	445	17	–	634
	(6)	(31)	(1)		(11)
4) Customary	88	–	–	–	88
payments	(3)				(2)
Works done	2146½	864	948	282	4238½
	(79)	(59)	(79)	(81)	(74)
1357–58					
Works due					
15v + 10c	2110	770	922	240	4042
Works allocated					
1) Feast days	296	120	102	15	53
	(14)	(16)	(11)	(6)	(13)
2) Illness	24	24	12	–	60
	(1)	(3)	(1)		(1)
3) Sales	451	136	106	60	753
	(21)	(18)	(11)	(25)	(19)
4) Customary	60	–	–	–	60
payments	(3)				(1)
Works done	1279	490	702	165	2636
	(61)	(64)	(76)	(69)	(65)
1371–72					
Works due					
13¾v + 7c	1671¾	747½	647	204	3270¼

	Winter	Summer	Autumn	Post-Autumn	Total
Works allocated					
1) Feast days	96	68¾	–	–	164¾
	(6)	(9)			(5)
2) Illness	–	–	–	–	–
3) Sales	393	295	107	168	963
	(24)	(39)	(17)	(82)	(29)
4) Customary	55	–	–	–	55
payments	(3)				(2)
Works done	1127¾	383¾	540	36	2087½
	(67)	(51)	(83)	(18)	(64)
1385–86					
Works due					
14v + 6c	1536	775	672	201	3184
Works allocated					
1) Feast days	154	84	28	14	280
	(10)	(11)	(4)	(7)	(9)
2) Illness	–	47	–	–	47
		(6)			(1)
3) Sales	176	189	127	55	547
	(11)	(24)	(19)	(27)	(17)
4) Customary	56	–	–	–	56
payments	(4)				(2)
Works done	1150	455	517	132	2254
	(75)	(59)	(77)	(66)	(71)
1386–87					
Works due					
13¼v + 6c	1619	622¾	643	192	3076¾
Works allocated					
1) Feast days	119	79½	79½	(?)	278(+?)
	(7)	(13)	(12)		(9)
2) Illness	–	–	8	8	16
			(1)	(4)	(.5)
3) Sales	166¾	141¾	146½	(?)	455(+?)
	(10)	(23)	(23)		(15)
4) Customary	53	–	–	–	53
payments	(3)				(2)
Works done	1280¼	401½	417	(?)	(2274¾)
	(79)	(65)	(65)		
1392–93					
Works due					
13¾v + 5c	1484¾	718¼	625½	172	3000½
Works allocated					
1) Feast days	151¾	55	27½	13¾	248
	(10)	(8)	(4)	(8)	(8)
2) Illness	38½	4½	16	–	59
	(3)	(1)	(3)		(2)

	Winter	Summer	Autumn	Post-Autumn	Total
3) Sales	170	152¾	120	58¼	501
	(11)	(21)	(19)	(34)	(17)
4) Customary	55	–	–	–	55
payments	(4)				(2)
Works done	969½	506	462	100	2137½
	(65)	(70)	(74)	(58)	(71)
1398–99					
Works due					
15¼v + 4c	1526¾	822¾	677½	204	3231
Works allocated					
1) Feast days	167¾	76¼	30½	15¼	289¾
	(11)	(9)	(5)	(8)	(9)
2) Illness	–	–	–	–	–
3) Sales	416	96½	164	106¾	783¼
	(27)	(12)	(24)	(52)	(24)
4) Customary	61	–	–	–	61
payments	(4)				(2)
Works done	882	650	483	82	2097
	(58)	(79)	(71)	(40)	(65)
(1403–04)					
Works due					
11½v + 4c	1150½	646½	520	159	2476
Works allocated					
1) Feast days	103½	57½	23	11½	195½
	(9)	(9)	(4)	(8)	(8)
2) Illness	–	–	–	–	–
3) Sales	451	308	179	30½	968½
	(39)	(48)	(34)	(19)	(39)
4) Customary	46	–	–	–	46
payments	(4)				(2)
Works done	550	281	318	117	1266
	(48)	(43)	(61)	(74)	(51)
1406–07					
Works due					
9½v + 4c	947½	523½	466	129	2066
Works allocated					
1) Feast days	123½	66½	57	9½	256½
	(13)	(13)	(12)	(8)	(12)
2) Illness	–	–	–	–	–
3) Sales	175½	165	48½	31½	420½
	(19)	(31)	(11)	(25)	(20)
4) Customary	38	–	–	–	38
payments	(4)				(2)
Works done	610½	292	360½	88	1351
	(64)	(56)	(77)	(68)	(65)

	Winter	Summer	Autumn	Post-Autumn	Total
1408–09					
Works due					
6½v + 2c	645	314	283	84	1326
Works allocated					
1) Feast days	52	39	–	–	91
	(8)	(12)			(7)
2) Illness	–	–	–	–	–
3) Sales	257	118	28	80	483
	(40)	(38)	(10)	(95)	(36)
4) Customary	26	–	–	–	26
payments	(4)				(2)
Works done	310	157	255	4	726
	(48)	(50)	(90)	(5)	(55)
1412–13					
Works due					
5½v + 1c	560	210	258	69	1097
Works allocated					
1) Feast days	71½	22	33	5½	132
	(13)	(10)	(13)	(9)	(12)
2) Illness	–	–	–	–	–
3) Sales	272	77	225	21	595
	(49)	(37)	(87)	(30)	(54)
4) Customary	22	–	–	–	22
payments	(4)				(2)
Works done	194½	111	–	42½	348
	(35)	(53)		(62)	(32)

Wistow

	Winter	Summer	Autumn	Post–Autumn	Total
1335–36					
Works due					
23v + 9½c + 5h	2637	885½	1086	250½	4859
Works allocated					
1) Feast days	253	138	23	–	414
	(10)	(16)	(2)		(9)
2) Illness	29	18	32	–	79
	(1)	(2)	(3)		(1)
3) Sales	–	54½	242	–	296½
		(6)	(22)		(6)
4) Customary	93	–	–	–	93
payments	(3)				(2)
Works done	2262	675	789	250½	3976½
	(86)	(76)	(73)	(100)	(82)

	Winter	Summer	Autumn	Post–Autumn	Total
[1350–51]					
Works due					
21½ v + 2c + 3h	2216	753	943	204	4116
Works allocated					
1) Feast days	322½	86	42	63	513½
	(15)	(11)	(4)	(31)	(12)
2) Illness	7½	–	–	–	7½
	(.3)				(.1)
3) Sales	–	137½	185½	102	425
		(18)	(20)	(50)	(10)
4) Customary	86	–	–	–	86
payments	(4)				(2)
Works done	1800	530	715	39	3084
	(81)	(71)	(76)	(19)	(75)
1351–52					
Works due					
21½ v + 3c + 4h	2427	561½	1027½	214½	4230½
Works allocated					
1) Feast days	409½	86	86	–	581½
	(17)	(15)	(8)		(14)
2) Illness	–	–	–	–	–
3) Sales	116	115½	378	65½	675
	(5)	(21)	(38)	(31)	(16)
4) Customary	86	–	–	–	86
payments	(4)				(2)
Works done	1815½	360	563	149	2887½
	(74)	(64)	(54)	(69)	(62)
1368–69					
Works due					
19v + 1c + 5h	2106	483	848	189	3626
Works allocated					
1) Feast days	209	76	38	57	380
	(10)	(16)	(5)	(30)	(10)
2) Illness	–	–	–	–	–
3) Sales	320	106	810	9½	1245½
	(15)	(22)	(95)	(5)	(38)
4) Customary	76	–	–	–	76
payments	(4)				(2)
Works done	1501	301	–	122½	1924½
	(71)	(62)		(65)	(50)
1379–80					
Works due					
17¾v + 1c + 5h	1771	651	828¾	177¾	3428½
Works allocated					
1) Feast days	177½	88¾	106½	–	372¾
	(10)	(14)	(13)		(11)

	Winter	Summer	Autumn	Post–Autumn	Total
2) Illness	1½	–	10	2	13½
	(.08)		(1)	(1)	(.4)
3) Sales	67	39¼	59	23¾	189
	(4)	(6)	(7)	(13)	(6)
4) Customary	71	–	–	–	71
payments	(4)				(2)
Works done	1454	523	.653	152	2782
	(82)	(80)	(79)	(86)	(81)
1388–89					
Works due					
18⅛v + 1c + 5h	2010⅝	461⅛	810⅜	181⅛	3463
Works allocated					
1) Feast days	217½	72½	36⅛	36¼	362½
	(11)	(15)	(5)	(20)	(10)
2) Illness	–	–	–	7	7
				(.4)	(.2)
3) Sales	110½	52½	132¼	3	298¼
	(5)	(11)	(16)	(2)	(9)
4) Customary	72½	–	–	–	78½
payments	+6 (heriot)				
	(3)				(2)
Works done	1604	336	642	135	2717
	(82)	(74)	(79)	(78)	(79)
1389–90					
Works due					
19⅛v + 1c + 5h	1983¾	603⅜	891⅝	190⅛	3669
Works allocated					
1) Feast days	210⅜	95⅝	114¾	19⅛	439⅞
	(11)	(16)	(13)	(10)	(12)
2) Illness	30	15	22½	4½	72
	(2)	(3)	(3)	(2)	(2)
3) Sales	160⅞	120¼	192⅜	26½	500
	(8)	(20)	(21)	(14)	(13)
4) Customary	76½	–	–	–	76½
payments	(4)				(2)
Works done	1506	372½	562	140	2580
	(75)	(61)	(63)	(74)	(71)
1393–94					
Works due					
18¼v + 1c + 5h	2006	464¼	797½	182¼	3450
Works allocated					
1) Feast days	216	91¼	73	36½	416¾
	(11)	(19)	(9)	(20)	(12)
2) Illness	48½	–	14	–	62½
	(2)	–	(2)	–	(2)

	Winter	Summer	Autumn	Post–Autumn	Total
3) Sales	165¾	90½	174	16¾	447
	(8)	(19)	(22)	(9)	(13)
4) Customary	73	–	–	–	73
payments	(4)				(2)
Works done	1503	282½	536½	129	2451
	(75)	(62)	(67)	(71)	(71)
1394–95					
Works due					
18¼v + 1c + 5h	1949¾	519	815¾	182¼	3466¾
Works allocated					
1) Feast days	255	73	36½	36½	401
	(13)	(14)	(4)	(20)	(12)
2) Illness	–	4½	20½	1½	25½
	(.8)	(3)	(.8)	(.7)	
3) Sales	190¾	80½	203¼	20¼	494¾
	(10)	(16)	(25)	(11)	(14)
4) Customary	73	–	–	–	73
payments	(4)				(2)
Works done	1431	361	555½	124	2471½
	(73)	(70)	(68)	(68)	(71)

The Tenurial Spread at Abbots Ripton, Upwood, and Wistow

The main purpose of this appendix is to add further information about the gradual transition to money rent from work service that was discussed in chapter 4. Since the work service owed declined radically from the late fourteenth century, these data become less significant in the fifteenth century. Furthermore, surviving account rolls become more scattered after the early fifteenth century. Even when account rolls do survive, the data to be found on them is often patchy. For example, from account rolls at Wistow we know that 13¾ virgates were still held by work service over 1419–25, but names of tenants are not listed. For the same manor, the names of those leasing demesne lands are not given in account rolls for 1413–15. Several account rolls survive for all these manors during some years around the mid-fifteenth century. But the listings of tenants and their holdings are very incomplete for this later period. Upwood, as the more complete list for this "Third Period," is given in the following table. The list of tenants for Abbots Ripton in 1456 seems to be largely confined to new tenants, thereby offering little for comparison with earlier tenant lists. The tenurial picture for larger landholders can be better appreciated through the sources employed for chapter 5.

The survival pattern of late fourteenth- and early fifteenth-century account rolls varies considerably from one of our five villages to another. For this reason, tenurial data from three villages not available elsewhere are given here in order to complement the whole picture. Although poorly served by survivals for the greater part of this period, the account records of Abbots Ripton give more information for the 1370s and 1380s than do any other of the five account series. Thus, Abbots Ripton most clearly indicates the focus upon the *ad opus* and *ad censum* at the beginning of the last quarter of the century. Data for Abbots Ripton also indicate the beginnings of engrossing by older families (Juell, Nicol, Onty [Outy], Robbes) and the introduction of new wealth (Jurdon, Ladde, Martyn, Shepherd) largely by taking advantage of the long-term money lease (*arrentatum*).

Upwood records are the most complete among these villages for the three decades between 1390 and 1420. Account rolls for Upwood are especially useful, therefore, in demonstrating the fairly complete transition to the *arrentatum*. This series of account rolls also shows how this transition took place rather later for some tenants (John Bigge, Robert Miles, William Payne, Thomas Peny).

Information from the account rolls for Wistow tends to be less concentrated and thereby adds to data from the two other villages. In addition, Wistow data do have their own characteristics. For this manor, long-term leases were not uncommon from the third quarter of the fourteenth century (Simon Asplond, Simon Augustyn, William Barker, William Benet, William Flexmor, Robert Gouler, John Gregge, Stephen Hiche, John Ivesson, Ralph Sabyn, Peter Waker). However, data designated "Second Period" for Wistow demonstrate a longer continuation of work-service tenure for what was left of the demesne. Indeed, work service continued in considerable amounts over the first half of the fifteenth century. As already noted, there were 13¾ virgates *ad opera* over the 1419–24 period. The shortened form "hide" employed in this list refers to the smallholding called a hidemanland.

For convenience, those serving in official tasks as reeve, beadle, and ploughman have been placed under the general designation of work service. One should recall, as noted in chapter 4, that many tenants show a remarkable versatility of skills and resource disposition. For example, Nicholas Hoberd of Abbots Ripton was a ploughman for a half-virgate as well as holding another half-virgate for yearly money rent over 1375–76; over 1378–79 he held 1 virgate for service; over 1384–85 he held as in 1375–76; over 1377–78 he held a half-virgate for services and another half-virgate for longer-term money rent; over 1389–90 a half-virgate was held for yearly money rent and another half-virgate for the longer-term money rent; over 1390–91, he held 1 virgate as reeve and the half-virgate for longer-term money rent; and, in the last recorded year of 1394–95, he held a half-virgate as beadle and 1 virgate for services. Such a pattern, and there are others for each manor, reminds us again that wealthier tenants could survive involvement even during the dying days of the "manorial system."

ABBREVIATIONS

o *ad opera*, work service or official tasks.
c *ad censum*, yearly commutation of work service to money rent.
a *ad arrentatum*, long-term commutation of work service to money rent.

No abbreviations have been entered for rentals of various small acreages of demesne, since the record does not employ any special term. These parts of fields were always leased for a number of years, though the exact number is not usually given unless a surviving entry is for the first year of the lease. These tables do not provide a complete list of demesne leases, since to do so would have required entries for smallholders and entries for wealthy tenants who held the major proportion of such lands in neighbouring villages. The total demesne leasing picture can be seen above, chapter 4, section iv. In short, references to demesne leasing in these tables merely provide some sample illustrations. Finally, the full date is given (as, for example, 1411, 1412 for Upwood, rather than 1411–12) when there is some doubt about the exact chronology of the records.

ABBOTS RIPTON, 1375–95

Attechurche, John sr.	½v (o) + ½v (c) 1379–80
Attechurche, John jr.*	1v (o) + ½v (c) 1375–76; ½v (o) 1379–80; 1v (o) 1384–87; ½v (c) + ½v (o) 1394–95
Attehill, Thomas of Hartford	Land 1375–76
Attehill, William of Stukeley	10a (life) 1387–88, 1394–95
Austyn, John	1 cot (a) + 1 cot (o) 1375–76, 1379–80, 1384–85, 1387–88, 1389–90
Bette, John	½v (o) + ¼v (c) 1375–76, 1379–80; 1v (o) 1384–85; 1v (o) + ½ v (c) 1387–88; 1v (o) 1389–90; ¼v (o) 1390–91, 1394–95
Bette, Philip	1 cottage 1375–84; 1 cot (life) 1384; 1v (o) + ½v (c) 1375–76, 1379–80
Bole, John	1v (o) 1379–80, 1384–85, 1387–88, 1389–90; ½ v (o) 1394–95
Bonde, Thomas	1v (o) 1375–76, 1379–80
Bouk, John	1v (o) 1375–76, 1379–80, 1384–85, 1387–88, 1389–90; ½v (o) 1390–91
Broun, John	cottage + parcel (life) 1384
Cademan, John	1v (o) 1394–95
Carter, John	1v (o) 1379–80, 1384–85, 1387–88, 1389–90, 1390–91; ½v (c) + ½v (o) 1394–95
Carter, William	½v (o) 1375–76, 1379–80
Cobbe, Andrew	1v (o) 1375–76, 1379–80, 1387–88; ½v (o) + ½v (c) 1384–85; ½v (o) + ½v (c) + ½v (a) 1389–90, 1390–91; 1v (o) + ½v (a) 1394–95
Colier, Andrew	1v (o) 1375–76, 1379–80, 1384–85
Cole, John	1 cot (o) + ½v (o) 1379–80; ¾v (o) 1384–85; ½v (c) + ½v (o) 1389–90, 1390–91

* Junior ceased to be added by 1387

Dicon, John	2a 1389–94; ½v (c) 1394–95
Ede, John	1v (o) 1375–76
Flecher, John	1a 1389; 1 cot (o) + 1 cot (a) 1390–91; 1 cot (o) 1394–95
Fuller, Thomas	1a 1387
Galt, William	1 cot (a) 1394–95
Gille, John	1 cot (o) 1375–95
Goteherde, John	1 cot (o) + 1 cot (a) 1387–88
Haulond, Agnes	½v (c) 1390–91
Haulond, John	1 mess (life) 1384–85; ½v (o) 1394–5
Haulond, Philip	¼v (c) + 1v (o) 1375–76; 1v (o) 1379–80, 1384–85, 1387–88, 1389–90, 1394–95; 1v (o) + ½v (o) 1390–91
Henry (Herry), Thomas	¾v (o) 1379–80; ¼v (c) + 1v (o) 1384–85; ¾v (o) 1387–88, 1389–90; ½v (a) 1390–91
Henry (Herry), William	1v (o) 1375–76; ¼v (o) 1379–80
Hiche, William	1v (o) + ½v (c) 1375–76, 1384–85, 1387–88, 1389–90
Hoberd, Nicholas	½v (c) + ½v (o) 1375–76; 1v (o) 1379–80; 1v (o) + ½v (c) 1384–85; 1v (o) + ½v (a) 1387–88, 1389–90, 1390–91, 1394–95
Howe, William	1v (o) 1375–76; ½v (c) + ½v (o) 1379–80; 1v (o) + ½v (c) 1384–85, 1387–88, 1389–90, 1390–91; 10a (2 years) 1387–88
Hulot, John	1v (a) with Robert Jurdon 1389–90
Huntingdon, Prior and Canon of	meadow 1375–76; 1 pasture in Houghton 1384
Hurst, Gilbert	¼v (o) + land 1375–76; ½v (o) 1379–80
Hurst, William de	ten. (10s) 1384–85
Juell, John	½v (c) + ½v (o) 1379–80; 1v (o) + ½v (c) 1384–85; 1v (c) + ½v (o) 1389–90; 1v (c) + ½v (o) + ½v (o) 1390–91; 1v (c) + ½v (o) 1394–95
Jurdon, Robert	1v (a) with John Hulot 1389–90; ¼v (a) with John Shepherd 1389–90; ½v (a) 1389–90; 1v (o) + ½v (a) 1394–95
Jurdon, William	½v (c) + 2¼v (a) 1375–76; 2 ¾ v (a) 1379–80, 1384–85, 1387–88, 1389–90
Ladde, Philip	½v (c) + 1v (a) + ½v (o) 1375–76, 1379–80; 1v (o) + 1v (a) 1384–85, 1387–88, 1389–90, 1390–91, 1394–95
Littlejohn	½v (o) + 1 cot (o) + 1 cot (a) 1375–76, 1379–80; 1 cot (o) + 1 cot (a) + 1v (o) 1384–85, 1389–90, 1390–91; ½v (c) + ½v (o) 1387–88; ½v (o) + ½v (c) with Thomas Nene 1379–80

Love, Thomas	1 cot (o) 1375–76, 1379–80, 1384–85, 1389–90
Martyn, John of the Green	½v (o) 1375–76; ¼v (c) 1387–88
Martyn, John sr.	1v (o) 1375–76, 1379–80, 1384–85, 1387–88
Martyn, John jr.	½v (o) + ½v (c) 1375–76
Martyn, John	½v (o) + ½v (c) 1387–88; 1v (o) 1389–90; ½v (c) 1390–91; ½v (c) + ½v (o) 1394–95
Martyn, Thomas	1v (o) 1379–80, 1384–85, 1387–88, 1389–90, 1390–91; ¾v (a) 1394–95
Martyn, William	1v (a) 1375–76; 1v (a) + ½v (c) 1379–80, 1384–85; 1v (a) + 1v (o) 1387–88, 1389–90; 1v (a) 1390–91; 1v (o) 1394–95
Martyn, William of Wennington	1v (o) + 1v (a) 1390–91; ½v (a) 1394–95
Martyn, William of Ripton	1v (o) 1390–91; 1½ v (o) + 1v (a) + 1 cot ? 1394–95
Merewyk, John	2a 1387–89
Nene, John	1v (o) 1375–76
Nene, Thomas	½v (c) + ½v (o) 1375–76; ½v (c) + ½v (o) with Littlejohn 1379–80
Newman, Thomas	½v (o) 1379–80
Nicol, John	1v (o) 1379–80, 1384–85; ½v (o) + ¾v (c) 1387–88; 1v (o) + ¼v (c) 1389–90; 1v (o) + 1¼v (c) 1390–91; 1½v (c) + ½v (o) 1394–95
Outy, Andrew	1v (o) + ½v 1379–80; ½v (c) + ½v (o) + ½v (o) 1384–85; 1v (o) + 1v (a) + ½v (c) 1387–88, 1389–90, 1390–91; 1v (o) + 1 ¾v (a) 1394–95
Outy, Thomas	1v (o) 1394–95
Prikke, John	¾v (o) 1375–76, 1379–80; ¾v (o) + ¼v (c) 1384–85; 1v (o) 1387–88; ½v + ½v (o) 1389–90
Prikke, William	1v (c) + ½v (o) 1375–76; 1v (o) 1379–80, 1384–85; ½v (a) + ½v (o) 1387–88; 1v (o) + ½v (a) 1389–90, 1390–91, 1394–95
Purquey, John	½v (o) 1394–95
Ravensdon, John	1 cot (o) 1389–90, 1390–91, 1394–95
Reve, John le	1v (o) 1375–76
Robbes, John sr.	½v (c) + ½v (o) 1384–85
Robbes, John jr.	1 cot (a) + 1v (o) + ½v (c) 1384–85
Robbes, John	1v (o) 1379–80; 1v (o) + ½v (c) + 1 cot (a) 1387–88, 1389–90; 1v (o) + ½v (c) 1394–95
Saly, John	1v (o) 1375–76
Sabyn, John	½v (c) + ½v (o) 1375–76, 1379–80; 1v (o) 1384–85, 1387–88, 1389–90, 1390–91, 1394–95
Sabyn, William	1v (o) 1375–76

Sarresson, Martyn	1v (c) + ½v (o) + land 1375–76
Stotland, John	1v (o) 1375–76, 1379–80, 1384–85, 1387–88, 1389–90
Sewell, John	3a (of 9a) 1384
Shepherd, Henry	½v (a) 1375–76, 1379–80, 1384–85, 1387–88, 1389–90, 1390–91, 1394–95
Shepherd, John	4s for land 1389–90; ¼v (a) with Robert Jurdon 1389–90, 1394–95; ¼v (a) 1390–91; ½v (a) 1394–95
Smith, Andrew	blacksmith shop 1375–76; ¼v (c) 1379–80, 1384–85; 12d land 1384–85
Smith, William	¼v (c) 1375–76, 1379–80, 1384–85; ¼v (c) + ½v (a) 1387–88, 1390–91
Son, Thomas	1 cot (a) 1375–76, 1379–80, 1384–85, 1387–88, 1388–89, 1390–91
Stevens, John	1v (o) + ½v (c) 1379–80, 1387–88; ½v (o) + 1v (c) 1384–85
Swan, Thomas	1 cot (a) 1394–95
Taylor, Nicholas	6a (of 9a life) 1384–85; ½v (a) 1394–95
Thacher, John	2a (life) 1394–95
Thedwar, John	1v (o) 1375–76, 1379–80, 1384–85; ½v (o) + ½v (o) 1387–88, 1389–90; 1v (o) 1390–91, 1394–95
Vernon, Robert	3s for ten. 1384–85
Vernon, Thomas	¼v (c) 1384–85
Wattes, Robert	1v (o) + ½v (c) 1375–76; ½v (o) 1384–85, 1387–88, 1389–90, 1390–91
Wattes, William	1v (o) 1394–95
Webester, John	3a (life) 1387–88
West, John	1v (o) + ½v (c) 1375–76; 1v (c) + ½v (o) 1379–80; 1v (o) + ½v (o) 1380–81; 1v (o) + ½v (c) 1384–85, 1387–88, 1390–91, 1394–95; 1v (c) + ½v (o) 1389–90
West, Thomas	1v (o) + ½v (c) 1375–76; 1v (c) + ½v (o) 1379–80
West, William jr.	½v (c) + ½v (a) 1384–85
West, William sr.	1v (o) + ½v (a) 1384–85; ½v (a) 1389–90; 1v (o) + ½v (c) + ½v (a) + ½v (o) 1387–88
West, William	½v (a) 1375–76, 1379–80; 1v (o) + ½v (a) 1389–90; 1v (o) + 1v (o) + ½v (a) 1390–91; 1v (o) + ½v (a) 1394–95
West, William of Wennington	1v (o) 1384–85, 1389–90; 1v (o) + ½v (a) 1394–95
White, William	1v (c) + ½v (o) 1389–90; 1v (o) + ½v (c) 1394–95
Wrighte, Andrew of Ripton	1v (o) + 1 cot (o) + 1 cot (a) 1394–95

UPWOOD 1371–1453

	First Period*	Second Period	Third Period
Albyn, Richard	½v (c) 1371–72; ¾v (a) 1385–86	¾v (a) 1392–93, 1401–02, 1406–07, 1411–12; 1 cot (a) 1401–02	
Albyn, John		1a (of 17a 3½r) 1388–9, 1403–4; 1a 1398–99, 1403–04, 1406–07; 1a (of 11a 1r) 1406–07, 1408–09, 1411–12, 1412–13	
Albyn, Nicholas		¾v (a) 1420–21	¾v(a)1446–47
Alcok, William	1v (o) 1371–72, 1385–86	1v (o) 1392–93, 1401–02; 1a 3r (of 9a 1r) 1398–99, 1403–04, 1406–07, 1412–13	
Aleyn, John		¼v (a) 1401–02, 1406–07; 1r 1406–07 ½cot (a) 1411–12, 1412–13; 1r (of 1a 3½r) 1406–07, 1408–09, 1412–13; 1r 1420–23; ½v (a) with William Aleyn 1420–22	1r 1446–56; ½v (a) 1446–47
Aleyn, Robert		¼ v (a) 1411–12, 1412–13; 1 cot (alias Newman) 1420–21; 15 butts + 1r + ¼v (a) 1420–23	

* As noted in the introductory remarks to this Appendix, the designation of periods for
  Upwood and Wistow is intended to assist in locating the different patterns of data employed
  for analysis of peasants' forms of tenure.

	First Period	*Second Period*	*Third Period*
Aleyn, Richard			½v(a) + ½v (a) + ¼v (a) 1446–49
Aleyn, William		1 cot (c) 1401–02; ¼v (a) 1412–13; ½v (a) with John Aleyn 1420–21	
Alston, Nicholas	½cot (o) 1385–86; 9a 1385–86, 1386–87	½ cot (o) 1392–93; ½ cot (a) 1401–02; ¼ v (a) 1406–07, 1411–12, 1412–13, 1420–21; 3a 33p (of 16a 3r) 1398–99, 1403–04; 4a (of 9a) 1398–99, 1403–04; 2a (of 14a 3½r) 1398–99, 1403–04; 4a (of 7a) 1398–99, 1403–04; 2s6d land 1420–23	
Andrew, John		½v (a) + ½v (a) 1420–21	1 forland 1446–53; ½v (a) + ½v (a) 1446–49
Andrew, Richard		1a + 1 cot (a) 1421–22	
Andrew, William		2a 1421–22; 1 mess 1421–23	
Atteforde, William	4a 1385–86		
Attestede, Walter	4a (of 6a) 1386–87		
Attestede, William		4a (of 6a) 1392–93; 2a 3½r with William Chamberlayn 1398–99; 4a (of 11a) 1398–99, 1403–04; 1a 1½r 10p 1403–04	
Attewell, John	1v (o) + ¼v (c) 1371–72, 1385–86		

	First Period	*Second Period*	*Third Period*
Attewelle, Richard		½ cot (a) + ½ cot (a) 1411–12; ½ cot (a) 1412–13; 1 cot (c) 1420–21; 2a (of 14a 3½r) 1406–07, 1408–09, 1411–12, 1412–13; 4a (of 9a 1r) 1406–07, 1408–09, 1411–12, 1412–13; 3a 30p (of 16a 3r) 1406–07, 1408–09, 1411–12, 1412–13; 4a (of 7a) 1406–07, 1408–09, 1411–12, 1412–13	
Attewelle, William	1v (o) + ¼v (c) 1371–72	1v (a) + 1 cot (o) 1401–02; 1 cot (o) 1406–07	1 forland + 1r + 1 parcel meadow 1446–53
Aubes, John	3a 1r + 2a 1385–86, 1386–87	2a 1392; 2a (of 11a) 1398–99, 1403–04, 1406–07, 1408–09, 1411–12, 1412–13	
Aubes, John sr.			½v (a) + ¼v (a) + ¼v (a) + 1 forland + 1 cot (a) 1446–49; 1 piece of demesne 2s 1446–53
Aubes, William		3a 3r + 3a 1r + 4½a 1392–93; 2a (of 9a 1r) 1398–99, 1403–04; 4½ a (of 8½ a) 1398–99, 1403–04, 1406–07; 3a (of 14a) 1398–99, 1403–04, 1406–	

	First Period	Second Period	Third Period
		07, 1408–09, 1411–12, 1412–13; 3½a (of 6a) 1398–99, 1403–04, 1406–07, 1408–09, 1411–12, 1412–13; 2a 1403–04; 3a + 3r mea. 1408–09, 1411–12, 1412–13; 3½a (of 8½a) 1408–09, 1411–12, 1412–13; 5s4d land with Adam Parvus of Wennington 1420–23	
Baker, John		½v (a) 1406–07, 1411–12; 2a 3r (of 17a 3½r) 1406–07, 1408–09, 1411–12, 1412–13	
Baker, Walter	½v (a) + 1 cot (c) 1371–72; ¼v (a) + ½ v (o) +1 cot (c) 1385–86; 1r + 3a +½a 1385–86; 1r 1386–87; 3a (of 8a) 1386–87; ½a (of 1a 3½r) 1386–87	¼v (a) + ½v (o) + 1 cot (a) + 1 cot (c) 1391–92; 1r 1392–93; 3a (of 8a) 1391–92; ½a (of 1a 3½ r) 1392–93; 2a (of 11½a) 1398–99, 1403–04; 1a (of 17a 3r) 1403; 1½a 1406	
Baker, William		¼v (a) + ½v (o) + 1 cot (a) + 1 cot (c) 1401–02; ¼v (a) + 1 cot (a) + 1 cot (c) 1406–07; ½v (o) + ¼ v (a) 1411–12, 1412–13; ¼v (a)	

	First Period	Second Period	Third Period
		1420–21; 2 cot (a) (thacher) with Peter Bray 1420–21; 4a + 2r with William Heryng jr. 1398–99, 1403–04, 1406–07; ½ a (of 15 butts) 1406–07; 1 r of mea. with William Heryng jr. 1406–07, 1408–09, 1411–12, 1412–13; 4a 2r with Richard Newman, 1406–07, 1408–09, 1411–12; 4a 2r with Robert Newman 1412–13; ½r 1420–23	
Baker, William jr.		½v (o) 1406–07	
Balde, Robert		mess of ½v 1420–23	
Baldock, Walter			2¼ v(a) 1446–49
Balle, Andrew		½v (c) + ¾v (a) 1411–1412, 1412–13; ½v (a) + ¼v (a) 1420–21	
Balle, Margaret, widow of Thomas		½v (o) + ½v (a) 1392–93	
Balle, Thomas	1v (o) + ¼v (c) 1385–86; 2½a 1385–86, 1386–87		
Baron, Richard			1 forland 1446–53; 1v (a) 1446–49
Bele, John	3a 1385–86; 6a with William West 1386–87	6a with William West 1392–93; 3a (of 14a) 1398–99, 1403–04, 1406–	

	First Period	*Second Period*	*Third Period*
		07, 1408–09, 1411–12, 1412–13	
Bigge, John	1v (o) 1371–72, 1385–86	1v (o) 1392–93; 1v (o) + ½v (a) + 1 cot (a) 1401–02; 1v (o) + ¼v (a) + 1 cot (a) 1406–07; ½v (o) + ½v (a) + ½v (a) + 1 cot (a) 1411–12; ½v (o) + ¾v (a) + ½ cot (a) 1412–13; ½v (a) + ¼v (a) + 1 cot (a) 1420–21	
Bracer, John		1a + 1a 1420–23; 3 cot (a) 1420–21	
Bracer, William	1a 1385–86; 1a (of 6a) 1386–87	1a (of 6a) 1392–93; 1a 1398–99, 1403–04, 1406–07, 1408–09, 1411–12, 1412–13; 1a (of 11a) 1398–99, 1403–04, 1406–07; ½v (a) 1420–21	
Bray, Peter		½v (o) + 1 cot (c) 1392–93; 1v (a) 1406–07, 1420–21; 1v (a) + 1 cot (a) 1411–12, 1412–13; 2 cot (a) with William Baker 1420–21; 1½a (of 9a 1r) 1398–99, 1403–04, 1406–07, 1408–09, 1411–12, 1412–13; 1a 1398, 1403–04	
Bronnote, John			1 cot (a) 1446–49

	First Period	Second Period	Third Period
Buckworth, John			½v(a) + ½v(a) + 1 cot (a) 1446–49
Buckworth, Richard	1v (o) 1385–86	½v (c) + ½v (o) 1392–93	
Buckworth, William	½v (o) 1371–72; ½v (o) + ¼v (a) 1385–86		
Burne, Richard			1 cot (a) 1446–49
Cademan, Ralph		1a (of 14a 3½r) 1398–99, 1403–04, 1406–07, 1408–09, 1411–12, 1412–13	
Chamberlyn, William		¼ v(o) 1392–93; ½v + ¾v (a) 1401–02, 1406–07; 2a 3½r with William Attestede 1398–99; 3a (of 11a) 1398–99, 1403–04; 1a 1½ r 10p 1403–04; 1a + 3a with Thomas Wardebusk 1403–04, 1406–07, 1408–09, 1411–12, 1412–13; 2a (of 11a) 1406–07, 1408–09, 1411–12, 1412–13	
Chaplain of Lt Stukeley		2a 1408–09, 1411–12, 1412–13	
Clerk, William	½ cot (a) 1271–72; 4a 3r 1385–86, 1386–87		
Collisson, John		2½ a (of 11a½r) 1398–99, 1403–04, 1406–07, 1408–09, 1411–12, 1412–13; 3a 1403–04	

	First Period	*Second Period*	*Third Period*
Collisson, William			1 forland + ½ pigsty + 3r 1446–53; ½v (a) 1446–49
Cook, John	¼v (a) 1371–72; ¼v (a) + 1 cot (c) + 1 cot (o) 1385–86	¼v (a) + 1 cot (c) + 1 cot (o) 1392–93; ¼v (a) 1401–02	
Cook, Walter	4a 1r with John Haukyn, 1385–86, 1386–87		
Cary (Cory), John		2a 1392–93; 2½ a + 2p mea. with William Flemyng 1398–99; 4a 3r (of 14a 3½r) 1398–99, 1403–04, 1406–07, 1408–09, 1411–12, 1412–13; 1a (of 7a) 1398–99, 1403–04, 1406–07, 1408–09, 1411–12, 1412–13; 2a (of 8½ a) 1398–99, 1403–04, 1406–07, 1408–09, 1411–12, 1412–13; 3a 3r 1406–07; 2½a (of 6a) 1406–07, 1408–09, 1411–12, 1412–13	
Cusse, William			1 forland + 1a 1446–53; 1½v (a) + ½ pigsty 1446–49
Daye, Walter	½v (a) +1 cot (o) + 1 cot (c) 1371–72; 3½a + 1 r mea. with William Newman 1385–		

	First Period	Second Period	Third Period
	86, 1386–87; 1r (of 1a 3½r) 1386–87; 1r (of 1 a 3½r) 1392–93		
Denyll, John	1 cot (o) 1385–86	1 cot (o) 1392–93; 2a with John Frounceys 1392–93	
Dicon (Decon), William		1 cot (a) 1401–02, 1406–07, 1411–12; 1a (of 17a 3½r) 1398–99; 1r with William Heryng jr. 1403–04; ½ cot (a) 1412–13, 1420–21	
Edward, John			2 butts + forland 1446–53
Edward, Robert	½v (o) + ¼v (a) 1371–72; ½v (o) + ¾v (a) 1385–86; 1a (of 8a) 1385–86, 1386–87	½v (o) + ¾v (a) 1392–93	
Edward, William		1v (o) 1401–02; 1v (a) 1420–21	1 forland 1446–53; ½v (a) + ¼v (a) 1446–49
Erl, William		1a 1398–99, 1403–04, 1406–07, 1408–09, 1411–12, 1412–13; 1a 1406–07; 2a (of 17a 3½ r) 1406–07, 1408–09, 1411–12, 1412–13; 1 cot 1420–21; 1a + 1a + 2½a + 2 parts meadow 1420–23; 1 cot (a) 1420–21	
Flemyng, John	1v (o) 1371–72, 1385–86		

	First Period	*Second Period*	*Third Period*
Flemyng, William	1 cot (o) 1371–72, 1385–86; 7a 3r 1385–86, 1386–87	1 cot (o) 1392–93, 1401–02; 7a 3r + 2½ a 1392–93; 2½ a + 2 p meadow with John Cory 1398; 7a 3r 1398–99; 2a 1398–99, 1403–04; 2½a (of 6a) 1398–99, 1403–04	
Forgon, Thomas	1a 1385–86; 1a (of 11a) 1386–87	1a (of 11a) 1392–93; 2a with Walter Baker 1398–99; 2a (of 11a) 1408–09, 1411–12, 1412–13	
Fraunceys, John	1 cot (c) 1371–72, 1385–86; 3r + 1a + ½a 1385–86; 3r 1386–87; 2a with John Holy 1386–87; ½a 1386–87	1 cot (c) 1392–93; 3r + 1a + ½a 1392–93; 2a with John Denyll 1392–93; 3r 1408–13	
Fraunceys, William		1 cot (c) 1401–02, 1406–07, 1411–12, 1412–13; 1 cot (a) 1420–21; 3r 1398–99, 1403–04, 1406–07, 1408–09, 1411–12, 1412–13	
Freeston, John			½a + 1 butt + 1 forland + 5 butts 1446–53; ½v (a) 1446–49
Galopyn, John	¼v (o) + ½v (c) + 1 cot (c) 1371–72, 1385–86, 1386–87	¼v (a) + ½v (o) + 1 cot (c) 1392–93, 1401–02, 1406–07, 1411–12, 1412–13; ½v (a) + ¼v (a) + 1	

	First Period	Second Period	Third Period
		cot (a) 1420–21; 2a ½ r (of 14a½r) 1398–99, 1403–04, 1406–07, 1408–09, 1411–12, 1412–13; 2a (of 9a) 1406–07, 1408–09, 1411–12, 1412–13	
Genge, Richard			1v (a) 1446–49
Gouler, John		½v (o) + ¼v (a) 1401–02, 1406–07, 1411–12, 1412–13; ¼v (a) 1420–21; 1a (of 11½a) 1398–99, 1403–04, 1406–07, 1408–09, 1411–12, 1412–13	
Gouler, Richard		1v (o) 1392–93, 1401–02; 1v (a) 1406–07, 1411–12, 1412–13; 1v (a) 1420–21	
Gouler, Thomas			½v (a) + ¼v (a) + ¼v (a) 1446–49; 2 forlands + 6s8d meadow 1446–53
Grime, Roger			½ cot (a) + 1 cot (a) + toft 1446–49
Haconn, William	½ cot (a) 1371–72; ½ of 2a 3½r 1385–86	½ cot (a) 1392–93	
Haukyn, John	1v (o) + ½v (a) 1371–72, 1385–86; ½ of 4a 1r 1385–86; 4a 1r with Walter Cook 1386–87		
Haukyn, Joan		1v (o) 1392–93	
Haukyn, Thomas	¼v (a) 1385–86		

	First Period	Second Period	Third Period
Haukyn, William	2a 3½r with Thomas Smyth 1386–87		
Hawat, Edward	½ cot (a) 1385–86; 3a 1385–86; 3a (of 11a) 1386–87	½v (a) + ½ cot (a) 1392–93; 1v (o) + ½v (a) + ½ cot (a) 1401–02; 4a 1r with William Heryng jr. 1392–93, 1398–99; 1a (of 17a 3½r) 1398–99, 1403–04; 3a (of 11a) 1392–93	
Henderson, John			½v (a) + ¼v (a) + ½ of a cot of 2a (a) 1446–49
Henderson, Nicholas		4a (of 11a) 1406–07, 1408–09, 1411–12, 1412–13; 2a (of 11½a) 1406–07; 1a 1½r 10p with William Heryng 1406–07, 1408–09, 1411–12, 1412–13; 4a ? 1408–09, 1411–12, 1412–13; 1a ½r + ¼r + 4a + 1a 1420–23; ½ cot (a) 1420–21	
Heryng, Richard		1v (o) 1406–07; ½v (o) + ½v (a) 1411–12; ½v (o) + 1v (a) 1412–13; ½v (a) + 1v (a) + 1 cot (a) 1420–21; 2a 1r (of 17a 3½r) 1406–07, 1408–09, 1411–12, 1412–13	

	First Period	Second Period	Third Period
Heryng, Richard jr.		1 cot (a) 1406–07, 1411–12, 1412–13	
Heryng, William	1v (o) + ½v (a) + + 1 cot (a) 1371–72, 1385–86	1v (o) + ½v (a) + 1 cot (a) 1392–93, 1401–02; 1v (o) + ½v (a) 1406–07; 2a 1r (of 17a 3½r) 1398–99, 1403–04; 1a 1½r 10p with Nicholas Henderson 1406–07, 1408–09, 1411–12, 1412–13	
Heryng, William jr.		½v (o) + 1 cot (c) + 1 cot (a) 1392–93; 1v (o) 1401–02; ½v (c) 1406–07; ½v (?) 1406–07; ½v (o) + ½v (a) + ½v (c) + ½v (a) 1411–12; 1r + 3½a + 1r +3a 1392–93; 1a (of 6a) 1392–93; 4a 1r with Edward Hawat 1392–93, 1398–99; 3a 1398–99, 1403–04, 1406–07, 1408–09, 1411–12, 1412–13; 1a (of 11a) 1398–99, 1403–04, 1406–07, 1408–09, 1411–12, 1412–13; 5a (of 17a 3½r) 1398–99, 1403–04; 4a + 2r with William	

	First Period	*Second Period*	*Third Period*
		Baker 1398–99, 1403–04, 1406–07; 1r with William Dicon 1398–99, 1403–04; 2a 3½ r 1403–04; 1r of meadow with William Baker 1406–07, 1408–09, 1411–12, 1412–13; 4a (of 17a 3½r) 1408–09, 1411–12, 1412–13	
Herry, John	1v (o) + ½v (a) 1371–72; ½v (o) 1385–86		
Hikkesson, John		1r 1398–99, 1403–04, 1406–07, 1408–09, 1411–12, 1412–13; 5s meadow (of 10s) 1398–99, 1403–04, 1406–07, 1408–09, 1411–12, 1412–13, 1420–23; ¼v (a) 1420–21	
Hikkesson, John sr.	1v (o) + 1v (a) + ½v (a) 1371–72; ½v (a) + ¼v (a) 1385–86		
Hikkesson, John jr.	¼v (a) 1371–72; ½v (o) 1385–86	½v (c) + ¼v (a) + ½v (o) 1392–93; 1v (o) + ½v (c) + ¼v (a) 1401–02; ½v (o) + ¼v (a) 1406–07, 1411–12, 1412–13	
Holy, John	1r + 1a 1385–86; 1r 1386–87; 2a with John		

	First Period Fraunceys 1386–87	Second Period	Third Period
Houghton, John		1a 1392–93	
Hurre, John	1 cot (o) + 1 cot (a) 1371–72; ¼v (a) 1385–86; 3a + 1a 1385–86; 3a 1386–87; 1a (of 6a) 1386–87	¼v (a) 1392–93; ½v (o) + ¼v (a) 1401–02, 1406–07, 1412–13; ½v (o) + ½v (a) 1411–12; 1a + ¼v (a) 1420–21	¼v (a) + ¼v (a) 1446–49; 1 forland 1446–53
Jerkyn, John	1 cot (c) 1371–72, 1385–86	½v (o) 1412–13; 1v (a) + 1 cot ?1420–21	1 cot (a) + 1 cot (a) 1446–49
Leche, John			¾v (a) 1446–49
Lone, John*	½v (o) + ½v (c) + ¼v (a) 1371–72	1v (o) + ½v (a) 1392–93; 1 cot (a) 1420–21; 1a + 3a with Thomas Wardebusk 1398–99, 1403–04, 1406–07, 1408–09, 1411–12, 1412–13; 1a (of 17a 3½r) 1406–07, 1408–09, 1411–12, 1412–13	
Lone, Alice, widow of John	1v (o) + ½v (a) 1385–86		
Loveday, John		1 cot (o) + 1 cot (a) 1392–93, 1401–02; ½v (o) + 1v (a) 1406–07, 1411–12, 1412–13; 6a 1½ r (of 16a 3r) 1398–99, 1403–04, 1406–07, 1408–09, 1411–12, 1412–13; 1a (of 17a	

* Very likely John jr holds these lands from 1392.

	First Period	Second Period	Third Period
		3½r) 1398–99; 2s6d (of 1s meadow) 1398–99, 1403–04, 1406–07, 1408–09, 1411–12, 1412-13, 1420–23	
Michell, Thomas		¼v (a) 1412–13, 1420–21	
Miles, John	½v (c) + 1v (a) 1371–72; ½v (o) + ½v (c) + 1v (a) 1385–86	1v (o) + 1v (a) 1392–93; 1v (a) 1411–12; ½v (a) 1412–13, 1420–21	
Miles, John jr.		1v (a) 1420–21	
Miles, Robert		1v (o) + 1v (a) 1401–02, 1406–07; ½v (o) + 1v (c) + 1½v (a) 1411–12; ½v (o) + 1½v (a) 1412–13; 1½ v (a) 1420–21	
Miller, John	15a 1385–86		
Newman, John		(alias Newman) ½ cot (a) 1420–21	½ v (a) + meadow 1446–53; 3 sellion 1446–53
Newman, Richard		2a 3r 1392–93; 2a 3r (of 17a 3½r) 1398–99, 1403–04, 1406–07; 1a (of 8½a) 1406–07, 1408–09, 1411–12, 1412–13; 1½a (of 3a) 1398–99, 1403–04, 1406–07, 1408–09; 2a (of 8½a) 1398–99, 1403–04, 1406–07, 1408–09; 2a (of 8½a) 1398–	

	First Period	Second Period	Third Period
		99, 1403–04; 3a ((of 11a) 1398–99; 4a 2r with William Baker 1406–07, 1408–09, 1411–12; 1¼v (a) 1406–07, 1411–12, 1412–13, 1420–21	
Newman, Robert		2s6d 1411–12; ½ cot (a) 1412–13; 4a 2r with Walter Baker 1412–13	½v (a) + ¼v (a) 1446–49; 1 forland + 10s meadow + 8 butts 1446–53
Newman, Thomas	1v (a) 1371–72; ½v (o) + 1v (a) + 1 cot (a) 1385–86	1v (a) 1392–93, 1401–02; 2a (of 7a) 1398–99, 1403–04, 1406–07, 1408–09, 1411–12, 1412–13; 4 forlands 1398–99, 1403–04	
Newman, William	½v (o) 1371–72; 2(a) + ½ of 3a + ½a + 1r + 1a 1385–86; 3½a + 1r mea with Walter Deye 1386–87; 1a 1386–87		
Othehill, Richard		2a (of 11a) 1398–99, 1403–04, 1406–07, 1408–09, 1411–12, 1412–13	
Onty, John	12a 1r 1385–86		
Parquay, William		1v (a) 1401–02; ½v (a) 1406–07, 1411–12, 1412–13, 1420–21; 1a 1406–07, 1408–	

	First Period	Second Period	Third Period
		09, 1411–12, 1412–13	
Parvus, Adam of Wennington	5a with William Smith of Wennington 1386–87	5a with William Smyth of Wennington 1392–93; 8a (of 14a) 1398–99, 1403–04, 1406–07, 1408–09, 1411–12, 1412–13; 5s4d land with William Aubes 1420–23	
Payne, William	1v (o) + ½v (a) 1371–72, 1385–86	1v (c) + ½v (a) 1392–93; 1v (o) + ½v (a) + 1½v (a) 1401–02; 1v (o) + 1¼v (a) 1406–07; 2¼v (a) 1411–12; ½v (o) 1412–13	
Payne, Richard		½v (o) 1406–07, 1411–12; 2¼v (a) 1412–13, 1420–21	
Peny, John	4a with William Wynde 1386–87		
Peny, Robert	1v (o) 1371–72, 1385–86; 2a + ½r 1385–86; ½ r (of 1a 3½r) 1386–87	1v (o) 1392–93; ½r (of 1a 3½r) 1392–93; 4a with William Wylde 1392–93	
Peny, Thomas		2a (of 11½a) 1398–99, 1403–04, (1406–07), 1411–12, 1412–13; 1v (o) + ¼v (a) + ½ cot (a) 1401–02; 1v (o) + ½v (a) + 1 cot (a) 1406–07; ½v (o) + ¾v (a) + ½ cot (a) 1411–12,	½v (a) + ¼v (a) + ½ cot (a) 1446–49

	First Period	Second Period	Third Period
		1412–13; ½ v (a) + ¼v (a) + ½ cot (a) 1420–21; ½r (of 1a 3½ r) 1398–99, 1403–04, 1406–07, 1408–09, 1411–12, 1412–13; 2a 1411–12, 1412–13; 1r 1420–23	
Peny, William	1a 1385–86; 1a (of 11a) 1386–87	1a (of 11a) 1392–93; 1a (of 3a) 1398–99, 1403–04, 1406–07, 1408–09, 1411–12, 1412–13; 1a (of 17a 3½r) 1408–09, 1411–12, 1412–13	
Pennyman, Thomas			1 forland + 1 forland + 1 forland + 1 forland + 1a 1446–53; 1½v (a) 1446–49
Pikeler, Matilda	½v (o) + ½v (c) 1371–72		
Pikeler, Stephen	½v (o) 1385–86; 3a 1385–86; 3a (of 11a) 1386–87	½v (o) 1392–93	
Ponder, Reginald	2a 3½r 1385–86		
Ponder, Roger	2a 3½r 1386–87		
Ramsey, John	1a 1385–86; 1a (of 11a) 1386–87	1a (of 11a) 1392–93; 1a (of 8a) 1392–93	
Robyn, John	1v (o) + ½v (c) 1371–72, 1385–86	1v (o) + ½v (c) 1392–93; 1v (o) 1401–02	
Robyn, John jr.		1v (o) + ¼v (o) 1392–93, 1401–02	
Rolf, Thomas		15a 1392–93; 3a 33p (of 16a 3r)	

	First Period	Second Period	Third Period
		1398–99, 1403–04, 1406–07, 1408–09; 5a (of 14a 3½r) 1398–99, 1403–04, 1406–07, 1408–09, 1411–12, 1412–13; 1 cot (a) 1401–02, 1411–12, 1412–13, 1420–21	
Sabyn, Alexander	3a 3r 1385–86, 1386–87		
Shepherd, Simon	1 cot (o) 1385–86		
Shepherd, Walter		3a + 3r meadow 1420–23	
Skinner, Henry			1a + ½r + ¼r 1446–53; ½v (a) 1446–49
Skinner, John	3a 1385–86, 1386–87; 10a with assoc. 1385–86, 1386–87	3a 1392–93; 10a with assoc. 1392–93; 1a (of 11a) 1398–99, 1403–04, 1406–07, 1408–09, 1411–12, 1412–13; 4a (of 16a 3r) 1398–99, 1403–04, 1406–07, 1408–09, 1411–12, 1412–13; 2s6d (of 10s meadow) 1398–99, 1403–04, 1406–07, 1408–09, 1411–12, 1412–13, 1420–23;* 1 cot (a) + 1 cot (c) 1401–02, 1406–07, 1411–12, 1412–13	

* Over this period John's portion of this meadow was held with Richard Skinner.

	First Period	Second Period	Third Period
Skinner, John jr.	4a 1385–86, 1386–87	4a 1392–93	
Skinner, Richard		3 cot (a) 1411–12, 1412–13; ¼v (a) + 1 cot (a) + 1 cot (a) + 2 cots (a) 1420–21; 1½a (of 3a) 1398–99, 1403–04, 1406–07, 1408–09; 3a (of 11a) 1398–99, 1403–04, 1406–07, 1408–09, 1411–12, 1412–13; 2s6d (of 10s meadow) 1420–23	
Skinner, William			½v (a) 1446–49; 1 forland + 1 forland 1446–53
Siwell, John	½ cot (a) 1371–72; ¼v (a) + ½v (a) 1385–86, 1386–87	¼v (a) + ½ cot (a)1392–93; ½ cot (a) 1401–02; 4a 3r 1392–93; 1r (of 1a 3½r) 1398–99, 1403–04	
Siwell, William	1 cot c(c) 1371–72		
Smith, Simon	forge 1385–86 1386–87	forge 1392–93 1398–99, 1403–04, 1406–07, 1408–09, 1411–12, 1412–13; 3a (of 11a) 1392–93	
Smith Robert			forge 1446–53
Smith, Thomas	2a 3 ½r with William Haconn 1385–86, 1386–87; 3a 1386–87	forge 1420–23	
Smith, William of Wennington	5a with Adam Parvus of Wennington 1385–86, 1386–87	5a with Adam Parvus of Wennington 1392–93	

	First Period	*Second Period*	*Third Period*
Stukeley, Nicholas de		6a with John Wyse 1392–93	
Sutter, John	½ cot (o) 1371–72; 12a 1r (with others) 1386–87		
Symond, William	1 cot (o) + 1 cot (a) 1371–72; ½v (o) + 1 cot (o) + 1cot (a) 1385–86	½ v (o) + ¼v (a) 1401–02, 1406–07	
Thacher, William (see Baker)		1a (of 17a 3½r) 1406–07, 1408–09, 1411–12, 1412–13; 1 cot (a) 1420–21	
Thurston, William		4s4d land 1420–23; 1a (?) 1406–07	
Thurston, William and John		4s2d land 1412–13	
Vernoun, John		3a 3½r (of 17a 3½r) 1398–99, 1403–04, 1406–07, 1408–09, 1411–12, 1412–13; 4a (of 11½a) 1398–99, 1403–04, 1406–07, 1408–09, 1411–12, 1412–13; 2a (of 3a) 1398–99, 1403–04, 1406–07, 1408–09, 1411–12, 1412–13; 5 butts of land 1398–99, 1403–04, 1406–07, 1408–09, 1411–12, 1412–13; 1a + 3a meadow with Thomas Vernoun 1420–23; ½ cot (a) 1420–21	
Vernoun, Thomas		1a + 3a meadow with John Vernoun 1420–21; ½v (?) + 1 cot (?) 1420–21	

	First Period	Second Period	Third Period
Walton, Thomas	6a 1385–86; 7a 1386–87		
Wardebusk, Richard	1a 1385–86; 1a (of 1a 3½r) 1386–87, 1392–93; ½v (c) + ½v (a) + 1 cot (c) 1371–72; ½v (c) + ½v (a) + ½v (o) + 1 cot (c) 1385–93		
Wardebusk, Thomas		½v (c) + ½v (a) + ½v (o) + 1 cot (o) 1401–07; 1v (o) + 1 cot (c) 1411–13; 1 cot (c) +½v (a) 1420–21; 1a + 3a with John Lone 1398–99; 1a (of 1a 3½r) 1398–1413; 1a + 3a with William Chamberlayn 1403–13; 7s6d 1408–1413	
Webester, Robert	1a 1385–86; 1a (of 11a) 1386–87	1a (of 11a) 1392–93; 2a (of 11a) 1398–99	
Webester, William		2a (of 11a) 1403–04; 3a (of 11a) 1406–07	
West, William	6a with John Bele 1385–86, 1386–87	6a with John Bele 1392–93; 3a (of 11a) 1406–1413	
White, Richard			1 forland 1446–53; ¼v (a) 1446–49
Willisson, Richard		1 piece of frisc' land 1420–21, 1422–23	
Wylde, Robert	¼v (a) 1401–02, 1406–07, 1411–		

	First Period 12, 1412–13, 1420–21	Second Period	Third Period
Wyse, John	½v (o) 1385–86	½v (o) 1392–93, 1401–02, 1406–07	
Wyse, Nicholas		½v (o) 1412–13	

WISTOW 1368–1424

	First period	Second period
Albyn, Agnes	1 hide (o) 1368	
Albyn, Richard	4½a (of 36a 2½r) 1381	
Aspelond, John	1v (o) 1368; ¾v (o) + ¼v (c) 1381, 1388–90	
Aspelond, Richard	¼v (o) 1389–90; 1v (o) 1393–95	1v (o) + ¼ v(a) 1413–15; ¼v (a) + hedge with Walter Shepherd, John Hiche and John Thacher 1419–24
Aspelond, Simon	½ v (o) 1368, 1381; ¾v (a) 1379–80; ½v (o) + ¼v (a) 1388–90; ¼v (a) 1393–95; 1v (a) with assoc. 1381	
Attegate John	1 hide (o) 1381, 1388–95; ½v (o) 1393–95; ½a 1381, 1388–95	½v (a) + 1 hide 1413–15; 1a 1419–24; 2 hides (o) with Robert Rede sr. 1419–24
Attegate, John jr., son of Robert		½v (a) 1419–24
Attegate, Robert	½v (c) 1388–90; ½v (o) 1388–89; ½v (c) + ½v (o) 1393–95	
Attegate, Stephen	½v (c) 1368; ½v (o) 1388–89; ½v (o) + ½v (c) 1381	
Attestede, William	5½a (of 36a 2½r) 1381	
Aubyn, William	2½a (of 34a) 1368–1395	
Augustyn, John	28a (life) 1393–95	
Augustyn, Simon	½v (o) 1368; ¾v (a) 1378–80, 1388–90, 1393–95; 1v (a) w. assoc. 1381	

	First period	*Second period*
Aylmar, John	1 cot (c) 1368	¼v (a) 1419–24
Aylmar, Robert		½v (o) + ¼v (a) 1413–15
Aylmar, Stephen	½v (o) 1389–90, 1393–95; 1a (of 9½a) 1381; 1 mess + 6a 1379–95	
Baker, Walter	4½a (of 36a 2½r) 1381	
Barker, Richard		½v (a) + 1½ cot (a) 1413–24
Barker, Robert		¼v (a) 1413–14
Barker, Simon	1 mess 1381	
Barker, William	½ cot (c) + 1 cot (a) + ½v (a) 1381; ½v (a) + 1½ cot (a) 1388–90, 1393–95; 3½a 1381; 2½a (of 3½a) 1393–95	
Baron, Aneta		1 cot (a) + ½ cot (c) 1413–14; ¼v (a) + ½ cot (c) + 1 cot (a) 1414–15; 1 place 1423; ¼v (a) + 1½ cot (c) 1419–24
Baroun, John	1 mess 1381; 1 place (3 cottages) 1379–95; ½v (a) 1368, 1381 ?, 1388–90, 1393–95; 1 cot (a) 1393–95; ½ cot (c) 1394–95	
Baroun, Richard		1½v (a) 1413–14; 1¼v (a) 1414–15, 1419–24
Baroun, Thomas	¾v (o) 1368; ½v (o) 1381, 1389–90	
Baseley, Margeria	1 cot (?) 1368	
Benet, Matilda	1v (o) + ¼v (a) 1389–90	
Benet, William	½v (c) 1368; ⅛v (o) + 1 mess + 1v(a) with assocs. + ¼v (a) + 1v (a) 1381; ¼v (a) 1379–80, 1388–89	
Bigge, John	4½ a (of 36a 2½r) 1381	
Blakwell, Robert		1 cot (a) 1414–15
Blakwell, Thomas		1 cot (a) 1413–14, 1419–24
Bokeland, John		1⅛v (o) 1414–15; 1a 1423–24

	First period	*Second period*
Bonk, Philip	1 cot (c) 1393–95	
Botiller, Thomas		1 hide (a) 1419–24
Brene(Brone?), Adam	½a 1379–80; 1 butt 1388–90	
Breselaunce, Thomas		½v (a) 1413–14; ½v (a) + 2 cot (a) 1414–15, 1419–24; windmill 1419–24
Bromnore, Adam	½v (o) 1368	
Bronnote, John	½a (of 6a) 1381; ½a (of 6a) with John Elliot 1381; ½a + ½a + 1 cot (c) + ½v (o) 1381; ½v (o) 1388–90, 1393–94; ½v (o) 1388–90; 1 cot (c) 1393–95	
Broughton, William de	9½a with William Newman (for 10 years) 1368	
Brunne, Adam	1v (o) 1368; ½v (o) + ½v (o) 1381	
Brunne (Bronne), Nicholas	¼v (c) 1394–95	1¼v (a) 1419–24
Catelyne, John	1a (of 3½a) 1393–95; 1 place 1379–95; 1 cottage (c) 1381	¼v (o) (alias Shepherd) 1415; 1 place 1423–24
Catelyne, Richard	1v (o) 1368; 3r 1381; 1 cot (c) + 1v (o) 1381	
Clerevaux, John	½v (a) + freehold 1389–90, 1393–95	
Cotte, William	½v (o) 1368	
Dekene, Robert	4a 3½r 1388–95; 1a 1393–95	
Derworth, William		1v (a) 1413–15, 1419–24
Elliot, John	¼v (o) with Richard Sabyn 1381; ⅛v (c) + ½v (o) + ⅝v (o) 1389–90; ½a (of 6a) with John Bronnote 1381–95	
Elliot, Thomas	¾v (o) 1368; ½v (o) + ⅛v (c) 1381; ½v (o) + ¼v (c) 1388–90 (dead)	
Elliot, Joan, wife of Thomas	1 mess + ¾v ?1390	
Elmyslee, John		¾v (a) 1414–15

	First period	Second period
Ely, Richard	1 mess 1381; 1a (of 9½a) 1379–95; 1r + 1r + ½a 1381–95; 1a (of 6a) w. William Sabyn 1381–95	
Flexman, William	½v (o) + ½ cot (a) 1368; ½ cot (a) 1381	
Fraunceys, Alice		¾v (o) 1413–15
Fraunceys, John	½v (o) 1381, 1388–89; ¾v (o) 1389–90, 1393–95	½ cot (a) 1413–14; 1½ cot (a) 1415; 2 lands + ½ cot (a) 1419–24; lands w. John Randolf 1423–24
Fraunceys, Thomas		¾v (o) 1413–15
Frere, John	¼v (a) 1419–24	
Gocce, Anna	1 toft (c) 1381	
Goulere, Alice	1v (c) 1381	
Goulere, Benedict	1v (c) 1368	
Goulere, John	¾v (o) 1388–89; ¾v (c) + ½v (o) 1389–90; ½v (o) with Emma Randolf 1381; ¾v (c) + ½v (o) 1393–95	
Goulere, Robert	½ v (a) 1368	
Goulere, Thomas	¼v (o) 1389–90; ½ cot + ½v (o) + ¼v (c) 1393–95	
Goulere, William	¼v (o) + ½ cot (c) 1368, 1381, 1388–89	
Grafham, William		1 place 1419–24
Grene, John	1a 1368, 1379–95	
Grigge, John	¼v (a) 1368, 1379, 1388–95	
Grymbalde, Isolda	1v (a) 1368	
Harsene, John	1 cot (c) 1381; 1 cot (c) + ⅛v (o) 1388–90	
Haukyn, John	½v (o) 1381, 1389–90, 1393–95	
Haukyn, William	½v (o) 1368	
Herrow (Harrow, Herron, Herod), Nicholas	½v (o) + ⅛v (c) 1381; ½v (o) + ¼v (c) 1368, 1388–89	
Hiche, Cristina	1v (o) + ¼v (a) 1394–95	
Hiche, Henry	⅛v (o) + ¼v (o) 1381; ½v (o) 1388–90; ½ cot (c) 1393–95	

	First period	*Second period*
Hiche, John	½v (o) + ¼v (c) 1389–90; ½v (o) + ¼v (c) 1393–94; ¾v (o) + ¼v (c) 1394–95	1v (o) + ½v (a) 1413–15; ¼v + ¼v ?1419–20
Hiche, John, son of John		¼v (a) 1419–22
Hiche, Robert	1v (c) 1368; ½v (c) + ½v (o) 1389–90, 1393–94; ¼v (o) + ½v (c) + ½v (o) 1394–95	
Hiche, Stephen	1 v (o) + ¼v (ao) 1368, 1388–90, 1393–94; 1v (o) + ⅛v (a) 1381	
Hiche, William		¼v (a) 1413–15
Hikkesson, Simon	½v (c) + ½ cot (c) 1368	
Hobbe, Richard	1v (o) + ¼v (c) 1368; ⅛v (o) + ⅛v (o) + ⅛v (o) + 1 cot (o) 1381; ¾v (c) + ½v (o) + 1 cot (a) 1388–89; ¾v (o) + ¼v (c) + 1 cot (a) 1389–90	
Holbech, Richard	½v (o) 1381, 1388–90; ¼v (o) 1394–95	
Hoo, Richard	1v (o) 1388–95	
Hunne, Godfrey		¾v (o) + ¼v (a) 1413–15; ¼v (a) 1419–24
Ivesson, John	1cot (a) 1368; ½v (a) 1368, 1379–80; 1½ cot (a) 1379–80; 3½a w. William Waryn, Richard Wode-koc, 1368, 1379–90	
Kendale, John	½ cot (a) 1388–89	
King, John	½v (o) 1381; ¾v (o) 1388–89, 1393–95; ½v (o) + ¼v (c) 1389–90	
Lache, William	28a 1p 1388–90	
Leighton, William	5a (of 34a) 1368–94	
London, John	5a (of 34a) 1368–94	
Lone, John	½v (o) 1381, 1388–90; ¼v (a) + ½v (o) 1393–95	¼v (a) + 1 hide (a) 1413–15; ¾v (a) + 1 hide (a) 1414–15; ¼v (a) + ½v (a) + 1 hide (a) + 1a + 3r + ½a 1419–24

	First period	*Second period*
Lowthe, Hugh		¼v (a) + ½v (a) + ½v (a) 1413–14
Marchant, John	½v (o) 1381, 1388–89	
Martyn, Nicholas	1v (o) 1388–90, 1393–95	
May, Alan	1 cot (c) 1368	
Mice, John	5a (of 34a) 1368–94	
Miller, Emma	4½a (of 34a) 1368–94	
Miller, Thomas of Haddenham	windmill 1381	
Mowyn, Avota	½v (o) 1368	
Newman, John		½v (a) 1413–20
Newman, Thomas	4a (of 36a 2½r) 1381	
Newman, William	9½a w. William de Broughton 1368	
Newman, William de Bury	5a 3½r 1368	
North, Robert	1a 1390–93	
Nottyng, Robert	½a (c) + 1 butt (c) + 1 cot (c) 1393–95; 2a 1394–95	1 cot (a) + 1 cot (c) 1413–14; 2 cot (a) + 1 cot (c) 1414–15; 1 place + 5a 3½r + 3a + 1 butt + 1 cot (c) + 2 cot (a) 1419–24; 1a 1423–24
Outy, John		1v (o) + ½v (a) 1414–15; 2½v (a) 1415; 1 ¾v (a) + ½v (a) + ½v (a) 1419–22
Outy, John de Raveley	1v (o) 1368, 1381, 1389–90; 1½v (o) 1393–95	
Outy, John, son of John		¼v (a) + ½ cot (a) 1414–24
Outy, John jr.		¼v (a) 1413–14
Outy, John, thatcher		2v (a) + 2 cot (a) 1413–14
Outy, Thomas	½v (o) 1381, 1388–89; ¾v (o) 1389–90; 1v (o) 1393–95	¼v (a) 1413–14; ¾v (a) 1414–24
Page, John	½v freehold 1381	
Philip, Agnes	1 mess 1381	
Prat, Thomas		1 hide (a) 1413–15
Prikke, William	3a (of 34a) from 1368 ?, 1381	
Pycard, Richard		1 cot (a) 1419–24
Ramsey, Thomas		¼v (a) 1419–24

	First period	*Second period*
Randolf, Emma	½v (o) + ½v (o) w. John Gouler 1381	
Randolf, John	4a (of 34a) 1368; ¾v (o) 1368;	¼v (a) + ¾v (o) + ¾v (a) 1413–15; 7a + 1a + ¾v (?) 1419–24; 1a 1423–24; land w. John Fraunceys 1423–24
Randolf, Robert	1v (c) 1388–90, 1393–95	1v (o) 1413–15; land 1419–20
Randolf, Thomas	½v (o) 1368; ⅝v (o) 1393–95	1⅛v (o) 1413–14
Rector of Wistow (Raymond)	6a (of 9½a) 1379–95	½v (a) 1419–24 (just Rector)
Rede, John the	⅛v (o) + ½v (o) 1381; ½v (o) 1393–95; ½v (o) + ¾v (o) 1388–90, 1393–95	
Rede, Richard		1v (o) 1413–15
Rede, Richard jr.		½v (o) 1413–14
Rede, Robert (alias Waryn)		½v (o) + ½v (a) 1413–15
Rede, Robert	½v (c) + 1 hide (o) 1368, 1381; 1a (of 9½a) 1381; 1 hide (o) + ½v (c) + ½v (o) 1389–90; 1 hide (o) 1393–95	1a + 3½a + 1a + 2 hides (?) with John Attegate 1419–24; ½a + 3a + land + ? 1423–24
Rede, Robert jr.		½v (a) 1413–14
Rede, Thomas	¾v (o) 1368	
Revesson, Richard	1v (o) 1368; ½v (o) 1381	
Ripton, John	1 hide (o) 1368	
Rode, Robert		1 hide (o) 1413–14; ½v (o) + ½v (a) 1414–15
Rolege, Walter	5a 3½r 1379–81	
Sabyn, Alexander	½ cot (o) + 1 cot (c) 1368	
Sabyn, John	½v (o) + ½v (c) + 1 cot (c) 1368; 1 cot (c) 1388–90	
Sabyn, Margeria, widow of Ralph	1 cot (c) 1393–95	
Sabyn, Ralph	½v (a) with John Grigge 1368, 1381; ¼v (a) 1388–90; lands (11s) 1381	

	First period	*Second period*
Sabyn, Richard	¼v (c) + 1 hide (o) 1368; ⅛v (o) w. John Elliot 1381; 1 hide (o) 1381; ½a (of 9½a) 1379–85; 20d demesne land w. Robert Smith 1379–95	
Sabyn, William	¼v (o) 1368; 1a (of 6a) w. Richard Ely 1381; 1 cot (a) 1379–80; ¾v (c) + ½v (o) 1388–89; ¼v (o) 1389–90, 1393–95	
Shepherd, John		¼v (o) + ¼v (a) + 1 hide (a) 1414–15; ¼v (?) + 1 hide (?) 1419–24; 1a 1419–20, 1423–24
Shepherd, Nicholas	1 cot (a) 1393–95	
Shepherd, Richard	1 cot (c) 1368, 1388–89; 1a (of 6a) 1379–95	
Shepherd, wife of Richard	1 cot (c) 1389–90	
Shepherd, William		34a w. assoc. 1419–24
Siwelle, John	4a+ (of 36a 2½r) 1381	
Smith, Andrew	1 hide (o) 1381, 1388–89, 1393–95; ⅛v (o) 1381–95; 2r (of 6a) 1381–95	
Smith, Robert	1 cot (c) + forge 1381; 1 cot (c) 1388–90; 20d demesne land w. Richard Sabyn 1379–95	
Smith, Thomas	5½a (of 36a 2½r) 1381	
Synne, John		¼v (a) 1413–14
Taylor, Robert	¼v (o) + 1 hide (o) 1388–90, 1393–95	
Taylor, William	¼v (o) + 1 hide (o) 1368, 1381; ½v (o) + 1 hide (o) 1388–90, 1393–95; ½v (o) with John de Welle 1381	
Vernoun (Gernoun), John	1v (o) + ¼v (c) 1368; freehold + ½v (o) + ½v (o) 1381; 1v (o) 1388–90, 1393–94	

	First period	*Second period*
Vernoun, Richard	½v (c) 1368	
Waker, Peter	¾v (c) + 1 cot (o) 1368; 1v (a) + 2 cots (a) 1379–80; 1v (a) w. assocs. + ½ v (a) + ⅛v (a) + ½v (c) + 1 cot (a) + 1 cot (o) 1381; ½v (c) + 1v (a) + 2 cots (a) + 1 cot (o) + ½ cot (c) 1388–89; ¼v (a) + ½v (c) 1393–94	
Waryn, Agnes		¼v (o) + ½v (a) 1414–15
Waryn, John	½v (o) + 1 cot (c) 1368; ½v (o) 1394–95	½v (o) + ¾v (a) 1413–14
Waryn, Robert	3r 1379–94	¼v (a) 1413–15
Waryn, William	1a (of 6a) 1381; 3½a with John Ivesson and Richard Wodekoc 1368–1395; 3a 1379–95; 3r 1393–95	
Waryn, William de Warboys	1v (o) (bailiff) 1388–90, 1393–95	
Waryn, William, and wife Emma	2 pieces of meadow 1379–95	
Webestere, William	1 cot (c) 1368, 1381	
Well, John de	½v (o) with William Taylor 1381	
Wennington, John	4½a (of 34a) 1381–95	
West, John	½v (o) 1393–95	1 cot (c) 1413–24
Willisson, John	½v (o) 1368; ⅓v (a) + 1 toft (a) + ½v (o) 1381; ¾v (a) + ½v (o) + ½v (c) 1388–90, 1393–94; ¾v (a) + ½v (c) + 1v (o) + 1 cot (a) 1394–95	½v (a) + ½ cot (a) 1413–14
Willisson, Richard		1v (o) + 1v (a) 1413–15; 1¼v (a) + 1 cot (a) 1414–15; 1¼v (?) + 1 cot (?) 1419–24; 1 mess 1419–20
Wodekoc, Richard	¾v (o) 1368; ½ v (c) + ⅛v (c) + 1 cot (a) 1381; 3½a with John Ivesson and William Waryn 1368–95;	¼v (a) 1413–15

	First period	*Second period*
	¾v (c) + 1 cot (a) 1388–90; ¾v (o) + 1 cot (a) 1393–94; 1v (o) + ¼v (c) + 1 cot (a) 1394–95	
Wodekoc, Robert		½v (a) 1414–15
Wold, William of the	½ freehold 1381	
Wrighte, John		¼v (a) 1414–24; ¾v (a) 1419–24
Wrighte, Richard		¼v (a) + ½ v(a) 1413–14; ½v (a) 1414–15; ¼v (?) 1419–24
Wrighte, William	1 cot (a) 1388–90, 1393–95	
Wyse, John	4½a (of 36a 2½r) 1381	

Notes

INTRODUCTION

1 R.H. Britnell, *The Commercialization of English Society, 1000–1500.*
2 James Masschaele, "Transport Costs in Medieval England."
3 *Agrarian History of England and Wales,* 2:136.
4 See, for example, at Ramsey Abbey, *Estates,* chaps. 2 to 4, and *Abbey and Bishopric of Ely,* 131.
5 M.M. Postan, *The Medieval Economy and Society,* 123.
6 Kosminsky, *Agrarian History,* 203.
7 Britnell, *Commercialization of English Society,* 45–6, 121–3; and Kosminsky, *Agrarian History,* 252, 319–20.
8 R.A.L. Smith, *Canterbury Cathedral Priory,* espec. chap. 2. I understand that Dr Rosamond Faith is now advancing the scholarship on the Anglo-Norman economy and questioning whether resumption of demesne farming from the late twelfth century was not simply a managerial revolution.
9 Kosminsky, *Agrarian History,* 86. There is also a question of evidence for continuation of farming practices for some manors of large estate complexes throughout the thirteenth and fourteenth centuries.
10 Dorothea Oschinsky, *Walter of Henley and Other Treatises on Estate Management and Accounting.*
11 Edward Miller and John Hatcher, *Medieval England,* 215.
12 Ibid., 217.
13 Ibid., 212.

14 Ibid., 222. For a wider perspective see Edward Miller, "England in the Twelfth and Thirteenth Centuries: An Economic Contrast?"

15 Kosminsky, *Agrarian History*, 112.

16 Ibid., 118.

17 Miller and Hatcher, *Medieval England*. Chap. 5 provides an excellent review of this historiography.

CHAPTER ONE

1 It is interesting that this point is disregarded by most of the contributors to vols. II (1042–1350) and III (1348–1500) of *Agrarian History*. More recent writers on topics related to local markets appear to omit all references to this topic.

2 Ellen Wedemeyer Moore, *The Fairs of Medieval England*, 99. Re St Giles Fair: "Why would the bishops of Winchester kill, or at least injure, the goose that laid the golden egg, by placing an extraordinary toll upon precisely those persons who brought products capable of attracting royal buyers and a good part of the rest of England to their fair?" The author continues with respect to the fairs at St Giles and St Ives, 200: "The last major element in fair income was the fair court itself. At St. Giles fair this item constituted around 3 percent, never more than 6 percent, of the total profits each year. At St. Ives fair, the annual profits were relatively small as well. For example, the £8 9s taken in 1287, although not a negligible sum, compares rather feebly with the £126 taken from stall and shop rentals alone just one year earlier, especially in light of the fact that a scribe and seven bailiffs had to be hired to assist in the work of the fair court and thus to earn the £8. It would be useful to re-examine the frequent claims by medieval historians that the right to hold court was an eagerly sought-after source of great profit among feudal leaders. That the abbot's fair was a profitable enterprise cannot be doubted, but it would seem that, for the abbot of Ramsey, the fair court was a rather burdensome ancillary to that fair." And in conclusion, 295: "The abbots and bishops involved with the running of the fairs of St. Ives and St. Giles were generally intelligent businessmen, careful organizers: well aware that they could derive greatest profit from their fairs only if they maintained the security and flexibility of the facilities which they could provide for fairgoers."

3 Few of these records are extant owing to the temporary nature of the agreement. See William Hale, ed., *The Domesday of St. Paul's*, which provides some good examples of these farm contracts.

4 M.M. Postan intuited the importance of capital as early as the study he promised in 1937. But the limited range of original studies available at that time precluded development of his project.

5 For the manors to be studied in this volume, the customaries appear in W.H. Hart and P.A. Lyons, eds., *Cartularium Monasterii de Rameseia*, hereafter cited as *Carts*. (Ramsey Cartulary), 3 vols. Rolls Series, 79, 1:305ff.

6 J.A. Raftis and M.P. Hogan, *Early Huntingdonshire Lay Subsidy Rolls*, 31–5. From his study of English parliamentary subsidies (1275–1334), Stuart Jenks has come to the conclusion that these surpluses would be employed for internal trade.

7 Information similar to the Hunts study of the previous note may be found for neighbouring Beds and Bucks. See Alexander T. Gaydon, ed., *The Taxation of 1297*, and A.C. Chibnall, *Early Taxation Returns*. The potential use of the Beds data is well demonstrated by Kathleen Biddick, "Medieval English Peasants and Market Involvement."

8 See n 3 above.

9 For the wider context of this entry, see J.A. Raftis, *Tenure and Mobility*, 66.

10 Ibid., 74.

11 Ibid., 73.

12 Ibid., 72. In January 1318 William Fyne was cited for allowing the buildings on the mondaymanland that he held in villeinage to fall and for taking his lumber to his free tenement. He was fined and pledged by two men of the vill to repair these buildings and keep them in repair.

13 *Carts*., I, 307.

14 W.J. Ashley, *An Introduction to English Economic History and Theory*, part II, 281. Acceptance by the lord of virtual inheritance rights by customary tenants would be another guarantee of capital maintenance. See Raftis, *Tenure and Mobility*, 48–52. Such a practice contrasts sharply with the escheating practices of the Crown.

15 J.M. Bennett, "Spouses, Siblings and Surnames: Reconstructing Families from Medieval Village Court Rolls." Owing to the lack of vital statistics, individuals and families must be identified through numerous references to their daily activities. Such references become much less frequent for smallholders and even more rare for the landless. Many questions that one might like to ask about the relevance of the actions of substantial tenants to the lives of other villagers cannot be addressed.

16 J.A. Raftis, "The Concentration of Responsibility in Five Villages," 93. These data come from the court rolls for Abbots Ripton (1274–1356), Upwood (1278–1353), Warboys (1290–1353), and Wistow (1278–1353). There was no great influx of new names for the first few years after 1348 – that is, by 1353 – but a continuation of the previous rate. Nearly all surnames of substantial tenants seem to have become fixed

on Ramsey estates earlier than for the estate complexes of some other lords. Various factors would be at play in such determination, such as administrative accuracy for lay-subsidy listings that involved "outside" clerks and the evidential purpose that lay behind retention of manorial-account and court-roll series from this time. None the less, there is an immense difference between the nominal system employed in the mid-thirteenth-century extents and the later system, so that references in the following paragraphs to individuals entering Ramsey estates prior to the court-roll series are merely presented as possible examples. But such identifications are not entirely impossible, as P.D.A. Harvey demonstrates by useful reflections on tracing the names of outsiders for this pre-court-roll period. See Harvey, *Cuxham Manorial Records*, 126–8.

17 Edmund King, *Peterborough Abbey*, 182.

18 Ibid., 184.

19 Ibid., 186.

20 For Ramsey estates, the findings reported in J.A. Raftis, *Warboys*, 216, 225ff., are typical. A useful recent review of relevant demographic studies may be found in Richard M. Smith, "Demographic Developments in Rural England, 1300–1348: A Survey", espec. 37–52. This study is in chap. 2 of B.M.S. Campbell, ed., *Before the Black Death*. The various studies summarized by Smith show that the mortality picture on Ramsey estates is not at all exceptional. Indeed, Ramsey replacement rates would appear to be considerably less than those for some places cited by Smith, 43–5. What is of relevance for this study of Ramsey manors, therefore, is not the necessity for replacement but the fact that replacement so often involved outsiders. Social as well as family replacement could also explain the disappearance of some families. At Warboys in 1301, Robert the son of Mabel was reported to have gone overseas, so that his virgate had to be taken into the custody of others. In 1290 at the same vill, one prominent family lost its place in the village when Ralph, son of William de London, murdered Henry, son of Albyn, and fled.

21 For example, Raftis, "The Concentration of Responsibility," 93, n 6, and E.B. DeWindt, *Land and People in Holywell-cum-Needingworth*, 175–6. The most striking evidence on this point comes after the Black Death. Among the much-studied Ramsey estates such as Broughton, Holywell, and Warboys there is no evidence at all that the numerous identifiable smallholding families pre–1348 became major tenants. As we shall see in chapter 4, smallholders could increase in numbers when more smallholdings became available. From the very detailed records of Halesowen, Zvi Razi has confirmed this criticism of Postan's assumption. See Razi, *Life, Marriage and Death in a Medieval*

Parish, 89ff., 14. For a more general critique of Postan and Lenin, see Christopher Dyer, *Lords and Peasants in a Changing Society*, 298–9.

22 Kosminsky, E.A., *Studies in the Agrarian History of England in the Thirteenth Century*, ed. R.H. Hilton, trans. Ruth Kisch, 214ff.

23 R.H. Hilton, *Medieval Society*, 114ff.

24 Elements of this question have been known for decades. For example, Kosminsky in chap. 3 of *Studies in the Agrarian History* struggles with the problem of the amount of money rent. Other scholars have clearly been surprised by the size of various payments, as, for example, M.M. Postan and J. Titow, "Heriots and Prices on Winchester Manors." But the implications for the supply of customary tenants has failed to be developed.

25 This figure is derived from all sources: account rolls, court rolls, and lay-subsidy rolls. Lay-subsidy rolls are less comprehensive but none the less revealing. See Raftis and Hogan, *Early Hunts Lay Subsidy Rolls*, 20.

26 Raftis, *Tenure and Mobility*, 20.

27 Ibid., 21. A useful review of Bracton's assessment of the legal possibilities that allowed a free person to enter a lord's domain and hold in villeinage may be found in Jean Scammell, "The Formation of the English Social Structure," 608.

28 *Agrarian History of England and Wales*, III, chap. 4.

29 Kathleen Biddick estimates that in the thirteenth century Ramsey Abbey sold only 10 per cent of its grain harvest. See Biddick, *The Other Economy*, 76.

30 J.P. Bischoff, "Fleece Weights and Sheep Breeds in Late Thirteenth- and Early Fourteenth-Century England," 143–60.

31 Ibid., 156.

32 Raftis, *Tenure and Mobility*, 23, and Raftis, *The Estates of Ramsey Abbey*, 149–51.

CHAPTER TWO

1 It is interesting that in their studies of late medieval and early modern Norfolk, Mark Overtun and Bruce M.S. Campbell have concluded that livestock had greater potential for commercial development than arable farming and that the livestock sector often emerged as the more dynamic branch of farming. See, for example, "Norfolk Livestock Farming 1250–1750," 377–96. According to Kathleen Biddick's seminal study *The Other Economy*, emphasis upon consumption brought the lords of Peterborough Abbey to "sell their potential resources to the peasants for cash" (98). Our preliminary findings for Ramsey (chap. 1, n 28) corroborate the Biddick observations.

2 Despite the decrease in entry fines from the late first quarter of the fourteenth century noted in chap. 1, there is no evidence to suggest that at this time, or after the Black Death, the main customary tenements were undercapitalized.

3 Chap. 3, and Judith Bennett in a forthcoming study.

4 I am grateful to Dr Anne DeWindt for this information about King's Ripton.

5 Subletting within families would not be likely to appear in records. P.D.A. Harvey suggests further that family ingenuity bypassed many exterior forms. See *The Peasant Land Market in Medieval England*, conclusion.

6 J.A. Raftis, "The Land Market at Godmanchester, *ca.* 1300."

7 It is to be hoped that as family studies become a major growth industry, more attention will be given to this question.

8 See *The Court Rolls of Huntingdon in the Fourteenth Century*, ed. John C. Parsons, intro. J.A. Raftis, forthcoming, intro.

9 J.A. Raftis, *Early Tudor Godmanchester*, chap. 3.

10 A future study of commercial activities of the region will address fully the question of petty tradespeople who were not in tithing.

11 R.E. Latham, *Revised Medieval Latin Word-List*, 21. George C. Homans, *English Villagers of the Thirteenth Century*, 136–7, 210–11, has given perhaps the most useful translation of this word to date. On page 211 Homans translates an entry from the Ely customal of 1227: "It is to be known that every undersettle or anilipiman or anilipiwyman, holding a house or a *bord*, no matter of whom he holds it." Perhaps the determined opposition to the notion of a peasant land market and subletting, as well as the paucity of references, has turned historians from further investigation of this term and its analogues.

12 Lori A. Gates, "A Glastonbury Estate Complex in Wiltshire," PhD, University of Toronto, 1991. I am grateful to Dr Gates for permission to refer to this work.

13 F. Pollock and F.W. Maitland, *The History of English Law*, 581. The authors were clear, however, about the lord's concern for "retaining his power."

14 The term "chevage" (*chevagium*) would seem to be more common among other estate complexes in England.

15 The point being pursued here is part of a much larger picture. In a forthcoming volume, *A Chronicle of All That Happens*, Sherri Olson has made abundantly clear that village government involved much more than a landholding elite and that a great variety of changes in the practice of village government occurred throughout the fourteenth and early fifteenth centuries.

16 The lord turned over to William le Moigne all fines from his people except for failure to appear in court and refusal to correct violations on the lands of others (purprestures). The classification of the men of Le Moigne is interesting: men not having lands or homes, non-residents, and those having lands and homes who were resident. One continues to be surprised at the lack of coordination in the lord's policies prior to the late thirteenth century. An arrangement similar to that of le Moigne had been made at Elton in the mid-century (*Carts.*, 1:491).

17 This list has been slightly changed from Raftis, *Tenure and Mobility*, 147.

18 Local clerks differed in style from manor to manor in the amount of detail recorded. Even this abbreviated form was sometimes reduced to *De capitagio dant*. The *capitagium* was not the only form of composition to be found on Ramsey estates. Sherri Olson notes that the customary tenants who farmed the Ramsey manor of Ellington had land-entry fines compounded in 1315 for £6, and thereafter until 1443, £6 was paid every seven years for these fines.

19 See Raftis, *Tenure and Mobility*, chap. 6, sect. 1. This control is most clearly articulated in court rolls with respect to wrongful gleaning. Here again one must note the considerable jurisdiction of local people over fellow villagers that is hidden from the historian.

20 Dower values could be considerable, as in the case cited by Homans, *English Villagers*, 140, for Broughton valued at 22s.4d. But again, for all fines to be abroad there was the pattern of change from heavier fines in the late thirteenth century (Raftis, *Tenure and Mobility*, 140: 40s.; 14s.6d.; 10s.) to nominal licence fees by the second quarter of the fourteenth century.

21 See chap. 5, sect. i.

22 Raftis, *Tenure and Mobility*, 129. Feudal society was quite capable of expanding the power of the lord to pursue, as in the well-studied peasant conflicts of late medieval Germany and Hungary. A useful view of the actual use of sheriffs in England can be found in the writ of excommunication. See F.D. Logan, *Excommunication and the Secular Arm in Medieval England*. For secular village affairs in England, however, it is important to keep in mind that the usual regulations of king's courts provide the model. See W.A. Morris, *The Frankpledge System*, 90ff.

23 That is to say, the lists above have combined both groups. The short-lived effort at more official pledging noted at the beginning of this paragraph is part of a general phenomenon that Sherri Olson calls a failed experiment by the lord at this time.

24 This rare reference to the reality of mobile causal labour would seem to have arisen because of the other charges in the local court or because Nicholas may have had property by this time.

25 By contrast, see the information available from the fifteenth-century *gersuma* rolls, below, chap. 4, sect. i.

26 Raftis, *Tenure and Mobility*, 151–2. Entries below are excerpted from 152.

27 Again, we draw attention to resolution by grant of licence and the petty nature of the fine by contrast with the value of chattels.

28 *Broughton*, chap. 2. Good detail is also provided on this point by Zvi Razi, *Life, Marriage and Death in a Medieval Parish*, 50ff.

29 Ibid., 60ff.

30 Unfortunately, available data about marriage from 12 Ramsey manors are largely concentrated in the first quarter of the fourteenth century and are highly selective, so that they are not readily comparable to movements of licensed and unlicensed people considered in this chapter. These data from account rolls are available for 112 women. Only 40 per cent of the women remained within their native villages, while the remaining 60 per cent married beyond their native place (either on another estate of the lord, as indicated by *super feodum*, or beyond the Ramsey complex, as indicated by *extra feodum*). The average fine for marriages *super feodum* was 2s.8d., while that for marriages *extra feodum* was 4s.6d., and that for marriages within the manor was 3s. The significant feature here, therefore, was the licence rather than a quid pro quo for loss of a potential villein family and the substantial dowry. This feature takes on more significance when it is noted that at least 95 of 108 individuals (in 4 cases details were not clear) were from main families.

CHAPTER THREE

1 Raftis, *Warboys*, 241.

2 Raftis, *Estates of Ramsey Abbey*, chap. x, sect. 11.

3 This phenomenon can be traced more completely among the bailiffs of the royal manor of Godmanchester, where the annual court-record series is almost complete. See Raftis, *Early Tudor Godmanchester*, 13–15.

4 See chap. 4, sect. ii.

5 In view of the perspective developed in this chapter, various references in mid-thirteenth-century account rolls (Raftis, *Estates*, 222, and nn 12 and 13) should likely be taken as only *ad tempus* information for the year of the document. The reader should also be cautioned about the meaning implied with respect to increased commutation values (ibid., 224, n 23), since inflation has not been taken into account. See, for example, P.D.A. Harvey, "The English Inflation of 1180–1220."

6 From the 1370s, when complete lists of property arrangements became available, *ad censum* would seem to indicate commutation of all services for most manors. But because of the bargaining aspect of all

service arrangements, one must be cautious on this point, in particular for the early fourteenth century. The little evidence we have (Raftis, *Estates*, 225, n 7) shows the villein challenging the lord's efforts to take advantage of changing economic conditions. Certainly by the time *opera* arrangements are detailed at the foot of account rolls – that is, from the late thirteenth century – periods of work exemption for feast days and illness have been firmly fixed.

7 See below, chap. 4, sect. iii.

8 *Carts.*, 1:312.

9 Ibid., 325.

10 Ibid., 337.

11 Public Record Office, London, sc2, portfolio 885, no. 30. This fragment has been annotated in the margin, likely by the auditor. The final revenue entry in the account roll for that year shows 42s.2d.ob. from the sale of work – that is, 4s.½d. less than the total given here.

12 M.P. Hogan, "The Labour of Their Days," 141ff.

13 For some of the best data on this point, see Raftis, *Warboys*, 159–61. In managing the preferential treatment described in this paragraph, it must have been a temptation for the manorial official to line his own pockets. The court of 1325 for Warboys charges that Godfrey the beadle was a poor servant of the lord and the community since he had accepted small gifts from customary tenants for sparing them from service they owed to the lord. He was fined 40d. and pledged by the reeve. Smallholders were no doubt quite willing to draw the attention of the court to such misdemeanours. As suggested above, smallholders would be less likely to have cash, and this no doubt explains their complaint at Elton in 1279 (Raftis, *Estates*, 225, n 26) that they had been obliged by the reeve to take money rents whereas richer tenants had bought off the reeve.

14 See Appendix iii, "The Structure of *Opera* Allocations."

15 Ibid.

16 Ibid.

17 Raftis, *Warboys*, 200.

18 See Appendix iii.

19 By far the greater part of the drama may have been within households. For example, Alice, the wife of Stephen, refused even to hire herself out in the autumn of 1318 at Abbots Ripton. The many who gleaned wrongly over the following decades likely also belonged to this category. Recalcitrant sons, such as those exemplified in chap. 2 above, were another important family group.

20 The surviving court rolls for Abbots Ripton and Broughton are fewer and less evenly spaced than for the other three manors – especially with so few for the 1320s and 1340s – so they are not tabulated here. At

Abbots Ripton there were large group refusals later (1334 in particular), but at Broughton earlier (22 once in 1299; 9 once and 17 on another occasion in 1308). Such variations highlight local decision-making rather than general patterns of response to economic conditions.

21 Although ploughing, somewhat comparable in capital equipment involvement to carrying, had a more consistent pattern of higher fines. But these pre-established fine scales obscure what must have been the costly correction of ploughing badly.

22 See chap. 1.

23 See Appendix II, "Preliminary Observations towards a Calculus of *Opera* Obligations."

CHAPTER FOUR

1 A useful recent updating of literature on this topic may be found in M. Mate, "Agrarian Economy after the Black Death."

2 *Estates*, 253–9.

3 The sale prices for three seasons of Broughton remained (ob., 1d., 2d.), see "Commutation in a Fourteenth-Century Village," 297.

4 These data are abstracted from the complete detail given in Appendix III, "The Structure of *Opera* Allocations."

5 See *Tenure and Mobility*, 63–5.

6 See below, App. IV.

7 See below, chap. 3, Warboys.

8 Broughton, chap. 2.

9 *Estates*, 259–66. Obviously the inferences I made throughout chap. 9 of *The Estates* about the negative impact of demesne management upon tenants must now be corrected in favour of the direct evidence for tenant policy to be found in this study.

10 *Estates*, 261.

11 B.M.S. Campbell, "Arable Productivity in Medieval England."

12 Farmer, *Agrarian History of England and Wales*, 451.

13 *Estates*, 263, 265. Again, the percentage of available work services sold, as noted in the listings in App. III, does not point to labour supply as a significant factor for the lord even if he had been able to control such a supply.

14 Examples are not given here from the village of Warboys since such data have already been published; for Abbots Ripton there are too many breaks in the court-roll series for this period to make possible a reasonably certain identification of family survival.

15 Families disappearing in this village around the time of the Black Death, with earlier noted members in brackets, were Attehall (5), Attewell (4), Baseley (3), Bishop (7), Cotes (4), Curteys (8), Daye (3),

Downham (3), Frere (12), Jowel (7), Lanerok (8), Mice (2), Sutor (12), Walter (11), White (4), Wysman (5).

16 Families disappearing from Upwood around 1348 were Ayse (5), Baron (10), Broun (15), Attechurche (6), Coupere (6), Crane (7), Curteys (7), Elliot (1), Elys (4), Frere (7), Fryth (2), Galyon (6), Geffrey (2), Gernoun (10), Godeson (8), Grenan (6), Heringmonger (10), Hilhyl (3), Lanerok (13), Man (7), Nicholas (6), Peretre (8), Richard (7), Sabyn (6), Suel (4), Sutbury (7), Wadilone (4), Walter (4), Waryn (7), Wauk (6), Wennington (9), Weston (5), William (5), Wodestrate (2).

17 Families apparently disappearing from Broughton around the time of the Black Death were Blosme (5), Carpenter (5), Edward (8), Gilbert (7), Hanecok (2), Henry (7), Heyneston (2), Hobbe (9), Horseman (7), Hugh (17), Le Bon (6), le Longe (3), Nunne (5), Roger (10), Waleboy (6), Woodward (5), Willymot (4).

18 And towards the end of the century a rent collector (bailiff) gradually supplanted the reeve. *Estates*, 263–4.

19 And see App. IV.

20 See M.P. Hogan, "Management Efficiency at Fourteenth Century Wistow." Identification and location of Wistow fields in the next four paragraphs are taken from this article.

21 Richard of Ely also held one-half of a 4½-acre unit at Warboys over the 1370s, the remainder being held by John Rede of Warboys.

22 Richard Sabyn also held 4 acres of demesne land at Warboys over 1374–79.

23 See, for example, *Warboys*, 162–5.

24 *Estates*, 275.

25 While this study focuses upon customary tenants rather than the land market as such, it may be noted that sources for these villages over the first half of the fifteenth century do not lend themselves to a thorough study of the land market. Andrew Jones has demonstrated from the good records available for Beds ("Bedfordshire: Fifteenth Century," in *The Peasant Land Market in Medieval England*, ed. P.D.A. Harvey, chap. 4) the continued role of small units of land (see espec. table IX, 208, for the Ramsey estate of Shillington) and the volatile nature of declining demand for land.

26 *Estates*, chap. 14, sect. I, espec. 253, 258.

27 See above, chapter 1.

28 Farmer, *Agrarian History of England and Wales*, 255–61.

CHAPTER FIVE

1 Edwin B. DeWindt has depicted the survival of even smallholders, especially up to the 1370s. See *Holywell-cum-Needingworth*, 100, 102, 112.

2 Given that the holdings of villagers could vary over a twenty- or thirty-year period, some selectivity has been required. In each case the largest amount of land accumulated by a villager has been taken as his representative holding for the period.

3 It should be noted that "family" is used here to indicate the agnatic kin group rather than simply the domestic unit. Information provided by sources covered in this chapter is more detailed than data from court rolls one hundred years earlier. At the same time, as is exemplified throughout this chapter, data from this later period do serve to corroborate the methodological conclusions of Judith Bennet noted in chap. 1, n 15.

4 Only in the case of Upwood is this pattern not dramatic, since the individual-family ratio is about the same for those holding 10–29 acres and those holding 30 acres or more. However, in both cases the individual-family ratio favours families to a much greater extent than in the case of those holding less than 10 acres.

5 *Tenure and Mobility,* chap. 2.

6 A special debt of gratitude is owed Edwin B. DeWindt for his edition of this court book, *The Liber Gersumarum of Ramsey Abbey, a Calendar and Index of B.L. Harley* MS *445.* The material employed in this study does not at all exhaust the information to be found in this exceptional record.

7 These seven marriages, plus one from a Broughton court roll of 1387, have been included with the 104 court-book marriages to give a total of 112 in Table 5.2. The almost total lack of marriage data in court rolls and account rolls in the period between 1350 and 1398, the first year of the extant court book, would seem to indicate that a record of marriages was kept in an earlier section of the court book that has not survived.

8 The connection between this amount of land and yeoman status has been advanced by H.E. Hallam in "The Agrarian Economy of South Lincolnshire in the Mid-Fifteenth Century," 93. Although prominent villagers were describing themselves as husbandmen in Hunts records, such as wills, from later in the fifteenth century, the more familiar term "yeoman" is employed here for convenience. The convenience lies in the perduring existence and national comparability of this class. See, for example, Gordon Baths in *Agrarian History of England and Wales,* IV:301–6.

9 The only other category not been mentioned as yet involves marriages in which women from yeoman families appear to be marrying men whose social and economic status seems to be below the lower limit established in this study for inclusion in the yeomanry (see Table 5.2). For example, in 1445 Margaret Olyver, widow of William Olyver and

daughter of Robert Raveley, married Robert Asshwell of Warboys. The only information we possess on Robert is that he acquired a half-virgate of customary land in Warboys from John Bereford in 1442. There is no indication in the court rolls that he participated in the administrative affairs of Warboys, and the half-virgate seems to have been the only land he held in the village. On the face of it, one would have to assume that Robert Asshwell was of a lower status and that Margaret Olyver married below her class in her second marriage.

CHAPTER SIX

1 For reasons of space, full detail on all emigrants is not given in an appendix as had been originally planned.
2 For Warboys villagers who migrated, see *Warboys*, 264–5, and clarifications, 147–50.
3 J.A. Raftis, *The Estates of Ramsey Abbey*, 291.
4 For the total debt figures from the account rolls for Broughton, Upwood, and Warboys, see Raftis, *Estates*, 297–9, and for details about officials, see below.
5 Raftis, *Estates*, 269, and *Warboys*, 270.
6 British Library, Additional Manuscript 29559.
7 While a strict comparison of tenants before and after the Black Death is not possible, since rent rolls are extant only from later in the fourteenth century, it can easily be deduced that main village families were tenants. For Broughton, 69 surnames of tenants in 1380 had the same surname as Broughton residents before 1348. For Wistow, of 45 customary tenants in 1380, only 13 had surnames not certainly pre-1348.
8 This may have been common in other parts of the country. C. Dyer, in "The West Midlands," in *Agrarian History of England and Wales*, III:636, cites evidence for increase in the size of holdings on the manors of Westminster Abbey and Worcester Cathedral Priory.
9 Raftis, *Tenure and Mobility*, 160ff.
10 Raftis, *Tenure and Mobility*, chap. IX, 1. Since we have the manumission price for only 10 of the 79 extant cases, it is not possible to give a fuller analysis of this phenomenon.
11 One wonders whether such large amounts included farm contract payments or some administrative role in Ramsey administration. But our references are usually mere account entries. Among the revenue items for the Upwood account roll of 1412–13 is the following: "Received for manumission, John Pyre of Setheford – £10, Curteys de Well – £20, John, son of Alexander Baldwin de Brancaster – £11.13s.4d., John, son of Thomas Accomer – £20 (of 100s.)." None of these was in fact an Upwood resident. John Pyre de Setheford may have been that John Pye

of Lyn, of Helgeye, enrolled later in the Ramsey Register under the date of 1445 (see Raftis, *Tenure and Mobility,* 184). Curteys de Well may be that Richard Curteys, the son of John of Helgeye, enrolled in the same register for 1444 (ibid.). In any case, the implication of changed address would be to suggest administrative or commercial activity.

12 For other concessions, see Raftis, *Tenure and Mobility,* chap. IX, sect. II.

13 Not many miles from Ramsey Abbey was Spalding Priory, where the pattern of fifteenth-century villein movements differed dramatically from that of Ramsey. Was this because of differing tenurial structure? R.H. Britnell has pointed out that 68 per cent of the tenants at Spalding had fewer than 5 acres ("Eastern England," *Agrarian History of England and Wales,* III:616). It is hoped that the current investigations of E.D. Jones can continue to throw further light on the Spalding evidence.

CHAPTER SEVEN

1 Professor North summarized his approach at a special lecture delivered at the University of Toronto, 6 Apr. 1995.

2 John Hatcher, *Rural Economy and Society in the Duchy of Cornwall, 1300–1500.* The variety of economic activities of lay lords is exemplified by the earls of Devon in coastal trade, now well documented by Maryanne Kowaleski, *Local Customs Accounts of the Port of Exeter, 1266–1321.*

3 H.E. Hallam, *Settlement and Society.*

4 I.S.W. Blanchard, "Seigneurial Entrepreneurship."

5 See chap. 1, n 2.

6 Searle, *Battle Abbey,* 143.

7 Barbara Harvey, *Westminster Abbey and Its Estates in the Middle Ages,* 315.

8 Alfred N. May's study "An Index of Thirteenth-Century Impoverishment? Manor Court Fines" is still useful for having drawn attention to lower fines as new to the late thirteenth century. One might notice especially his conclusion: "Business in manor courts was not particularly lucrative" (390). Unfortunately, his assumption that poverty was the reason for these lower fines was not proven. Certainly poverty does not explain why lower fines were applied to substantial customary tenants in Ramsey estates.

9 Kathleen Biddick and Catrin Bijlevield, "Agrarian Productivity on the Estates of the Bishopric of Winchester in the early thirteenth century," in *Land, Labour and Livestock,* points to the possibilities for updating traditional estate histories along these lines.

10 The study of Sandra Raban, *Estates of Thorney and Crowland,* is an especially useful description of the shift in new resources accruing to religious institutions.

11 The study given in n 9 above gives dramatic evidence on this point.
12 The most thorough study to date of the operation of these accounting practices is to be found in the introduction to *Cuxham Manorial Records* by P.D.A. Harvey.
13 F.R.H. De Boulay, *The Lordship of Canterbury*, 197.
14 E. Miller, "England in the Twelfth and Thirteenth Centuries: An Economic Contrast?"
15 Variations in types of demesne farming on the estates of Ramsey over the early fifteenth century may be seen in a forthcoming study by Michael Osmann.
16 An excellent introduction to recent work is now available in *Land, Labour and Livestock*, ed. Bruce M.S. Campbell and Mark Overtun, especially in the two chapters written by the editors.
17 D. McCloskey, "English Open Fields as Behavior towards Risk," in *Research in Economic History* (1976).
18 C.J. Dahlman, *The Open Field System and Beyond*.
19 John Langdon, *Horses, Oxen and Technological Innovation*.
20 John H. Munro, "The Medieval Scarlet and the Economics of Sartorial Splendour."
21 *The Cambridge Economic History of Europe*, vol. III, *Economic Organization and Policies in the Middle Ages*, 287.
22 *The Cambridge Economic History of Europe*, vol. II, *Trade and Industry in the Middle Ages*: see M.M. Postan, "The Trade of Medieval Europe: The North," 171.
23 Ibid., Robert S. Lopez, "The South," 324. A recent example of this per-during point of view may be found in *Before the Black Death*, ed. B.M.S. Campbell, in the introduction by Barbara F. Harvey, 12–13. The forthcoming study "Peasants, Merchants and Markets: Inland Trade in England, 1150–1350," by James Masschaele, will be of special importance in redressing this imbalance. It should also be acknowledged that research has begun to "move inland" from the traditional focus upon ports of export. The study of R.H. Britnell, *Growth and Decline in Colchester, 1300–1525*, holds a pioneer role in this regard. Moreover, a completely new methodology may now be seen at hand in the recent study by Maryanne Kowaleski, *Local Markets and Regional Trade in Medieval Exeter*, especially in the primary emphasis upon the regional economy (pt 1) and the use of the prosopographical approach (appendices 1 and 2).
24 This lack of investment assumption was one of the main themes of M.M. Postan and generally accepted by others. For a summary of Postan's final views, see *The Medieval Society and Economy*, espec. 43–4.
25 Raftis, *The Estates of Ramsey Abbey*, 234ff.
26 Ibid., 237ff.

27 Harvey, *Westminster Abbey*, 206.

28 Searle, *Battle Abbey.*

29 *Peterborough Abbey*, 110–25.

30 Anne DeWindt, "Peasant Power Structures in Fourteenth-Century King's Ripton."

31 Anne DeWindt, "A Peasant Land Market and Its Participants: King's Ripton 1280–1400."

32 Edward Miller, *The Abbey and Bishopric of Ely*, 131.

33 Ibid., 136.

34 *Agrarian History of England and Wales*, III:590–1; 597; 601; 636–8; 662–4; 706–7; 723–4.

35 *The Abbey and Bishopric of Ely*, 129.

36 Kosminsky, *Agrarian History*, chap. 1, gives an excellent example of this point by his reconstitution of the historical validity of the hundred rolls.

37 Peter Laslett, *The World We Have Lost*, 44.

38 R.M. Smith, "Families and Their Land in an Area of Partible Inheritance, Redgrave, Suffolk 1260–1320," in *Land, Kinship and Life-cycle*, ed. R.M. Smith, 135–95. See also the work of Smith's student, L.R. Poos, *A Rural Society after the Black Death: Essex 1350–1525.*

39 Nils Hybel, *Crisis or Change*, 294.

40 Robert Brenner may be seen as grossly imprecise in his remarks footnoted by reference to *Tenure and Mobility* (139–44), but in light of this current volume his statement must be considered simply incorrect on all counts: "What is telling, however, is the sudden change in the lord's approach to villein mobility which followed immediately after the Black Death and the sudden shortage (as opposed to plethora) of tenants. For this period there is ample evidence for the distraining of villeins to become tenants and take over obligations; for much heavier fines for licence to leave the lord's manor; for a remarkable increase in the number of pledges required for those permitted to leave the manor; for a sharper attitude concerning fugitives from the domain; and for limitations on the number of years the villein was allowed to be away from the manor." See Brenner, "Agrarian Class Structure and Economic Development in Pre-Industrial Europe," in *The Brenner Debate*, ed. T.H. Ashton and C.H.E. Philpin, 27.

41 In particular, *The Economic Development of Some Leicestershire Estates in the Fourteenth and Fifteenth Centuries; The English Peasantry in the Later Middle Ages; A Medieval Society: The West Midlands at the End of the Thirteenth Century.*

42 Especially C. Dyer, *Lords and Peasants in a Changing Society.*

43 *The Gulag Archipelago, 1918–1956*, 55.

44 For a summary, see H.E. Hallam in *Agrarian History of England and Wales*, 11:846–9.

45 Anne De Windt, "Peasant Power Structure in Fourteenth-Century King's Ripton."

46 R.A. Dobson, *The Peasants' Revolt of 1381*, 235–6. The following observation of Blanchard is an apt portrayal of this mentality: "The peasantry, whether in medieval England, early modern eastern Europe or nineteenth-century Russia, although subject to changing forms of social organization, remained steadfast in their acceptance of an enduring value-system which exalted the virtues of a land-based hierarchy and accorded the individual a sense of place or identity within his community on the basis of his family's landholding. Family members thus worked, in ways determined by the amount of land they held, to achieve objectives which were conditioned by their place within the village land-based hierarchy." I.S.W. Blanchard, *Labour and Leisure in the Historical Perspective, Thirteenth to Twentieth Centuries*, 12.

47 Of course, the individuality of families emerges much more clearly when social factors are added to the economic. See, for example, the use of networks for one Hunts village of Ramsey as presented by Judith Bennett, *Women in the Medieval English Countryside*. Almost intuitively, English scholars from the late nineteenth century, through F.M. Powicke's "Observations on the English Freeholder in the Thirteenth Century" (1938) to Alan Macfarlane's *The Origins of English Individualism*, have engaged in an intellectual protest against the negative categorization of their forebears. An anachronistic focus upon freedom has distracted attention from the genuine economic development by their countrymen. The limited perspective of certain disciplines no doubt goes far to explain the permanence of such notions, as a recent study reports: "Our sense is that the social sciences have been too timid in proposing and exploring what might be termed the sociocultural and psychological dimensions … they have been relatively reticent to address the role of group and individual selves and identities." Richard Shweder and Hazel Markus, "Culture, Identity and Conflict," in *Items*, 11–13.

48 For the first half of the fourteenth century a most useful summary may be found in J.R. Maddicott, *The English Peasantry and the Demands of the Crown, Past and Present* Supplement, 1. A.R. Bridbury provides a review of the traditional economic-history interpretation of the last half of the century in "The Black Death."

49 The late nineteenth-century appearance of the extents of Ramsey estates, with their long lists of services in the Rolls Series volumes on Ramsey materials, influenced scholars of the time like Paul Vinogradoff.

But there was still no more precision behind the remarks of M.M. Postan by the 1970s – "So great was the economic burden of the villeins," in *The Medieval Economy and Society*, 145 – than there was to statements of Vinogradoff such as those in *The Growth of the Manor*, 342.

APPENDIX ONE

1 By Anne Reiber DeWindt and Edwin Brezette DeWindt, 2 vols. Toronto: Pontifical Institute of Mediaeval Studies 1981. See 1:84–5.

2 See, for example, R.B. Goheen, "Peasant Politics? Village Community and the Crown in Fifteenth-Century England."

3 *Broughton:* British Library Additional Charters: 33189 (ca 1290), 33190 (ca 1300), 33191 (1315), 33192 (1322), 33193 (1329), 33194 (1336), 33195 (1339), 33196 (ca 1346).
Upwood: British Library Additional Charters: 33186 (ca 1340), 34107 (ca 1285), 34108 (1285), 34109 (1327), 34110 (1331), 34111 (1338).
Warboys: British Library Additional Charters: 34176 (ca 1300), 34177 (ca 1324), 34178 (1318), 34179 (1303), 34180 (1318), 34182 (1325), 34183 (1328), 34184 (1328), 34185 (1334), 34186 (1341), 34187 (1342). Public Record Office: E40 A5156 (1293), E326 B5494 (1330), E326 B6224 (1331).
Wistow: British Library Additional Charters: 34209 (1310), 34210 (ca 1315), 34211 (1315), 34212 (1324), 34213 (ca 1335), 34214 (1342). Dates preceded by ca are only approximate. These charters have been dated by means of court-roll data on the activity periods of the various witnesses.

4 See C.N.L. Brooke and M.M. Postan, eds., *Carte Nativorum*, and also Edmund King, *Peterborough Abbey, 1086–1310*, 99–125.

5 According to Professor Postan, some of the Peterborough charters involved customary land. See Brooke and Postan, ibid. xxix.

6 F. Pollock and F.W. Maitland, *The History of English Law*, 1:421.

7 John de Raveley was described as a freeman in 1279.

8 John Unfrey was described as free in the roll of 1299.

9 Each was described as *miles* in charters. On the relationship between freedom and knighthood, see Pollock and Maitland, 1:429.

10 The only Hugh de Croft who can be identified in the Ramsey and Upwood area around 1340 was the royal justice. The likelihood that this was the royal justice is strengthened by the fact that he appears as a witness with William le Moigne and John de Deen. For the other activities of Hugh de Croft, see *Carts.* 1:174, 178, 199.

11 Ibid., III:79, II:61, respectively.

12 Ibid., 1:376; Nicholas de Stukeley was described as a steward in the Broughton court rolls of 1333 and 1334.

13 Both Ralph Norreys and William Mowyn appear as extensive freeholders in the Hundred Rolls. See W. Illingworth and J. Caley, eds., *Rotuli
Hundredorum tempore Henrici III et Edwardi I*, II:600–4, 624, respectively.

14 Pollock and Maitland, *History of English Law*, II:628–9.

APPENDIX TWO

1 Eleanor Searle, *Lordship and Community*, 170, 171.

2 This point could only be fully appreciated with the appearance of the
splendid edition and study *Walter of Henley and Other Treatises on Estate
Management and Accounting*, by Dorothea Oschinksy.

3 *Medieval Households*, 155.

4 See Edmund King, *Peterborough Abbey, 1086–1310*, 160–6.

5 Lori Gates, "A Glastonbury Estate Complex."

6 *Kibworth Harcourt*, 235.

7 12–16.

8 "Labour Productivity in English Agriculture, 1300–1860," in *Land,
Labour and Livestock*, 235.

9 "Culture, Identity, and Conflict," in *Items* (March 1995): 11.

Bibliography

ARCHIVAL SOURCES

Court Rolls

Public Record Office, Special Collections 2 (s.c.2 179/)
British Library Additional Charters and Rolls (e.g., 39586)

ABBOTS RIPTON

1274	39586	1332	179/26	1404	179/49
1292	34337	1339–40	179/30	1405	39477
1294	39597	Edward III	179/28	1407	179/50
1295	179/9	Edward III	39738	1410	179/52
1296	179/9	1343	179/31	1411	34819
1299	179/10	1350	179/34	1423–24	179/57
1301	179/11	1356	179/36	1428	34370
1306	34895	1365	39860	1430	39480
1306	179/12	1369	179/38	1434	179/62
1307	179/15	1370	39580	1440	179/63
1308–09	39739	1395	179/44	1443	179/64
1313	179/17	1398	34817	1452–53	34827
1318	179/18	1400	179/45	1455	179/67
1321	179/20	1399–1400	179/45	1462	39729
1321	179/21	1402	179/47	1465	179/70

BROUGHTON

1288	175/5	1290	39754	1291	39849

1292	34335	1334	39762	1400	34920
1294	34894	1334–35	179/28	1402	179/47
1294	39597	1337	34899	1403	39861
1297	179/9	1339	34808	1405	179/50
1299	179/10	1339–40	179/30	1405	39477
1301	34913	1354–56	39471	1406	39478
1301	39913	1359	39583	1409	179/52
1306	39459	136?	179/37	1410	179/52
1306	34902	1360	39472	1411	34819
1307	34916	1365	39860	1412	39769
1308	34304	1369	39473	1418	179/55
1309	34342	1369	179/38	1420	34821
1311	34305	1371	39858	1421	39479
1313	34768	1373	179/39	1423–24	179/57
1314	39463	1375	179/40	1424	179/57
1316	39464	Richard II	39859	1425	34308
1317	34803	1378	179/41	1428	34370
1319	34804	1382	34306	1430	39480
1320	39759	1384	34901	1430?	179/60
1321–22	179/20	1386	179/42	1434	179/62
1322	39466	1387	179/43	1437	39481
1322	39467	1387–88	39474	1446	39867
1325	179/22	1390	34817	1451	39482
1329	39468	1390–91	39475	1452	179/66
1331	39469	1391	179/43	1455	179/67
1332–33	34363	1398	34817		
1333	39470	1399	39476		

KING'S RIPTON

1279–80	39595	1321–22	179/20	1396	179/44
1292	34336	1322	39467	1405	39477
1294	39597	1331	39469	1409	179/52
1294	34769	1332–33	34363	1411	179/53
1297	179/9	1333	39470	1412	179/53
1297	179/6	1347	179/32	1419	179/56
1299	179/10	1350	179/34	1419	179/55
1301	179/11	1357	179/36	1421	39479
1303	179/6	1360	39730	1422?	179/57
1306	179/12	1365	179/37	1423–24	179/57
1306	39459	1366?	179/37	1428	179/59
1309	34342	1384	34901	1429	179/60
1309	34770	1386	34771	1434	179/62
1312	34768	1390–91	39475	1453	34828
1316	39464	1395	179/44	1455	179/67

UPWOOD	Greater detail is given for this village as an illustration.	
1279–80	Monday, 3 Nov.	34911
1280	Aug./Sept.	179/4
1294	Saturday, 4 Dec.	34769
1295	Wednesday, 7 Dec.	179/9
1297	Monday, 4 Nov.	34798
1299	Thursday, 3 Dec.	179/10
1301	Thursday, 23 Nov.	179/12
1306	(heading missing)	34361
1307	Tuesday, 31 Jan.	34799
1307	Monday, 4 Dec.	179/15
1308	Monday, 4 Nov.	34801
1311	Wednesday, 3 Nov.	34802
1313	(heading missing)	34917
1318	Saturday, 7 Jan.	34803
1320	Monday, 14 Jan.	34804
1322	Monday, 18 Oct.	34805
1325 (1)	Jan.	34806
1325 (2)	Tuesday, 5 Nov.	39851
1326	Wednesday, 17 Dec.	34807
1329	Saturday, 1 Jan.	39852
1331	Monday, 16 Dec.	34321
1332	Friday, 18 Dec.	39582
1333	Monday, 6 Dec.	34810
1334	Monday, 28 Nov.	34809
1339	Thursday, 7 Jan.	34808
1339–40	(heading damaged)	34811
1344	Tuesday,? Jan.	39854
1347	Wednesday, 28 Nov.	34849
1349	Thursday, 12 Nov.	34850
1350	Friday, 29 Oct.	179/34
1353	(Tuesday, 29 Oct.?)	39855
1360	Saturday, 24 Oct.	34812
1365 (1)	Saturday, 26 July	39860
1365 (2)	Saturday, 18 Oct.	179/37
1369 (1)	Friday, 13 July	39473
1369 (2)	Saturday, 21 July	39765
1372	Thursday, 28 Oct.	39766
1373	Thursday, 3 Nov.	179/39
1375	Monday, 5 Nov.	179/40
1378	Tuesday, 14 Dec.	179/41
1382	Thursday, 14 Nov.	34306
1386	Monday, 1 Oct.	34813
1387	Friday,? Mar.	179/42

1390	Tuesday, 4 Oct.	34814
1391 (1)	Tuesday, (18 July?)	34815
1391 (2)	Saturday, 28 Oct.	34816
1395	Saturday, 30 Oct.	179/44
1398	Monday, (8 July?)	34817
1402	Thursday, 20 July	179/47
1403?	(heading missing)	179/48
1405	(heading damaged)	34818
1406	Friday, 19 Nov.	39478
1409	Thursday, 14 Nov.	179/52
1411 (1)	Friday, 12 June	34819
1411 (2)	Tuesday, 22 Dec.	39863
1413	Monday, 30 Oct.	34820
1418	Saturday, 5 Nov.	179/55
1420	Thursday, 11 Apr.	34821
1421	Tuesday, 28 Oct.	34368
1422	Saturday, 3 Oct.	34369
ca 1424	Saturday, (?) Aug.	34800
1424	Tuesday, 17 July	179/57
1425 (1)	Monday, (8 Oct.?)	39645
1425 (2)	Saturday, 27 Oct.	39745
1427	Monday, 27 Oct.	34370
1428 (1)	Monday, 2 Aug.	34370
1428 (2)	Monday, 18 Oct.	179/59
1429	Saturday, 25 June	179/59
ca 1430	Saturday, after 18 Oct.	39859
1430	Saturday, 22 July	39646
1430	Saturday, 28 Oct.	34822
1435	Monday, 24 Jan.	34371
1438	Thursday, 9 Jan.	34823
1439	Wednesday, 16 Dec.	34824
1441	Saturday, 28 Oct.	39866
1443	Thursday, 10 Oct.	34825
1448	Saturday, 2 Nov.	34826
1450	Saturday, 31 Oct.	39746
1452	Thursday, 2 Nov.	34827
1453	Monday, 29 Oct.	34828
1454	Saturday, 23 Nov.	34829
1456	Saturday, 6 Nov.	34830

WARBOYS

1290	39754	1294	34894	1301	39850
1292	34335	1294	39597	1301	179/11
1294	39755	1299	179/10	1305	34774

1306	39756	1347	39856	1400	34920
1306	35895	1347–48	34900	1402	179/47
1309	34342	1349	39763	1403?	179/48
1313	34910	1350	170/34	1404	179/49
1313	34324	1353	179/35	1405	39862
1316	34896	1360	39764	1410	39768
1316	34897	1363	39857	1411	179/53
1318	39757	1365	39860	1412	39769
1320	39758	1369	39765	1418	179/55
1320	39759	1369	39473	1421	39770
1320	34918	1371	39858	1423–24	39864
1322	34777	1372	39766	1424	39865
1322	179/20	1373	179/39	1427	34370
1325	34898	Richard II	39859	1428	179/59
1325	39851	1375	179/40	1430	39480
1326	39760	1382	34306	1434	179/62
1331	39761	1384	34901	1440	39771
1332–33	34363	1387	179/43	1440	39772
1333	39470	1387–88	39474	1448	39773
1333	34919	1390	34814	1455	39774
1334	39762	1390	34815	1458	179/68
1337	34899	1391	179/43	1462	39729
1339	39853	1398	34817		
1343	179/31	1400	179/45		

Note: For the Wistow court rolls, see *Tenure and Mobility,* 288–9. Account rolls formed the base of the study *Estates of Ramsey Abbey* but have been used infrequently here.

Charters

London, British Library, Additional Charters: 34107–34111, 34176–34180, 34182–34187, 34189–34196, 34209–34214
London, Public Record Office E40 A5156, E326 B5459, E326, B6224

Editions

Brooke, C.N.L., and Postan, M.M., eds. *Carte Nativorum: A Peterborough Abbey Cartulary of the Fourteenth Century.* Oxford: Oxford University Press 1960.
Cartularium Monasterii de Rameseia. Ed. W.H. Hart and P.A. Lyons. Rolls Series 79. 3 vols. London 1884–93.
Early Taxation Returns: Taxation of Personal Property in 1332 and later. Ed. A.C. Chibnall. Buckinghamshire Record Society 14, 1966.

Rotuli Hundredorum tempore Henrici et Edwardi I. Ed. W. Illingworth and J. Caley. 2 vols. London 1818.

The Domesday of St. Paul's. Ed. William Hale Hale. The Camden Society, no. 69. London 1857.

The Taxation of 1297: A Translation of the Local Rolls of Assessment for Barford, Biggleswade and Flitt Hundreds, and for Bedford, Dunstable, Leighton Buzzard and Luton. Ed. A.T. Gaydon. Publications of the Bedfordshire Historical Society 39, 1959.

SECONDARY SOURCES

Ashley, W.J. *An Introduction to English Economic History and Theory.* Pt II. London: Longmans 1901.

Aston, T.H., and C.H.E. Philpin, eds. *The Brenner Debate.* Cambridge: Cambridge University Press 1985.

Batho, Gordon. "Noblemen, Gentlemen and Yeomen." In *The Agrarian History of England and Wales*, IV, *1500–1640.* Cambridge: Cambridge University Press 1967. 276–305.

Bennett, J.M. "Spouses, Siblings and Surnames: Reconstructing Families from Medieval Village Court Rolls." *Journal of British Studies* 23, no. 1 (1983): 26–46.

– *Women in the Medieval English Countryside.* Oxford: Oxford University Press 1987.

Biddick, Kathleen. "Medieval English Peasants and Market Involvement." *Journal of Economic History* 45 (1985): 823–31.

– *The Other Economy: Pastoral Husbandry on a Medieval Estate.* Berkeley and Los Angeles: University of California Press 1989.

– with Catrina Bijleveld. "Agrarian Productivity on the Estates of the Bishopric of Winchester in the Early Thirteenth Century." In Campbell and Overtun, eds., *Land, Labour and Livestock.* 95–123.

Bischoff, J.P. "Fleece Weights and Sheep Breeds in Late Thirteenth- and Early Fourteenth-Century England." *Agricultural History* 57, no. 2 (1982): 143–60.

Blanchard, I.S.W. "Seigneurial Entrepreneurship: The Bishops of Durham and the Weardale Lead Industry, 1406–1529." *Business History* 15, no. 2 (1973): 97–111.

– *Labour and Leisure in Historical Perspective, Thirteenth to Twentieth Centuries.* Wiesbaden: Steiner 1994. Introduction, 9–38.

Brenner, Robert. "Agrarian Class Structure and Economic Development in Pre-Industrial Europe." In *The Brenner Debate*, ed. T.H. Aston and C.H.E. Philpin. Cambridge: Cambridge University Press 1985. 10–63.

Bridbury, A.R. "The Black Death." *Economic History Review*, 2nd ser., 26, no. 3 (1973): 577–92.

Britnell, R.H. *Growth and Decline in Colchester, 1300–1525.* Cambridge: Cambridge University Press 1986.

- "Tenant Farming and Farmers: Eastern England." *The Agrarian History of England and Wales*, III, *1348–1500*. Cambridge: Cambridge University Press, 1991. 611–24.
- *The Commercialisation of English Society, 1000–1500*. Cambridge: Cambridge University Press 1993.

Britton, Edward. *The Community of the Vill: A Study in the History of the Family and Village Life in Fourteenth-Century England*. Toronto: Macmillan 1977.

Campbell, Bruce M.S., with Mark Overtun. "Arable Productivity in Medieval England: Some Evidence from Norfolk." *Journal of Economic History* 43 (1983): 379–404.
- and Mark Overtun, eds. *Land, Labour, and Livestock: Historical Studies in European Agricultural Productivity*. Manchester: Manchester University Press 1991.
- with Mark Overtun. "Productivity Change in European Agricultural Development." In *Land, Labour and Livestock*, 1–50.
- "Land, Labour, Livestock and Productivity Trends in English Seignorial Agriculture, 1208–1450." In *Land, Labour and Livestock*, 144–82.
- "Norfolk Livestock Farming 1250–1750: A Comparative Study of Manorial Accounts and Probate Inventories." *Journal of Historical Geography* 18 (1992): 377–96.

Clark, Gregory, "Labour Productivity in English Agriculture." In Campbell and Overtun, eds., *Land, Labour and Livestock*. 211–35.

Dahlman, Carl. *The Open Field System and Beyond: A Property Rights Analysis of an Economic Institution*. Cambridge: Cambridge University Press 1980.

DeWindt, Anne, "Peasant Power Structures in Fourteenth-Century King's Ripton." *Mediaeval Studies* 38 (1976): 236–67.
- "A Peasant Land Market and Its Participants: King's Ripton 1280–1400." *Midland History* 4, nos. 3 & 4 (1978): 142–59.
- and Edwin. *Royal Justice and the Medieval English Countryside*. 2 vols. Toronto: Pontifical Institute of Mediaeval Studies 1981.

DeWindt, Edwin B. *Land and People in Holywell-cum-Needingworth*. Toronto: Pontifical Institute of Mediaeval Studies 1972.
- *The Liber Gersumarum of Ramsey Abbey, a Calendar and Index of B.L. Harley MS 445*. Toronto: Pontifical Institute of Mediaeval Studies 1976.

Dobson, R.A. *The Peasants' Revolt of 1381*. New York: St Martin's Press 1970.

DuBoulay, F.R.H. *The Lordship of Canterbury*. London: Nelson 1966.

Dyer, Christopher. *Lords and Peasants in a Changing Society: The Estates of the Bishopric of Worcester, 680–1540*. Cambridge: Cambridge University Press 1980.
- "Tenant Farming and Farmers: Western Midlands." *Agrarian History of England and Wales*, III, *1348–1500*. Cambridge: Cambridge University Press 1991. 636–45.

Farmer, David L. "Marketing the Produce of the Countryside, 1200–1500" and "Prices and Wages, 1350–1500." In *The Agrarian History of England and Wales*, III, *1348–1500*. Cambridge: Cambridge University Press 1991. 324–430, 431–95.

Gates, Lori A. "A Glastonbury Estate Complex in Wiltshire: Survival and Prosperity on the Medieval Manor, 1280–1380." PhD, University of Toronto 1991.

Goheen, R.B. "Peasant Politics? Village Community and the Crown in Fifteenth-Century England." *American Historical Review* 96 (Feb. 1991): 42–62.

Hallam, H.E. *Settlement and Society: A Study of the Early Agrarian History of South Lincolnshire*. Cambridge: Cambridge University Press 1965.

– "The Agrarian Economy of South Lincolnshire in the Mid-Fifteenth Century." *Nottingham Mediaeval Studies* 11 (1967): 86–95.

Harvey, Barbara. *Westminster Abbey and Its Estates in the Middle Ages*. Oxford: Clarendon 1977.

– Introduction to *Before the Black Death: Studies in the "Crisis" of the Early Fourteenth Century*. Ed. B.M.S. Campbell. Manchester: Manchester University Press 1991.

Harvey, P.D.A. *A Medieval Oxfordshire Village, Cuxham, 1240 to 1400*. London: Oxford University Press 1965.

– "The English Inflation of 1180–1220." *Past and Present* 61 (1973): 3–30.

– *Manorial Records of Cuxham, Oxfordshire, circa 1200–1359*. London: HM Stationery Office 1976.

– ed. *The Peasant Land Market in Medieval England*. New York: Oxford University Press 1984.

Harvey, Sally. "Domesday England." In *The Agrarian History of England and Wales*, II, *1042–1350*. Cambridge: Cambridge University Press 1988. 45–138.

Hatcher, John. *Rural Economy and Society in the Duchy of Cornwall, 1300–1500*. Cambridge: Cambridge University Press 1970.

Herlihy, David. *Medieval Households*. Cambridge, Mass.: Harvard University Press 1985.

Hilton, R.H. *The Economic Development of Some Leicestershire Estates in the Fourteenth and Fifteenth Centuries*. London: Oxford University Press 1947.

– *A Medieval Society: The West Midlands at the End of the Thirteenth Century*. New York: Humanities Press 1966.

– *The English Peasantry in the Later Middle Ages*. Oxford: Clarendon 1975.

Hogan, M.P. "The Labor of Their Days: Work in the Medieval Village." *Studies in Medieval and Renaissance History* 8 (1987): 77–186.

– "Clays, *Culturae* and the Cultivator's Wisdom: Management Efficiency at Fourteenth-Century Wistow." *Agricultural History Review* 36 (1988): 117–32.

Homans, George C. *English Villagers of the Thirteenth Century.* Cambridge, Mass.: Harvard University Press 1941.

Howell, Cicely. *Land, Family and Inheritance in Transition: Kibworth Harcourt, 1280–1700.* Cambridge: Cambridge University Press 1983.

Hybel, Nils. *Crisis or Change: The Concept of Crisis in the Light of Agrarian Structural Reorganization in Late Medieval England.* Aarhus University Press 1989.

Jones, Andrew. "Bedfordshire: Fifteenth Century." In P.D.A. Harvey, ed., *The Peasant Land Market in Medieval England.* 179–251.

King, Edmund. *Peterborough Abbey, 1086–1310: A Study in the Land Market.* Cambridge: Cambridge University Press 1973.

Kosminsky, E.A. *Studies in the Agrarian History of England in the Thirteenth Century.* Ed. R.H. Hilton, trans. Ruth Kisch. New York: Kelley and Millman 1956.

Langdon, John. *Horses, Oxen and Technological Innovation.* Cambridge: Cambridge University Press 1986.

Laslett, Peter. *The World We Have Lost.* London: Methuen 1965.

Latham, R.E. *Revised Medieval Latin Word-List.* London: Oxford University Press 1965.

Logan, F.D. *Excommunication and the Secular Arm in Medieval England.* Toronto: Pontifical Institute of Mediaeval Studies 1968.

Lopez, Robert S. "The Trade of Medieval Europe: The South." *The Cambridge Economic History of Europe,* II, *Trade and Industry in the Middle Ages.* Cambridge: Cambridge University Press 1963.

McCloskey, O. "English Open Fields as Behavior Towards Risk." *Research in Economic History: An Annual Compilation of Research* 1. Ed. Paul Uselding. Greenwich, Conn.: JAI Press 1976. 124–170.

Macfarlane, Alan. *The Origins of English Individualism.* Cambridge: Cambridge University Press 1978.

Maddicott, J.R. *The English Peasantry and the Demands of the Crown 1294–1341.* *Past and Present* Supplement 1. Oxford: Oxford University Press 1975.

Masschaele, James. "Transport Costs in Medieval England." *Economic History Review* 46, no. 2 (1993): 266–79.

Mate, M. "Agrarian Economy after the Black Death: The Manors of Canterbury Cathedral Priory, 1348–1391." *Economic History Review* 38 (1984): 341–54.

May, Alfred N. "An Index of Thirteenth-Century Impoverishment? Manor Court Fines." *Economic History Review* 26 (1973): 389–402.

Miller, Edward. *The Abbey and Bishopric of Ely.* Cambridge: Cambridge University Press 1951.

– "The Economic Policies of Governments: Introduction." *The Cambridge Economic History of Europe,* III, *Economic Organization and Policies in the Middle Ages.* Cambridge: Cambridge University Press 1963. 281–9.

- "England in the Twelfth and Thirteenth Centuries; An Economic Contrast?" *Economic History Review* 24 (1971): 1–14.
- and John Hatcher. *Medieval England: Rural Society and Economic Change: 1086–1348.* New York & London: Longman 1978.

Moore, Ellen Wedemeyer. *The Fairs of Medieval England: An Introductory Study.* Toronto: Pontifical Institute of Mediaeval Studies 1985.

Morris, W.A. *The Frankpledge System.* New York: Longmans, Green, & Co., 1910.

Munro, John H. "The Medieval Scarlet and the Economics of Sartorial Splendour." In *Cloth and Clothing in Medieval Europe,* ed. N.B. Harte and K.G. Ponting. London: Heinemann Educational Books 1983. 13–70.

Olson, Sherri. "A Chronicle of All That Happens: Voices from the Village Court in Medieval England." Toronto: Pontifical Institute of Mediaeval Studies, forthcoming.

Oschinsky, Dorothea. *Walter of Henley and Other Treatises on Estate Management and Accounting.* Oxford: Oxford University Press 1971.

Parsons, John C., ed. "The Court Rolls of Huntingdon in the Fourteenth Century." Intro. by J.A. Raftis. Forthcoming.

Pollock, F., and F.W. Maitland. *The History of English Law,* vol. 1. Cambridge: Cambridge University Press 1978.

Poos, L.R. *A Rural Society after the Black Death: Essex 1350–1525.* Cambridge: Cambridge University Press 1991.

Postan, M.M. "The Trade of Medieval Europe: The North." *The Cambridge Economic History of Europe,* 11, *Trade and Industry in the Middle Ages.* Cambridge: Cambridge University Press 1963.
- *The Medieval Economy and Society.* London: Weidenfeld & Nicolson 1972.

Raban, Sandra. *Estates of Thorney and Crowland.* Cambridge: Cambridge University Press 1977.

Raftis, J.A. *The Estates of Ramsey Abbey.* Toronto: Pontifical Institute of Mediaeval Studies 1957.
- *Tenure and Mobility: Studies in the Social History of the Mediaeval English Village.* Toronto: Pontifical Institute of Mediaeval Studies 1964.
- "The Concentration of Responsibility in Five Villages." *Mediaeval Studies* 27 (1966): 92–118.
- "The Structure of Commutation in a Fourteenth-Century Village." *Essays in Medieval History presented to Bertie Wilkinson.* Ed. T.A. Sandquist and M.R. Powicke. Toronto: University of Toronto Press 1969. 282–300.
- *Warboys: Two Hundred Years in the Life of an English Mediaeval Village.* Toronto: Pontifical Institute of Mediaeval Studies 1974.
- and M.P. Hogan, *Early Huntingdonshire Lay Subsidy Rolls.* Toronto: Pontifical Institute of Mediaeval Studies 1976.
- "The Land Market at Godmanchester, ca. 1300." *Mediaeval Studies* 50 (1988): 311–23.

– *Early Tudor Godmanchester*. Toronto: Pontifical Institute of Mediaeval Studies 1990.

Razi, Zvi. *Life, Marriage and Death in a Medieval Parish*. Cambridge: Cambridge University Press 1980.

Scammell, Jean. "The Formation of the English Social Structure: Freedom, Knights and Gentry, 1066–1300." *Speculum* 68 (1993): 591–618.

Searle, Eleanor. *Lordship and Community: Battle Abbey and Its Banlieu, 1066–1538*. Toronto: Pontifical Institute of Mediaeval Studies 1974.

Shweder, Richard, and Hazel Markus. "Culture, Identity, and Conflict." *Items* 49, no. 1 (1995): 11–13.

Smith, R.A.L. *Canterbury Cathedral Priory: A Study in Monastic Administration*. Cambridge: Cambridge University Press 1969.

Smith, Richard M. "Families and Their Land in an Area of Partible Inheritance, Redgrave, Suffolk 1260–1320." In *Land, Kinship and Life-cycle*, ed. R.M. Smith. Cambridge: Cambridge University Press 1984. 135–95.

– "Demographic Developments in Rural England, 1300–1348." In *Before the Black Death: Studies in the "Crisis" of the Early Fourteenth Century*, ed. Bruce M.S. Campbell. Manchester and New York: Manchester University Press 1991. 25–77.

Solzhenitsyn, Alexsandr L. *The Gulag Archipelago, 1918–1956*. Trans. Thomas P. Whitney. New York: Harper & Row, 1973.

Vinogradoff, Paul. *The Growth of the Manor*. London: George Allen & Unwin 1904.

Index of Villagers

Abbot family, 69
Ace, Roger, 136
Acolt: Agnes, 21, 22;
  Thomas of, 21; William
  of, 21
Adam, John son of, 46
Agace (Agath, Egace):
  family, 69; Robert, 53,
  54, 57
Alan: family, 19; William
  son of, 136
Albyn: Agnes, 189;
  Henry son of, 202n20;
  John, 166; Nicholas,
  166; Richard, 113, 166
Alcok, William, 166
Aleyn: family, 111; John,
  87, 166; Richard, 167;
  Robert, 57, 166; Will-
  iam, 87, 167
Alot: family, 45; Richard,
  61; Robert, 45
Alston, Nicholas, 167
Andrew: Geoffrey, 136;
  John, 25, 167; Richard,
  167; William, 167
Arnold: Dionysia, 32;
  Thomas, 32
Aspelond (Aspelon): fam-
  ily, 30; John, 33, 113,

136, 189; Richard, 76,
  189; Robert (alias
  Ploughwright), 113;
  Simon, 161, 189; Tho-
  mas, 33; William, 96,
  116; William (alias
  Ploughwright), 113
Asshwell: Robert, 210n9
Athewold, Thomas, 73
Attebrigge: Thomas, 33;
  William, 33
Attebrok: Christine, 30;
  Robert, 30
Attechurche
  (Attechirche): Andrew,
  25; family, 73, 209n16;
  John jr., 162; John sr.,
  162
Attedam (atte Dam): fam-
  ily, 69; John, 24, 136;
  Oliver, 25
Atteforde, William, 33
Attegate (Ategate): John,
  77, 113, 189; John jr.
  son of Robert, 189;
  Robert, 189; Stephen,
  24, 189
Attehall (Atehale): fam-
  ily, 208n15; Thomas,
  136

atte Hide, William of
  Bury, 111
Attehill (Atehile): family,
  69; Ralph, 24, 33;
  Thomas of Hartford,
  77, 110, 162; William
  of Stukely, 162
atte Snap: family, 69;
  John, 29; Richard, 29;
  Roger, 29; Thomas, 29
Attestede: Walter, 167;
  William, 76, 167, 189
Attewell (Attewelle): fam-
  ily, 208n15; John, 167;
  Richard, 168; William,
  168
Attewode: John, 95; Mat-
  ilda, 57
Aubes: family, 111; John,
  168; John sr., 168; Will-
  iam, 168
Aubyn, William, 76, 189
Augustyn (see Austyn):
  John, 189; Simon, 161,
  189
Aula, Stephen de, 136
Austyn (see Augustyn):
  family, 69; John, 77, 162
Aylmar (Alimer, Aly-
  mar): John, 93, 94, 190;

General Index